Going South

Why Britain will have a
Third

Larry Elliott

and

Dan Atkinson

palgrave
macmillan

First published 2012 by
PALGRAVE MACMILLAN

Palgrave Macmillan in the UK is an imprint of Macmillan Publishers Limited,
registered in England, company number 785998, of Houndmills, Basingstoke,
Hampshire RG21 6XS.

Palgrave Macmillan in the US is a division of St Martin's Press LLC,
175 Fifth Avenue, New York, NY 10010.

Palgrave Macmillan is the global academic imprint of the above companies
and has companies and representatives throughout the world.

Palgrave® and Macmillan® are registered trademarks in the United States,
the United Kingdom, Europe and other countries

ISBN: 978-0-230-39254-0   paperback

This book is printed on paper suitable for recycling and made from fully
managed and sustained forest sources. Logging, pulping and manufacturing
processes are expected to conform to the environmental regulations of the
country of origin.

A catalogue record for this book is available from the British Library.

A catalog record for this book is available from the Library of Congress.

10 9 8 7 6 5 4 3 2 1
21 20 19 18 17 16 15 14 13 12

Printed and bound in Great Britain by
CPI Antony Rowe, Chippenham and Eastbourne

Contents

We dedicate this book to our parents.

Acknowledgements

We would like to thank Ivan Mulcahy, our agent, and his business manager Stephanie Cohen, Taiba Batool, our editor at Palgrave Macmillan, Claire Morrison, trade marketing manager at Palgrave Macmillan, Ellie Shillito, who did a fine job of obtaining permissions, and Susan Curran of Curran Publishing Services, who copy edited, typeset and indexed the book.

Dan Atkinson and Larry Elliott
May 2012

The authors and publisher wish to acknowledge with thanks the following for permission to reproduce copyright material:

The Random House Group for permission to reproduce material from *The Complete Yes Minister* by Jonathan Lynn and Antony Jay © BBC Books 1984

Penguin Books Ltd and Ed Victor Literary Agency for permission to reproduce material from *The Big Sleep* by Raymond Chandler, Penguin, 2011, © The Estate of Raymond Chandler 1939.

John Wiley & Sons Ltd. for permission to reproduce material from 'National self-sufficiency' by John Maynard Keynes, *The Yale Review*, Vol. 22, No. 4, June 1933, © The Estate of John Maynard Keynes, 1933.

Viking Children's Books, a division of the Penguin Group USA, for permission to reproduce material from *The Singing Tree* by Kate Seredy, Viking Children's Books, 1939 © Kate Seredy, 1939, 1966.

Acknowledgements

Faber and Faber and Houghton Mifflin Harcourt Publishing Company for permission to reproduce material from 'The Waste Land' taken from *Collected Poems* by T. S. Eliot, Faber and Faber, 2002 © Estate of T. S. Eliot and Harcourt Inc. 1922, 1964. All rights reserved.

The Wylie Agency for permission to reproduce material from *The Return of Eva Peron* by V. S. Naipaul, Penguin, 1980 © V.S.Naipaul, 1980.

Guardian News and Media Ltd for permission to reproduce material by Peter Jenkins, writing on 27 September 1978 © Guardian News and Media Ltd.

The Random House Group for permission to reproduce material from *The Bonfire of the Vanities* by Tom Wolfe, Jonathan Cape, 1987 © Tom Wolfe, 1987.

Paramount Pictures Corporation for permission to reproduce an extract from *The Italian Job* © Paramount Pictures Corporation, 1969. All rights reserved.

Abner Stein Agency and The Penguin Group USA for permission to reproduce material from *The Joy Luck Club* by Amy Tan, GP Putnam's Sons, 1989 © Amy Tan, 1989.

Ian Fleming Publications Ltd, London, for permission to reproduce material from YOU ONLY LIVE TWICE © Ian Fleming publications Ltd 1964 www.ianfleming.com

Faber and Faber Ltd and Farrar, Strauss and Giroux LLC for permission to reproduce material from 'Aubade' from *Collected Poems* by Philip Larkin, first published in the *Times Literary Supplement*, 23 December 1977 © Estate of Philip Larkin 1988, 2003.

The Random House Group and the Wylie Agency for permission to reproduce material from *Money* by Martin Amis, Jonathan Cape, 1984 © Martin Amis, 1984.

The Random House Group for permission to reproduce material from *Damaged Gods* by Julie Burchill, Century Hutchinson, 1986 © Julie Burchill, 1986.

Souvenir Press and Nancy Stauffer Associates for permission t(
reproduce material from *The Moneychangers* by Arthur Haile
Doubleday, 1975 © Arthur Hailey, 1975.

Ed Victor Literary Agency for permission to reproduce material fr(
The Book and the Brotherhood by Iris Murdoch, Chatto & Windus, 1(
© Iris Murdoch, 1987.

Pan Macmillan for permission to reproduce material from
Remorseful Day by Colin Dexter, Pan Macmillan, London, 19(
Colin Dexter 1999.

Guardian News and Media Ltd for permission to reproduce m;
by Sir Paul Newall, writing on 22 January 1994 © Guardian
and Media Ltd.

City A.M. for permission to reproduce material by David
Norman, writing on 31 May 2011 © City A.M.

Introduction

One hundred all out

'Come away; poverty's catching.'

Mrs Aphra Behn (1640–1689)

'Minister,' said Humphrey, 'I beg you not to refer to it as a tin-pot African country. It is an LDC.'
    LDC is a new one on me. It seems that Burunda is what used to be called an Underdeveloped Country. However, this term has apparently become offensive, so then they were called Developing Countries. This term apparently was patronising. Then they became Less Developed Countries – or LDC, for short.

Jonathan Lynn and Antony Jay,
The Complete Yes Minister, 1984

Plenty has made me poor.

Ovid (43 BC–17 AD)

In the hundred years from 1914 to 2014, the century since the outbreak of the First World War, the United Kingdom will have declined from pre-eminent global superpower to developing country, or 'emerging market', part of the Global South. The symptoms of this vertiginous plunge in the world's rankings are already starkly apparent: a chronic balance of payments deficit, a looming shortage of energy and food, a dysfunctional labour market, volatility in economic growth and a painful vulnerability to external events.

Then there is the large number of unproductive workers engaged in supervisory or 'security' roles, on the streets, in public parks, on the railways and at airports, their prestige apparently directly related to the inconvenience (and sometimes worse) that they are able to inflict on the public. There are the wars fought without the proper resources to do so, and the awareness among military commanders that in the absence of any military conflict their forces will be shrunk further, there being no attempt objectively to assess the nation's enduring defence needs. There is the ramshackle infrastructure existing in parallel with procurement contracts that run billions of pounds over budget and are then cancelled.

If these are the big indicators of imminent relegation to the third world, the smaller ones are too numerous fully to catalogue. Thus the UK government has unveiled a 'tourism strategy', in the manner beloved of developing countries the world over; the annual allocation of places at state schools has disclosed such an enormous shortage of well-regarded institutions that the authorities have resorted to lotteries and other forms of rationing, rather like the 'rolling blackouts' seen in post-colonial countries that have allowed their power stations to decay; there have been suggestions that the government's 'growth strategy' could be capsized by its planned controls on immigration, the unemployed among the native workforce being incapable of gainful employment.

On 21 March 2012, Chancellor George Osborne, in his Budget speech, acknowledged that the United Kingdom was now in competition not with Germany or the United States but with emerging economies:

> Do we watch as the Brazils and the Chinas, and the Indias of this world power ahead of us in the global economy; or do we have the national resolve to say: 'No, we won't be left behind. We want to be out in front'?

Elsewhere in his speech, he made this telling aside:

> [We are] working to develop London as a new offshore market for the Chinese currency.[1]

Not only is the United Kingdom supposedly averse to offshore financial centres, believing them to be hotbeds of tax evasion and money laundering, but deliberately setting out to create one has been the act of developing nations round the world from Panama to the Seychelles, not of mature, developed economies.

So stark is the evidence that it is our contention that the United Kingdom's looming relegation is not in doubt. The names change with intellectual fashion – the developing world, the third world, less developed countries, 'emerging markets' or simply the Global South. But the destination is the same.

We are Going South – rapidly.

And we argue further that a developing country needs a development model, and suggest some ideas.

The fruits of such a model, if indeed it is adopted, are some way off. More immediately, we suggest that the notion of the United Kingdom as an emerging – or at present, submerging – economy provides a useful perspective through which investors, both private and institutional, can profitably gauge their asset allocation strategies.

This is not a book of hot investment ideas. Nor do investors, or indeed the general reader, need to buy into our concept without reservation. We argue simply that it is a valuable tool with which to assess the economic and social situation of our time. We hope also that this book will be an enjoyable and stimulating read.

Assuming that the United Kingdom faces up to its plight, there is no easy model for the redevelopment of the national economy. Whichever path is taken will be a hard one. The age of the quick fixes is over.

The southbound carriageway: what do we mean by it?

In terms of economic geography, the United Kingdom has been Going South for more than a century. The centre of gravity of the economy shifted towards London and the Home Counties in the first half of the twentieth century, and the regional disparity between a rich south and a poor north has widened over time. On the eve of the First World War, when our story begins, the cotton mills of Lancashire ensured that income per head in the north-west was higher than in the south-east. The United Kingdom's poorest region at that time was East Anglia; Scotland had the second-highest living standards after London. Prosperity and population have been sucked southwards for the past hundred years or more. The latest official figures show that in 2010 income per head in London was 70 per cent above the national average while in every other region apart from the south-east it was below the national average. London and the south-east were as rich as anywhere in the European Union; other parts of the United Kingdom, such as Wales, the north and Cornwall, ranked with southern Italy. Only oddities such as East Sussex and the Isle of Wight recalled the down-at-heel nature of much of the south-east in 1914.[2]

In another sense, too, there have been signs of the United Kingdom Going South. Changes to weather patterns linked by climate scientists to global warming have raised the possibility that before too long it will no longer necessary for Britons to suffer the indignities of modern air travel to enjoy a Mediterranean climate: they will able instead to head down the M23 to Brighton or take the train from Waterloo to Bournemouth. Oenophiles are looking forward to the days when the hillsides of the Downs and the Weald are carpeted with vineyards turning out British vintages that will compare with the best that Burgundy can offer.

It remains to be seen whether Kent or Sussex will soon be able to boast their own Volnays and Chambertins, since there are climate experts who believe that global warming will divert the Gulf Stream to the north and so make Britain colder rather than warmer. Even so, there were warnings in early 2012 that Britain, following two exceptionally dry winters, was in danger of suffering its worst drought since 1976, when the reservoirs dried up and water rationing was imposed. That sweltering summer provided the backdrop to a sterling crisis that eventually prompted the arrival of an International Monetary Fund (IMF) mission which forced the then Labour government to cut public spending in return for financial assistance. Arousing a certain degree of scepticism, the New Economics Foundation think-tank said in its 2004 report *Chasing Progress* that life in Britain had never been as good again as it had been in 1976, once rising crime, pollution, environmental degradation and higher unemployment were added to the traditional measure of gross domestic product to form a broader measure of well-being.[3]

What we are talking about in this book, however, is not a comparison between the bustle of Canary Wharf and the derelict foundries and mills of the north (although that is part of our story). Nor is our theme the threat of energy shortages and global warming (although they too feature). Rather, it is the sense that the United Kingdom is going backwards, de-developing, heading for third world status.

The United Kingdom has never suffered the indignity of a return visit from an IMF 'hit squad', although three members of the European Union – Greece, Portugal and Ireland – have found themselves in that unfortunate position in the aftermath of the financial crisis and recession of the past five years. There have, however, been three severe recessions, two raging booms and one subsequent sterling crisis in 1992, even more dramatic than that of 1976. The long period of steady growth and falling unemployment was the exception, not the rule.

There is an assumption that, while deep, the damage caused by the Great Recession will be temporary. This book makes a different argument. Our contention is that the events of the past five years bring to a head trends of the past hundred years: industrial hollowing out has been exacerbated by globalization; the growth of the financial sector provided credit to feed Britain's debt habit; the end of the cold war hardened attitudes towards welfare and the division of economic spoils.

The *Economist* newspaper constructed what it called a Proust index to assess how much time had been lost by a number of countries as a result of the Great Recession.[4] In Greece, the clock had been turned back to the 1990s; in the United Kingdom the economic time in 2012 was 2004. According to the Institute for Fiscal Studies average living standards in the three years from 2010 to 2012 were likely to fall by more than 7 per cent, unprecedented since the stagflation of the mid-1970s.[5] In the subsequent 35 years, the cracks in the UK economic edifice were papered over by North Sea oil, cheap imports and debt. The oil wells are now running dry, the appetite for credit has been sated, and a 25 per cent depreciation in the value of the pound has made imports dearer and caused higher inflation.

Game off? What big public events tell us about banana-republic Britain

The London Olympics of 2012 were to showcase the new United Kingdom. It was the third time that the Games had been held in London. On the first occasion in 1908 the United Kingdom was the world's superpower and there was public clamour to build enough Dreadnought battleships ('we want eight and we won't wait') to win the naval arms race with Germany. On the second occasion in 1948, the United Kingdom was the one country in Western Europe not completely devastated by six years of total war, but it came a poor third to the United States and the Soviet Union in geopolitical influence. By 2012, the United Kingdom had joined the ranks of the nations that saw the Games as a way of showcasing themselves or of getting the taxpayer to fund extravagant regeneration schemes that would not have been seen as financially viable in other circumstances. Neither Herbert Asquith nor Clement Attlee felt the need, as David Cameron apparently did at the Davos meeting of the World Economic Forum in January 2012, to cajole business leaders to come to the United Kingdom for the 16 days of the London Games so that they could eye up investment opportunities. Mr Cameron was nothing if not consistent: in one of his first speeches as prime minister he had said he wanted to make sure 'the Olympics legacy lifts East London from being one of the poorest parts of the country to one that shares fully in the capital's growth and prosperity'.

The festivities would be on a smaller scale than the

no-expense-spared event in Beijing four years earlier, but would still be the biggest sporting occasion held in the United Kingdom since the 1966 World Cup. Other cities, most notably Montreal in 1976, had been bankrupted by the Olympics, although there was no chance of this happening in the case of London, since the Games were underwritten by the Treasury. Instead, the aim was to prove that the United Kingdom could deliver a major infrastructure project, raise the spirits of the nation and leave a sporting, economic and regeneration legacy.

Critics said the legacy of the Games would be 'eight sheds' in East London, and that the only way the United Kingdom had managed to bring the Games in on budget was by almost quadrupling the original cost estimate of £2.4 billion arrived at when the Games were awarded by the International Olympic Committee in 2005. In other ways, too, the Games seemed to illustrate the United Kingdom's position as a putative banana republic: the warnings that the underground system in East London would only be able to cope if 60 per cent of the area's normal workforce absented themselves for the duration of the Games; the £500 fines for use of the designated stretches of chronically congested roads for Olympic VIPs, dubbed Zil lanes for their resemblance to the way apparatchiks were whisked around Moscow under Stalin and Brezhnev; the closure of thoroughfares such as the Mall and Whitehall.

Even before the United Kingdom had decided to bid for the games, the House of Commons Committee for Culture, Media and Sport had warned about escalating costs and stressed that, while it was desirable that London should host the event, 'it should not do so at any price'.[6] MPs considered on the basis of a report by the consultants Ove Arup that the true cost would be closer to £5 billion and the public subsidy £2.5 billion.

Other studies showed that the benefits of hosting the Games tended to be exaggerated, ignoring costs such as the deterrence effect on tourists who would normally be coming to London and the fact that heavy spending on infrastructure would result in less money being available for other projects.

The *Daily Mail* reported that only 9 per cent of the 194 pieces of Olympics memorabilia would be made in Britain. Chinese factories would be responsible for 62 per cent of the items on sale.[7]

The other big planned celebration in 2012 was that to mark the Queen's diamond jubilee. Only one previous monarch, Victoria, had attained such a milestone, but there was quite a difference between the Imperial Britain of 1897 and the country that 115 years later had just fallen behind Brazil in the international league tables. The United Kingdom was, of course, a much richer country: people were fitter, healthier, lived longer and in less squalid housing. But it had been more than a century of relative decline, brought to a climax by the financial crisis of 2007.

Elizabeth II's diamond jubilee was the third jubilee of her reign. There was a marked difference between the United Kingdom of the silver jubilee in 1977 (punk rock, the National Front, IMF bailout programmes) and that of the coronation year of 1952 (pre-Beatles, pre-Suez, just emerging from rationing). The golden jubilee in 2002 coincided with a period when there was widespread belief that the United Kingdom had 'cracked it' – found a way of thriving in a post-industrial globalized economy. The 'third way' of Tony Blair was designed to ensure that limited, smart intervention knocked some of the rough edges off the market economy and otherwise left private enterprise – especially financial enterprises – to deliver the goods.

By the time of the diamond jubilee, such optimism had been proved unfounded.

Both sides now: prosecution and defence

You can heat water for a very long time before it boils and turns into steam. Until that moment, it is merely hot water; afterwards, it has become something quite else. Is the United Kingdom nothing more than a first-world economy with lots of problems, or is it in the process of transforming into something very different? Put another way, is a quantitative change about to become a qualitative change? Are we approaching our own boiling point?

Let us briefly examine the case against, the argument that would place the United Kingdom as a troubled developed economy – a very troubled developed economy, perhaps – but a developed economy nonetheless. In Chapter 6 we look in depth at the argument that the United Kingdom's economic difficulties have been blown out of proportion and are reflective more of a national talent for self-flagellation than of any proper analysis. Suffice it to say here that third world countries do not commonly enjoy permanent representation on the United Nations Security Council, or have global diplomatic and military responsibilities, whether a worldwide chain of bases and overseas territories or a strategic nuclear capability. Nor do they boast universities whose reputation genuinely deserves that over-used epithet 'world class'. They tend not to produce leading companies in finance, medicine, aerospace and defence.

Furthermore, British eccentricity ought not to be confused with incipient third world status, eccentricity ranging from some of the more bizarre questions in the driving theory test for would-be motorists (not to mention those questions, selected apparently at random, that do not apply to candidates in Northern Ireland) to the ability of the justice secretary to lay down the heavy burden of office to make a series of radio programmes about the lives of great jazz musicians. Similarly, British hypocrisy – whether the swing-round from police indifference to a huge 100-detective-plus inquiry in the 'phone hacking' affair, or the effortless transformation in official discourse as to the nature of the Taliban in Afghanistan, from a bearded version of the wartime SS to our invaluable future negotiating partner – does not automatically denote un-developing country status.

It is indeed hard to assemble one jury-swaying 'Exhibit A' that proves beyond doubt that economic de-development is upon us. Ultimately, perhaps, this does not matter. Jean-Jacques Rousseau once wrote that there was no such thing as love, only evidence of love. We would argue the same is true of third world status. We believe the evidence is thick on the ground, and we intend to present it in this book, written as the centenary approaches of the United Kingdom's last moment of undisputed world supremacy.

It is our view that the United Kingdom is facing a moment of truth. One hundred years after the guns of August 1914 marked the beginning a century of decline, the long slide from great power status to that of developing country is nearly complete. The quick fixes with which we have sought to disguise our shrinking economic performance – imperial preference, European Community membership, North Sea oil, financial deregulation, asset stripping, and periodic property and house price bubbles – are all used up.

This would spell big trouble at any time in economic history. But with the centre of industrial and commercial gravity moving from west to east, the United Kingdom's problems will be greatly magnified. A brutal age of adjustment is at hand.

Indeed, it has started. In the years leading up to 1914, the Liberals were in power, as they are today. But there are few other similarities, beyond perhaps the lengthy holidays taken by statesmen. Then, the United Kingdom was able to afford both a fleet of Dreadnought warships and the beginnings of the welfare state, with pensions and national insurance. Today, we can afford neither aircraft carriers with aircraft (at least for a decade) nor the welfare state as it has been constituted – child and housing benefits are being cut.

As 2014 comes closer, it is nearly the midnight hour, the time of reckoning, in London. One hundred years of decline will reach their climax not in the relatively balmy economic climes of the near quarter-century that followed the 1985 appointment of Mikhael Gorbachev as general secretary of the Soviet Communist Party, an appointment that brought to a sudden halt the last, terrifying phase of the cold war, but at a time of ferocious global competition for energy, food, markets, minerals and money.

After decades of dinner-party chatter about the United Kingdom's third-rate status, relegation looms to what used to be called the third world.

Let nobody say it cannot happen. To recall Lebanon and Argentina in the 1970s is to remind oneself that the machinery for relegation is well-oiled and efficient. Taking a longer view, Spain and Portugal, two superpowers that once divided the New World between them, went into many centuries of real and painful decline, during which time they languished as mere appendages of Europe.

The immediate trigger launching the United Kingdom into its moment of truth will be the second financial crisis in a decade, one caused by the failure of politicians adequately to deal with the weaknesses exposed by the first crisis. But even without this trigger, the United Kingdom's 100-year odyssey from Great Power status in 1914 would be ending in the developing world anyway. There are quite simply no more quick fixes to be had. The cupboard is bare.

Once the workshop of the world, the United Kingdom is now deeply in debt, with a workforce that is not only poorly educated and unproductive but also, thanks to large-scale immigration, considerably in excess of the economy's medium-term needs. Downward mobility is inevitable.

It is instructive to run through the to-do list routinely handed by IMF teams sent in to basket-case countries seeking financial assistance. The supplicant is told to export more; to consume less; to get its current account into balance; to sort out its public finances and purge unproductive parts of the public sector, with special attention to political sinecures; to bring its military commitments into line with its resources; to downsize its internal security apparatus so that it costs less and confronts real, as opposed to imaginary, threats; and to sort out its dysfunctional school system. Do the problems identified here remind you of anywhere?

There are different models that can be followed by a developing (or redeveloping) country as it seeks to build (or indeed rebuild) its economic base. They involve a greater or lesser role for the state, for private enterprise, for foreign investment, for public welfare, and so on. We shall examine them in greater detail later.

There is a case for choosing one model or another. But make no mistake, a choice has to be made.

There is no case at all for 'choosing' all of them.

And there is no case at all for choosing none of them.

Chapter 1

June 1914
A snapshot as the storm breaks

The inhabitant of London could order by telephone, sipping his morning tea in bed, the various products of the whole earth – he could at the same time and by the same means adventure his wealth in the natural resources and new enterprise of any quarter of the world – he could secure forthwith, if he wished, cheap and comfortable means of transit to any country or climate without passport or other formality.

John Maynard Keynes,
The Economic Consequences of the Peace, 1920

Jansci leaned down from his horse. 'It's nothing. I mean, not to us. He was just telling Father that Francis Ferdinand had been shot this afternoon – somewhere in Bosnia.'

'Oh,' sighed Kate, relieved that nothing more serious had happened. 'Francis ... what? Funny name for a horse ...'

'Horse nothing. He was the Crown Prince or something.'

Kate Seredy, *The Singing Tree*, 1940

I looked down at the chessboard. The move with the knight was wrong .... Knights had no meaning in this game. It wasn't a game for knights.

Raymond Chandler, *The Big Sleep*, 1939

The scene: the servants' quarters in the country seat of a member of the peerage. The date: 31 July 1914. The credits roll as the cook ladles out the stew and the butler explains to the staff that the master and his important chums are in a flap about some 'archduke who has got himself shot in foreign parts'. The United Kingdom's declaration of war against Germany is just days away, and as the ratings constantly prove, there is nothing the television addict likes better, with the sole exception perhaps of a full-blown Jane Austen adaptation, than a story of how the horrors of the Western Front brought an end not just to the long Edwardian summer but to the United Kingdom's century of global dominance.

Few of us can resist the episodes in which one of the well-bred daughters of the duke joins the suffragettes and chains herself to the railings in Downing Street, falls for the Irish chauffeur battling for Home Rule or discovers a social conscience after visiting the slums in which her father's mill hands live. We wait in expectation for the moment when it is announced that one of the leading men has gone down on the *Titanic*, giving up his place in the lifeboat so that a woman and her child can be saved. And when the butler provides his intelligence about the worrying news from upstairs, we know that next week's episode will have the lantern-jawed hero decked out in khaki and maids sobbing as their loved ones answer the call to serve king and country.

Yet tempting though it is to try to emulate *Downton Abbey* or *Upstairs Downstairs*, our story does not begin by highlighting the different worlds inhabited by the rich and poor in a United Kingdom even more scarred by inequality than it is today. Nor does it start in Sarajevo on 28 June 1914, when Gavrilo Princip, a 19-year-old Bosnian Serb, ushered in what Eric Hobsbawm has called the short twentieth century when he shot Franz Ferdinand and his wife Sophie from a range of five feet. There had already been one attempt on Franz Ferdinand's life that morning from a group of six conspirators including Princip, but after the driver of the archduke's car took a wrong turning and then stalled upon realizing his mistake, this one did not fail. Within

38 days, Austria had declared war on Serbia, Russia had come to Serbia's aid, Germany had invaded Belgium, and the Triple Entente of the United Kingdom, France and Russia was lined up against Germany and Austria-Hungary in the first conflict involving all the major European powers for 99 years.

High noon at the centre of the world

Dramatic though the scenes in Sarajevo were, to understand why the United Kingdom has clearly been Going South for the past century (and in reality for longer than that), we have to ask our readers instead to imagine themselves on the steps of the Royal Exchange at the very heart of the City of London on the last day of July 1914. Two miles away stands the Palace of Westminster, seat of government for the largest empire the world has ever known, more than 12 million square miles of territory including the cotton fields of India, the rubber plantations of Malaya and the gold mines of South Africa, these last won with much difficulty and at great cost in the Boer War a dozen years earlier.

The true heart of the empire, and indeed the pre-1914 world, is where we stand, with the imposing doors of Sir John Soane's Bank of England to our right and Lombard Street, home to the cream of British commercial banking, to our left. The Old Lady of Threadneedle Street is responsible for the operation of the gold standard, the monetary system that binds the world economy together. The countries that belong to the gold standard ensure that their currencies can be exchanged for gold, and the undisputed reserve currency in June 1914 is sterling. No other country comes close to matching the United Kingdom as a financial centre; it has only been a year since the rapidly growing United States created its own central bank, the Federal Reserve. For a century, gilt-edged stock issued by the UK government has been a safe haven for investors when, as in 1848, continental Europe has been convulsed by revolution. It is a scene of solidity and order that belies the short-term threat to the United Kingdom posed by the growing tensions in the Balkans, and the longer-term threat posed by the challenge from the rapidly growing economies of the United States and Germany.

Outside the Bank a chauffeur is sitting in a Rolls-Royce Silver Ghost, waiting for the chairman of one of London's discount houses to emerge from a meeting with Lord Cunliffe, the governor of the Bank for the past year. The chauffeur notices during the wait for his boss that there are more cars in the streets of the Square Mile than there were a year ago, and wonders how long it will before horse-drawn carriages disappear altogether. It is a time of both technological and cultural change: the revolutionary impact of the cinema, the aeroplane and the motor car were matched in the first decade and a half of the twentieth century by Sigmund Freud's *The Interpretation of Dreams* published in 1899, by cubism in art and the modernist movement in literature. Stravinsky's *Rite of Spring* had been premiered in Paris the previous year.

None of this matters to Cunliffe, who is a worried man, having sniffed the panic in the banks, the discount houses and on the floor of the stock market. Although shares in Vienna had started falling by mid-July, the City had not woken up to the impending crisis until 27 July, the day before Austria declared war on Serbia. Even a month after the assassination at Sarajevo, bond yields failed to reflect the risk that the United Kingdom was about to go to war. Previous potential flashpoints, including one in the Balkans the previous year, had been defused, and the City's initial response had been to downplay Franz Ferdinand's death as yet another localized problem.

Certainly the emollient words of the chancellor, David Lloyd George, to bankers in his Mansion House speech on 17 July 1914 went unmatched for complacency until Gordon Brown in 2007 hailed the dawning of a new golden age for the City just six weeks before the world began its rapid descent into the most severe financial crisis since the Wall Street Crash ushered in the Great Depression of the 1930s.

'There are always clouds in the international sky', Lloyd George said:

> You never get a perfectly blue sky in foreign affairs. There are clouds, even now, but having got out of the greater difficulties last year, we feel confident that common sense, the patience, the goodwill, the forbearance which enabled us to solve the greater and more urgent problems last year will enable us to pull through these problems at the present moment.[1]

To be fair, Lloyd George was not the only one caught unawares. In Cambridge, John Maynard Keynes admitted that his punt on shares in Canadian Pacific and Rio Tinto was 'courageous', but justified the investment to himself by noting, 'The odds appear to me slightly against Russia and Germany joining in.'[2]

Keynes was a better economist than he was military strategist (or speculator, for that matter), and on Sunday 2 August he was summoned to the Treasury by an official, Basil Blackett, so that his brains 'could be picked for your country's benefit'.[3] He travelled down to London in the sidecar of his brother-in-law's motor-cycle to find the stock market closed for an extended bank holiday, interest rates raised to the emergency level of 10 per cent, and the London accepting houses – the first division of the merchant banks – facing ruin. The prime minister, Herbert Asquith, by now resigned to a European war, described the City as being in a 'terrible state of depression and paralysis'. Lloyd George was no longer as sanguine as he had been a fortnight earlier, noting in his war memoirs:

> I saw Money before the war, saw it immediately after the outbreak of war. I lived with it for days and days and did my best to steady its nerve, for I knew how much depended on restoring confidence and I can say that Money was a frightened and trembling thing.[4]

Shocks to finance are always greater when they follow long periods of benign market conditions. That was true during the long boom of 1992 to 2007, and it was true of 1914, which followed two decades of calm. The City had its share of banking crises, most notably the collapse of Overend and Gurney in 1866, and the crisis at Baring in 1890, but for the next 24 years there was little to trouble the grandees of the Square Mile. Indeed, the arrival of large quantities of South African gold from 1893 onwards made it a good time to run a bank or a discount house. The United Kingdom's commercial banks had dwindled in number but increased in size in the second half of the nineteenth century, and they regulated the flow of credit in line with the disciplines of the gold standard, since the money supply could grow only if gold reserves increased. The assumption was that the system of fixed exchange rates would last forever, since it provided certainty for investors and acted as a bulwark against inflation. The cost of living in Britain was lower in 1914 than it had been in 1815, and both sterling and the dollar were fixed

in terms of gold, and therefore against each other, at
£1 = \$4.86.

'Between 1890 and 1896 the Bank's total bullion and
coin reserve doubled,' Douglas Jay wrote in his book
Sterling: A plea for moderation. 'The mid-1890s were the
years, not merely of the highest real value of the pound,
but also of the lowest short-term and long-term interest
rates, and of the highest gilt-edged prices, in the whole
of the 19th Century and for a long time afterwards.'[5]
Replicated a century later in the late 1990s and early
2000s, the strength of the pound drew investors to
London, and made imports cheaper and exports dearer.
As ever, it took something special to shock the City out of
its complacency.

Some City panics appear irrational, but this was one
of the occasions when there was good reason for alarm.
Following Austria's declaration of war against Serbia,
German banks started to withdraw deposits from London,
anticipating that Vienna's uncompromising line with
Belgrade would escalate into a full-scale European war.
Still worse, as far as the City was concerned, it became
obvious that discounted bills worth £350 million would
not be honoured by foreign investors. As in the sub-prime
mortgage crisis more than 90 years later, there was a risk of
systemic damage. The fear in 1914 was that the acceptance
houses would not have enough liquid assets to remain
open for business, and that their failure would have a
domino effect through the entire global financial system.
The Bank responded by raising the cost of borrowing and
by bailing out the discount houses. Parliament rushed
through legislation that allowed the Bank to print new
£1 and 10 shilling notes that were not backed by gold.
Members of the public were legally entitled to exchange
this hastily printed cash into gold at the Bank of England,
but were asked not to do so out of patriotic duty. There

was no run on the United Kingdom's bullion reserve, and sterling never officially left the gold standard. The stock exchange was eventually reopened, but not until early 1915, by which time 1600 men had volunteered for the Stock Exchange Battalion of Royal Fusiliers. There are no records of whether Keynes's 'courageous' punt proved successful.

Into the maelstrom: war and aftermath

For all the Great Powers, the declaration of war on Tuesday 4 August 1914 marked the end of one era and the beginning of another. By 1918 the Austro-Hungarian empire had been broken up; the Bolsheviks were in power in Russia; a Kaiser-less Germany was an unstable democracy. But the contrast was particularly marked in the United Kingdom. Before the 'lights went out all over Europe', as the foreign secretary, Sir Edward Grey put it, the United Kingdom was the most important country in the world, if no longer as clearly pre-eminent as in 1870. The City's global dominance befitted a country that had spawned the industrial revolution in the mid-eighteenth century, been the unchallenged workshop of the world in the mid-nineteenth century, and still exported more goods than any other country by the time war broke out. In the nineteenth century the Pax Britannica, enforced by the Royal Navy, had prevented all the great European powers from becoming involved in a world war.

On 4 August 1914 the United Kingdom was a country with little more than a night watchman state, and in which there were few restrictions on the liberty of the individual. Lloyd George's so-called People's Budget of 1909 had prompted a constitutional crisis, after the Conservative-dominated House of Lords rejected plans to pay for old age pensions by higher taxes on the wealthy, including a land tax. Asquith's Liberal government was pursuing a 'guns and butter' approach, seeking both to build new Dreadnought battleships in the naval arms race with Germany and to increase welfare spending. By modern standards, the commitments were easily affordable: the Exchequer's tax take in the last full year of peace, 1913–14, was just £200 million, and while non-military spending was on the rise it was still modest, particularly for a country with the United Kingdom's wealth and strategic reach. Defence still accounted for almost half of central government spending, but even with the naval arms race with Germany in full swing, defence made up only 3.1 per cent of national output, half its level in the mid-1960s.

The small state pension was payable only to those who achieved their full biblical span of three score years and ten, but even so it had made a marked impact on the number of old people living in penury; there was a 75 per cent drop in pauperism among the elderly between 1906 and 1914. The state paid also for the education of children until they were 13, and by the time war broke out there was a rudimentary system of national insurance to protect against ill-health and unemployment. Government debt as a share of gross domestic product (GDP) was low and falling, reaching 27.6 per cent in 1913. National debt was lower in nominal terms than it had been in 1815. Bond yields had risen but were still low. British government bonds, or 'gilts', were the equivalent of German bunds today: the safe haven that all investor sought at times of international tension.

A. J. P. Taylor once described how until August 1914 an Englishman who obeyed the law and showed a modicum of common sense could exist perfectly happily without noticing the existence of the state beyond the post office and the policeman:

> He had no official number or identity card. He could travel abroad or leave his country forever without a passport or any sort of official permission. He could exchange his money for any other currency without restriction or limit. He could buy goods from any country in the world on the same terms as he bought goods at home. For that matter, a foreigner could spend his life in this country without permit and without informing the police.[6]

A licence was required to drive a car, but as Kenneth Grahame illustrated with the road hog activities of Toad in *The Wind in the Willows*, there was no need to pass a test. Prewar scares about German spies infiltrating the United Kingdom had been fanned by popular fiction, such as *The Riddle of the Sands* by Erskine Childers and William Le Queux's *The Invasion of 1910*, and the state had responded by setting up a Secret Service Bureau in 1909. This initially amounted to just two officers, Mansfield Cumming and Vernon Kell, working out of unprepossessing offices in Victoria. The two men eventually became the heads of two separate organizations, the Secret Intelligence Service, responsible for operations abroad, and MI5, in charge of domestic security, but they ran their operations on shoestring budgets. A police state to rival Tsarist Russia it was not.

By the time the lights came on again in November 1918, the United Kingdom was an unrecognizable place from the one it had been in 1914. It would never have crossed Grey's mind to have proposed passports for travel abroad, since as a foreign secretary who much preferred to go fly fishing at his home in Hampshire than to attend an international meeting, he could never understand why anybody would want to leave the United Kingdom in the first place. But on Armistice Day they were required, and have been so ever since. The state was far bigger than in 1914, far more intrusive and far deeper in debt. Conscription had been introduced, and labour had been directed to increase the production of munitions and to prevent the United Kingdom from being starved into submission. For the first time, there were licensing laws designed to prevent drunkenness from impairing the war effort. Whitehall now even interfered with the time the sun rose and set.

The United Kingdom had lost her role as the world's only superpower to the United States, and the City had a rival in Wall Street. Old industries started to struggle, and it was not until the United Kingdom came off the gold standard permanently in 1931 that the conditions for economic recovery were put in place. Internationally the prewar balance of power collapsed, and the war was followed by a period in which the rise of aggressive militarist states was matched by the decline of both the Hapsburg and Ottoman empires and the liberal democratic powers of Western Europe, the United Kingdom and France. The two countries with the might to curb the ambitions of Germany, Japan and Italy – Russia and the United States – chose not to do so until both were forced into action in 1941. It took 31 years, from August 1914 to the Japanese surrender in August 1945, for a stable balance of power to re-emerge.

By the time those 31 years had passed the United Kingdom was no longer an economic superpower. Indeed, by 1945 the guns and butter strategy of the Attlee government – the welfare state plus the atomic bomb – could only be afforded thanks to American largesse. The United Kingdom went south rapidly between 1914 and

1945, decades marked by bursts of inflation, high levels of unemployment and tepid growth. It would be wrong, however, to imagine that the empire upon which the sun never set was lost in the Flanders mud. The United Kingdom would have seen her power and influence diminish in the twentieth century even had the Asquith government chosen to remain aloof from the military struggle in 1914, which was never a realistic option given the United Kingdom's role throughout history of opposing attempts by continental land powers to become too powerful, from Phillip II's Spain to Napoleon's France. The pace of decline would have been slower but the trend would have been the same. The United Kingdom had already been eclipsed economically by the United States and Germany by 1914; the First World War hastened a process that was happening anyway.

We should start with a brief snapshot of what life was like for our forebears in 1914, and make it plain that we are talking here about relative and not absolute decline. The United Kingdom is an immeasurably better off country, in almost every respect, than it was when Ireland was struggling for home rule and women did not have the vote.

Life expectancy at birth had increased by ten years since the 1850s, largely because improvements to sanitation and public health had removed the threat of waterborne diseases like cholera. The Great Stench of 1858, when the sewage in the River Thames became so vile that MPs had to stop work, had been a seminal moment, forcing Parliament to confront the epidemics that were rife in fast-growing and overcrowded industrial towns. Even so, a child born in 1914 would have expected to live only until England won the World Cup in 1966, and the extent of poverty was considered a national scandal. Seebohm Rowntree, reporting in 1901, found that there were two groups living in poverty: 13 per cent of the population was living in 'primary poverty', where families lacked sufficient earnings to 'obtain the minimum necessaries for the maintenance of merely physical efficiency', and a further 14 per cent in secondary poverty, where total earnings would 'be sufficient for the maintenance of merely physical efficiency were it not that some portion of it is absorbed by other expenditure, either useful or wasteful'.[7]

The Boer War from 1899 had brought home just how badly the working classes had been affected by long hours of work in factories and living in slums. Many showed stunting and other growth deficiencies; ill health was rife, and although the height of the average worker had increased as working and living conditions improved, the soldiers that sought to cluster round King Harold on Senlac hill in 1066 were taller than those that marched off to fight in Sir John French's British Expeditionary Force in 1914.

No novel set in the Edwardian era is complete without a depiction of just how materially deprived the working classes were in comparison with the poor of today. That was true not just of socialist tracts such as Robert Tressell's *The Ragged-Trousered Philanthropists* but of D. H. Lawrence's description of the miner Walter Morel in *Sons and Lovers*. For most families, there were few creature comforts: no central heating, gas lighting only, and inside flushing lavatories were a rarity. The thriller writer Ken Follett has a graphic account of the state of what would now be considered the third-world level of the United Kingdom's sanitation in his novel *Fall of Giants*, with the miners in a South Wales pit village only able to do their ablutions at a block halfway down the street:

A low brick hut with a corrugated iron roof was built

over a deep hole in the earth. The hut was divided into
two compartments, one for men and one for women.
Each compartment had a double seat, so that people
went to the toilet two by two. The smell was suffocating,
even when you experienced it every day or your life.
Billy always tried to breathe as little as possible while
he was inside, and came out gasping for air.[8]

Towards the end of Victoria's long reign there had
been a residential property boom, with a growing middle
class drifting out to suburbs built on the western edge of
cities, where they were upwind of the pollution from the
factories. But this was not an era when the newspapers
were dominated by stories about the property market:
90 per cent of the population rented their homes,
primarily from private landlords. There was far more
debate about the state of Britain's jerry-built housing
stock, since much of it consisted of slums thrown up to
house the miners, foundry workers and mill hands of
the industrial revolution. The years between the death
of Queen Victoria in 1901 and the outbreak of war saw
real house prices fall by 20 per cent, and the modern
concept that property values should always go up was
unknown.[9] The priority, illustrated by Lloyd George's
post-war election slogan of a 'land fit for heroes', was to
tackle squalor.

Losing ground: economic decline in the long view

Concern about the military threat posed by Germany was
reflected in the newspapers, which as today were prone
to 'sexing up' a story. The *Daily Mail* agreed to serialize Le
Queux's book, only to discover that his account had the
German army advancing through rural villages rather

than the big urban conurbations where the bulk of the paper's readers lived. Christopher Andrew's history of MI5 notes drily that in the interests of circulation this was tweaked to ensure that the Germans terrorised every major town in England from Sheffield to Chelmsford.[10]

The economic challenge posed by Germany and the United States was less remarked upon. This was a time when economic statistics were scarce and not especially reliable; the first attempt at measuring inflation through the retail prices index was not available until 1914, and there were no annual – let alone quarterly – growth figures. Modern historians have managed to piece together a comprehensive picture of an economy displaying signs of sclerosis, especially when compared with the advances of rival countries.[11] In France, the equivalent of the Edwardian Summer was *l'age d'or*, or the Golden Age, and it was appropriately named, because the French economy hummed along in the two decades before the outbreak of the First World War. The British economy, with the exception of the City, was going backwards: growth was 2.5 per cent a year between 1882 and 1899, dropping to just 1.1 per cent a year between 1899 and 1913.

The productivity growth rate declined from 1.4 per cent a year in mid-Victorian Britain to 0.5 per cent a year on average in the final four decades before the First World War. Real GDP per worker fell from 1.43 per cent a year between 1882 and 1899 to 0.31 per cent between 1899 and 1913. The United Kingdom's share of world trade fell as new challengers emerged. According to one account:

> In addition, imports of a wide range of goods increased as manufacturing industry developed overseas. In some fields, such as machine tools, chemicals and electrical

goods, other countries and particularly Germany and the United States appeared to demonstrate greater skills of invention and innovation and Britain increasingly bought their machinery and the goods which they made.[12]

In 1896, the United States had slightly higher steel production (just over 5 million tonnes) than the United Kingdom. By 1913, US steel production had increased sixfold to 32 million tonnes, while British steel production had less than doubled to just under 8 million tonnes. Even in industries in which the United Kingdom was the world leader, such as coal, there was a marked reluctance to use more modern methods. Half the coal mined in the United States was extracted using machinery; 92 per cent of the coal from British mines was hacked out of seams by colliers using picks.

The United Kingdom also lagged in terms of use of electricity – producing 2.5 gigawatt hours by 1913 against the 24.75 gigawatt hours of the United States and the 8 gigawatt hours of Germany. The United Kingdom's output of sulphuric acid – a proxy for the performance of the chemical industries and science-based industries more generally – was poor. As Andrew Tylecote notes in his book on economic cycles, the gap between the new big two and the United Kingdom was growing. 'In terms of size and technical capacity, the United States's only real rival should have been Germany. Britain, clearly, was no longer in contention, having performed on almost every yardstick very badly since 1870.'[13]

There are those who say this weakness should not be overstated. The United Kingdom had a smaller population than either the United States or Germany, and was not blessed with an abundance of natural resources, apart from coal and seas rich in fish. Only an accident of history could explain why the United Kingdom had produced a third of the world's manufactured goods in 1870, and it was inevitable that bigger, more populous and better endowed countries, such as the United States and Germany, would eventually forge ahead.

Just as the United States today can point to its pre-eminence in aerospace, computer hardware and film making, so in textiles and shipbuilding, the United Kingdom was still a world leader in 1914. UK shipyards on the Clyde and the Tyne were busy, and launched 60 per cent of the world's merchant shipping tonnage in the decades leading up to the First World War. Nor was it the case that the British economy was entirely dependent on the staples of coal, cotton and ships. In the early 1890s, before the arrival of the motor car, there were 5000 separate firms making bicycles. British entrepreneurs were also quick to grasp the potential of the car. Rolls-Royce was founded in 1903, Herbert Austin founded his company two years later, and production began at William Morris's Cowley plant in 1913. Further, the notion that the United Kingdom in the Edwardian era was an economy set in aspic is false. Incomes were rising, the middle class was growing in size, and the arrival of the cycle, the motor car and the suburban railway had encouraged people to move out of city centres. The two decades leading up to 1914 saw the emergence of retail chains: there were 1000 branches of WH Smith by the outbreak of war, while the chemist Boots and Freeman Hardy Willis, the footwear chain, could each boast 500 outlets.

Even one of the great financial scandals of the twentieth century – the Marconi affair – can be given a positive gloss, illustrating that the United Kingdom could be a pioneer of the new high-tech industries that emerged in the two decades before the First World War.

Seeing the potential for the growth of a firm that had quickly become a world leader in wireless telegraphy after its creation in 1897, Asquith's solicitor general, Rufus Isaacs, secretly bought shares in the American sister company of Marconi, which was due to be floated on the stock market in London on 19 April 1912. The flotation was already likely to be a success, but was given an unexpected boost when the *Titanic* issued a mayday on the new Marconi wireless system as it sank beneath the icy waves of the North Atlantic on 15 April. Isaacs sold some of his shares to two of his political chums, the chancellor, David Lloyd George, and the Liberal Party's chief whip, Alexander Murray. The shares duly soared, rising by 15 shillings on their first day of trading, although none of the three ministers made money because in their greed for still higher profits they hung on to their stakes for too long.

This was not the first time, and nor was it the last, that ministers of the Crown had found it hard to resist financial temptation. Of greater long-term significance was that Marconi provided an early glimpse of what would become a British trait over the next 100 years: the self-delusional belief that the brilliance of one individual was evidence of an industrial potential waiting to be tapped. Marconi, Austin, Morris, Messrs Rolls and Royce: these were all entrepreneurs of verve and imagination. Yet they were the exception rather than the rule, and they were working within the confines of an economy that was displaying the structural weakness familiar to this day: an over-dependence on the City, a lack of innovation, a dearth of skilled labour. German industry was much more alert to the importance of research and development, with many companies seeing the employment of science graduates as vital to their future prosperity, and the country created the institutions to train the new cadre of technocrats. By

1914, the United Kingdom had 9000 full-time scientists; Germany had 58,000. There were three times as many trained chemists in Germany as in the United Kingdom, a fact of far greater long-term significance than the United Kingdom's ability to unearth the odd maverick entrepreneur.[14] The advantages of being the first nation to have industrialized were tossed away by a failure to adapt to changing economic circumstances and to much stiffer competition, in the final third of the nineteenth century.

Indeed, the United Kingdom's loss of industrial dominance had been predicted for more than half a century before first the United States and then Germany swept past. There had been warnings as early as the 1830s that the Americans, who since Alexander Hamilton's period as treasury secretary in the 1790s had displayed an ambition to do more than exchange agricultural produce for British industrial goods, needed to be watched. In the 1850s and 1860s, in the immediate aftermath of the showcasing of the United Kingdom's industrial supremacy in the Great Exhibition, Dr Lyon Playfair said decline was inevitable without a change in approach. Playfair had an explanation for the failure of UK manufacturers to scoop as many awards at the Paris exhibition of 1867 as they had when Joseph Paxton had erected the Crystal Palace in Hyde Park 16 years earlier: 'The one cause of this inferiority upon which there was most unanimity is that France, Prussia, Austria, Belgium and Switzerland possess good systems of industrial education for the masters and managers of factories and that England possesses none.'[15]

By the 1880s, a Royal Commission reported that the Europeans had surpassed the United Kingdom in science-based industries and were more efficient in the way they organized their manufacturing processes: 'The one point in which Germany is overwhelmingly superior to England is in schools, and in the education of all classes of the people. The dense ignorance so common among workmen in England is unknown' [16]

At first these weaknesses were disguised, with the US rise to industrial pre-eminence delayed by the civil war of 1861–65 and the unification of Germany occurring only after Bismarck's victory in the war against France in 1871. But gradually the loss of competitiveness did become evident, and it was starkly illustrated when the United Kingdom had to put the economy on a war footing in 1914. The UK share of world trade in manufactures had fallen from 31 per cent in 1870 to 14 per cent in 1914, by which time Germany was producing twice as much steel as the United Kingdom. Huge imports of US steel alone prevented Germany from inflicting a knock-out blow against the United Kingdom by 1916, according to official records. This vulnerability explains why Lloyd George was moved from the Treasury to run the Ministry of Munitions in 1915. Confronted with the possibility of military defeat, lessons were learned. According to Correlli Barnett:

> The munitions crisis in the first years of the Great War brought home to the government just how dependent Britain had become on foreign imports of advanced technology – machine-tools, aero-engines, sparking plugs, ball-bearings, magnetos, dyes and drugs, scientific instruments and much else.[17]

Britain being Britain, however, the lessons were just as quickly forgotten once the crisis was over.

Germany had achieved industrial take-off in the 1870s, but had not been content simply to close the gap with the United Kingdom in the industries that had formed the basis for the first industrial revolution in the mid-eighteenth century. Coal and steel production in the Ruhr valley were important, as were the shipyards of Kiel, but Germany was also much more alert to the opportunities afforded by the next stage of technological development. The electrical and chemical industries showed particularly impressive growth. Werner Siemens had invented the electric dynamo in 1866, and German companies were much quicker to exploit this new form of energy and light than their British counterparts. By the outbreak of war, half the world's trade in electrical products had begun in German factories, dominated by two fast-growing companies, Siemens-Schuckert Werke and AEG.

The close links between science and industry paid off, spawning new products – some of which, such as the discovery of synthetic ammonia needed to provide nitrates for munitions, were vital during the war when the Royal Navy's blockade prevented the imports of raw materials. The modern shape of German manufacturing was established during this period, with a growing emphasis on high-quality finished goods, many of them for export. In 1873, less than 40 per cent of German exports were finished manufactured products; by 1913 this had risen to almost two-thirds.

Barnett is one of the many historians who have contrasted Germany's dynamism with the sluggishness of the UK response. Two out of five workers in the United Kingdom were employed in manufacturing on the outbreak of war in 1914, but there were three times as many men in domestic service as in factories producing chemicals. As they had been for the past century and more, textiles and clothing were the biggest industrial employers:

In the early 1890s, only five per cent of the United Kingdom's industrial labour force were working in the new technologies, which accounted for seven per cent of her exports; 25 per cent of her labour force was locked up in older technologies such as coal, iron and steel, and textiles, which still accounted for 70 per cent of her exports. She had begun to retreat from the highly competitive but fast-growing markets of the industrial world such as Europe and North America into the refuges offered by less exacting but slow-growing markets in backward regions of the world, such as the British Empire or South America.[18]

Britain was looking south as well as Going South.

There were a number of lessons to be learned from Germany, had business and policy makers been less hidebound. It was not just that Germany had a large, growing and mobile population. There were close links between industry and finance; the state was ready to promote industrial growth through tariffs and subsidies; the country was blessed with a happy combination of a skilled, educated workforce and an innovative management willing and eager to learn from international best practice. Britain, by contrast, was slow to move with the times, clinging on to old industries and outmoded practices.

As with the Asian tiger economies in the postwar era, German industrial expansion was fostered by the encouragement of cartels, something frowned upon in laissez-faire Britain. In the chemicals and electrical engineering sectors, cartels led to larger firms, which found it easier to raise the capital necessary for expensive new product development. The United Kingdom's early industrial lead had been achieved with only modest levels of investment: around 10 per cent of national output was spent in the early nineteenth century on digging the coal mines and equipping the cotton mills. The next generation of products being developed at the end of the nineteenth century and the early years of the twentieth century needed higher levels of capital. Germany and the United States both outspent the United Kingdom, devoting a higher share of national output to manufacturing investment during this period. The long, depressing history of British companies sweating assets, even when obsolete, dates back to this period. For a long time the United Kingdom had invested a far smaller share of its national output than rival countries: at 9 per cent of GDP its investment rate was half that of the United States, Germany and France.

Those familiar with the United Kingdom's post Second World War economic history often point despairingly to the products – like the jet engine – that were invented in Britain but exploited elsewhere. What is less well known is that this had been happening since the second half of the nineteenth century. Coal tar dyes were discovered in Britain but by the time of the First World War Germany had forged an unassailable lead in the production of them, as well as in associated products such as explosives and pharmaceuticals. Economic historians have noted that this was no innate reason why this should have been so, since the raw materials needed for the manufacturing process were as available in Britain as in Germany, and that the United Kingdom's poor performance was the result of a lack of chemists and entrepreneurs.

Worse still was the case of the Solvay ammonia-soda process, clearly superior to the older Leblanc process of alkali production, yet neglected by British firms while the rest of the advanced world changed over.

Brunner Mond, a firm founded by immigrants, did
adopt the newer process, but most other British firms
stuck to their traditional method, and attempted to
hold up their declining market share by combining in
one near-monopoly firm, United Alkali.[19]

The United Kingdom certainly invested a great deal in
the pre-First World War decades, but much of the capital
flowed overseas. Overseas investments rose from £1.2
billion in 1870, with an income stream of £44 million, to
£4 billion by 1914, generating £200 million in income.
The United Kingdom was responsible for 44 per cent of
foreign investment in 1914, with the proceeds helping to
mask the underlying problems of an economy in which
there was no new generation of managers and technocrats
coming through with the ability to challenge the status
quo. The glories of the Edwardian summer were lost
on the 2.4 million people who left the country between
1900 and 1914. The United Kingdom exported people
as well as money, helping to explain the economy's lack
of dynamism.

By the time of Sarajevo, the financialization of the
British economy was well under way. The eclipse of the
United Kingdom's manufacturers was accompanied
by the hegemony of her financiers, who accounted for
almost half of the foreign investment around the globe.
Profits on these overseas investments meant the balance
of payments was in healthy surplus, but the hollowing
out of UK manufacturing had already started.

The United Kingdom had nothing to compare with
the scientific and technological institutes already set
up in the United States, Germany and Switzerland,
although a National Physical Laboratory was proposed
at the end of the nineteenth century, and there was a
greater degree of urgency about the United Kingdom's

perceived deficit in education, compared with not just Germany but France too.

Despite the jingoistic mood, these developments did not go entirely unremarked, and reforms were not only proposed, but in some cases acted upon. Sharpened by the pyrrhic victory in the Boer War, the loss of export markets to US, German and French rivals prompted a limited degree of national self-criticism. Just as American bookshops were awash with books warning of the rise of Japan in the 1980s and the threat posed by China's growing industrial strength in the 2000s, so at the end of Victoria's reign and in the early Edwardian period books were published with titles such as *Made in Germany* and *American Invaders*.

Joseph Chamberlain had decided that Birmingham should have a university that would provide a new form of higher education designed to service the need for graduates comfortable with industry and technology. Even then, there was a big gap between state funding of higher education in the United Kingdom and Germany. In 1897, the United Kingdom provided grants of £26,000 to universities; Prussia alone spent £476,000. Despite the breast-beating, the gulf was never bridged.

There was no state-funded education in the United Kingdom until 1902, and by the time of the First World War three-quarters of the young people in England and Wales were receiving no full-time or part-time education and no training.[20] The economic model that had served the United Kingdom well for 150 years was breaking down, but it is in the nature of things that those responsible for running a country that considers itself a cut above the rest have difficulty in recognizing, or admitting, that something is going wrong. To understand why that should be, it is necessary to look briefly at why the United Kingdom had been the first country to industrialize.

Why us? Causes and legacy of the industrial revolution

Estimates vary of when the United Kingdom achieved
economic 'take off', but most accounts point to the wave
of technological advance – the steam engine, the water
mule, the spinning jenny – of the eighteenth century.
Josiah Wedgwood pioneered mass-production factories
and modern marketing techniques in the 1770s, and
this was followed by more than half a century of rapid
industrial expansion.

In truth, the origins of the industrial revolution go back
much further, to the Reformation of the 1530s and the
civil war of the 1640s. It was Henry VIII's lack of money
to fight expensive wars, as much as his anger at Rome
for attempting to prevent his divorce from Catherine of
Aragon, that prompted the seizure of church lands in
the dissolution of the monasteries and their disposal to
a new merchant class. Hilary Mantel's study of Thomas
Cromwell in her novel *Wolf Hall* shows how the coming
men were as adept at adding up a row of figures as they
were at handling a sword, and were loathed for it by
the families that could trace their lineage back to the
Norman conquest. 'Love your neighbour. Study the
market. Increase the spread of benevolence. Bring in
better figures next year', Cromwell says at one point.[21]

An even bigger obstacle to industrialization was
removed when Parliament defeated the Crown in the
civil war. Christopher Hill says the conflict was pivotal
in the development of modern British capitalism,
because it removed the ability of a conservative
aristocracy to resist pressure for economic change.[22]
By the mid-seventeenth century, the United Kingdom
was a constitutional monarchy with a capitalist class
that had access to money, land and power. Whereas
potential rivals – France, Prussia, Russia – remained

autocratic and feudal monarchies, the United Kingdom started to piece together the building blocks for rapid advance: a system of property rights, a central bank, and crucially, protection for its infant industries. The British variant of capitalism proved to be different from those that came later: the break with Rome in the sixteenth century and the strength of the noncomformist tradition meant there was a suspicion of centralized authority. British industrialists were pragmatists and empiricists, preferring to do things their own way and inclined to stick to a winning formula. There were links between science and industry, but there was a tendency to rely on the ability of the self-made man to solve problems through trial and error.

Being first to industrialize proved to be both an advantage and a curse. The advantage was that the United Kingdom exerted more power and influence for longer than would have been warranted by a small nation of her size. In the years immediately after the battle of Waterloo, there was genuine industrial dynamism, even if the social costs were high. Factory output grew at an average annual rate of 4 per cent between 1820 and 1840, then slowed slightly to 3 per cent a year on average in the next three decades.

The curse was that by the middle of the nineteenth century Britain was stuck with an industrial model that relied heavily on old technology – steam, coal and iron. In retrospect, the challenge facing the magnates of Victorian Britain was plain. They could ditch the exhausted model rapidly, and use their position as world leaders to adopt the new materials and production techniques becoming available, or they could wait until other countries had made a go of the 'newfangled ideas' and only respond when it was too late. Britain took the latter course. Its economic hegemony was at its zenith at around the time of the Second Reform Bill in 1867, but in the 1870s and 1880s there was a marked decline in the growth rate of manufacturing, with industrial output rising at only 1.5 per cent a year on average, far slower than Germany or the United States. Worse was to follow: when adjusted for inflation, output per worker grew at just 0.3 per cent a year between 1899 and 1913, its slowest rate for a century.

In retrospect, what is remarkable about the century from Waterloo to Sarajevo is that it took so long for evidence to appear that the economy was Going South. The explanation lies in the stable balance of power, guaranteed by the United Kingdom's maritime strength, which ensured this was a century of peace in which the classical doctrines of free movement of capital, goods and people held sway. The end of the Napoleonic war left the United Kingdom holding the ring in a Great Power system in which no continental country could achieve or even seek dominance. Formally through the congress system and the concert of powers, and informally using her naval power, she could ensure that any wars that took place were local affairs.

Historians have noted the contrast between the lack of generalized conflict in the nineteenth century and the bellicosity of the 1914–45 period. Eric Hobsbawm, for instance, commented:

> In 1914 there had been no major war for a century, that is to say, a war in which all, or even a majority of, major powers had been involved, the major players in the international game at that time being the six European great powers (Britain, France, Austria-Hungary, Prussia – after 1871 enlarged into Germany – and, after it was unified, Italy), the USA and Japan. There had been only one brief war in which more than two

of the major powers had been in battle, the Crimean War (1854–6) between Russia on one side, Britain and France on the other. Moreover most wars involving major powers at all had been comparatively quick. Much the longest of them was not an international conflict but a civil war within the USA (1861–65). There had been no world wars at all. All this changed in 1914. The First World War involved *all* major powers and indeed all European states except Spain, the Netherlands, the three Scandinavian countries and Switzerland.[23]

The era of the classical gold standard came at the end of this period: it only really applied to the three or four centuries before the First World War. Niall Ferguson has noted that it was characterized by fixed exchange rates, nearly balanced budgets, converging interest rates and – beyond the confines of the British Empire – rising protectionism: 'The key to the relative stability of the entire edifice was no mystery. It was the absence of a major war; for it was war which more than any other factor – including harvest failure – traditionally unbalanced budgets.'[24] The Napoleonic Wars had wrecked the United Kingdom's public finances, leaving the country with a national debt that was 250 per cent of GDP, four times as high as that of today. A century of peace, growth and government frugality led to a steady improvement, and in only four years from 1815 to the end of the nineteenth century did the United Kingdom run a budget deficit of more than 1 per cent of GDP.

Ferguson's reference to rising protectionism is important. Protectionism hastened the economic growth of Germany, the United States and Japan, and this strength put the nineteenth-century balance of power at increasing risk. Instead of a stable system, with Great Britain the global hegemon above a number of European states of similar size and influence, there was a growing disparity between the major powers. As we have seen, the United States had overtaken the United Kingdom as an economic superpower by the end of the nineteenth century, having used an aggressive system of tariffs to industrialize. The unification of Germany, the end of serfdom in Russia and the Meiji revolution in Japan all signified countries that were on the rise. By contrast, the Austro-Hungarian and Ottoman economies were in decline. What one historian has called a 'grave and shifting inequality in the distribution of effective power between the leading states of the world' created the conditions for two world wars in the first half of the twentieth century, because Germany was able to use its growing strength to become Europe's master.[25] But it also meant that the weaknesses of the British economy –its narrow range of products, its lack of flexibility, its dysfunctional labour relations, its lack of management skills – were finally, and brutally, exposed.

Paul Kennedy has noted that after 1870, the shifting of the balance of global forces eroded British supremacy in two ways. The first was that the United Kingdom, as the established superpower, had more to lose in relative terms than any other country from the economic and military clout that rapid industrialization provided to her rivals. 'The second, interacting weakness was less immediate and dramatic, but perhaps even more serious. It was the erosion of the United Kingdom's industrial and commercial pre-eminence, upon which, in the last resort, its naval, military and imperial strength rested.'[26]

Other countries learned lessons from the methods used by the United Kingdom to encourage her own manufacturing strength from the sixteenth century onwards. Wool exports were banned in the reign of Elizabeth I, making it harder for the Dutch to compete with British clothmaking. The Navigation Act stipulated that all trade with Britain should be carried in British ships. The first prime minister, Robert Walpole, brought in legislation in 1721 that protected British manufacturing from foreign competition. In a period when the British economy was going north – from 1700 to 1850 – protectionism was used actively, and the benefits of doing so were not lost on other countries. Indeed, as one economist has noted, the British route to industrial take-off, which relied in 1820 on manufacturing tariffs of 45–55 per cent at a time when those in continental Europe ranged between 8 and 20 per cent, has been followed slavishly to this day:

> Tariffs on imported manufactured goods were significantly raised, while tariffs on raw materials used for manufacture were lowered or even dropped altogether. These policies are strikingly similar to those used with such success by the 'miracle' economies of East Asia such as Japan, Korea and Taiwan, after the Second World War.[27]

It was only from the repeal of the Corn Laws in 1846 that protectionism was replaced by free trade, because by this stage Britain's domination seemed unassailable. The United States, too, waited until it was indisputably the most powerful economy in the world before embracing free trade, although the conversion was never as absolute as it was in mid-Victorian Britain. What happened over time was that high tariffs priced British goods out of the US and European markets, and eventually UK firms also saw themselves squeezed out of their home market by cheaper imports. In 1880, the United Kingdom's share of world manufacturing output stood at 23 per cent; by 1913 this had dropped by ten percentage points. There was a similar decline – from 23 per cent to 14 per cent – in the UK share of world trade: 'In terms of industrial muscle, both the US and Germany had moved ahead. The "workshop of the world" was now in third place, not because it wasn't growing, but because others were growing faster.'[28]

The United Kingdom believed in free trade but her rivals did not. The United States had overtaken the United Kingdom as the world's biggest manufacturer using an industrial tariff that reached almost 50 per cent in the second half of the nineteenth century. In 1902, when free trade was challenged by Joseph Chamberlain's tariff reform movement, manufacturing tariffs were 131 per cent in Russia, 73 per cent in the United States, 34 per cent in France and 25 per cent in Germany. 'There was a growing sentiment within the commercial community as well as sections of the Foreign Office that Britain was entering a new era of international rivalry with one arm tied behind its back.'[29]

The United Kingdom sat back and expected other nations to see the benefits of free trade for themselves. Unlike the United States after 1945, it did not use its economic strength to force down tariffs, and nor did it have at its disposal the international organizations set up after the Second World War, in particular the General Agreement on Tariffs and Trade (GATT), to help force the issue. To the United Kingdom's dismay, most of her rivals proved strangely resistant to the idea of free trade in the decades running up to the First World War, a period that was marked by frequent tit-for-tat bouts of tariff escalation. All the major nations apart from the United Kingdom – the United States, Germany, France, Italy, Russia and Canada – were involved.

Protectionism was not always an advantage. The pioneering work of Daimler and Benz in the motor industry did not prevent France from taking an early lead over Germany in car production. As with the Common Agricultural Policy, high prices for the domestic market were accompanied by the dumping of excess output abroad. So while German car makers were paying 140 marks a tonne for their steel, firms abroad could buy it for 100 marks a tonne.

Yet the United Kingdom had perhaps the worst of all worlds. Free trade opened up domestic manufacturing to foreign competition, but industry tended to behave as if it were protected, and by 1914 the economy was labouring under the weight of five significant weaknesses. The first was that it was slow to change. Indeed there may have been deep-seated historic and cultural factors that made British industry particularly unsuited to developing the large-scale industrial complexes that were coming to the fore in the late nineteenth century and blossomed as the 'Fordist' method of mass production in the first half of the twentieth century. While Britain was producing exquisite Rolls-Royces for a tiny pre-war elite, Henry Ford had worked out how to mass produce cars and ensure that those who made them could drive what was coming off their own assembly lines.

The second weakness, the conservatism of Britain's business elite, compounded the first. The safe option was to stick to what Britain had done best: hew coal out of the ground; import cotton from India and America for the cotton mills of Lancashire; build ships and other bits of heavy machinery. Rather than reinvest the profits from the first industrial revolution in new plant and machinery at home, the capital was increasingly exported abroad where returns looked juicier. At home, there was a tendency of management and workers to collude, preferring a quiet life rather than take the risks involved in adapting to new technologies.

This was all the more dangerous in a global economic environment where the United Kingdom was committed to free trade and her rivals were not. As Trentmann puts it:

> Britain could do little to strip its main trading partners and geo-political rivals in the late 19th Century of their neo-mercantilist strategies. Trade was, indeed, not a level playing field, but it was increasingly Britain which was finding itself at the lower end. And, from, the 1890s, the naval supremacy which had supported Britain's Free Trade Empire was being threatened by foreign gunboats and submarines.[30]

This was the third reason for the more far-sighted Edwardians to suspect that there could be trouble ahead.

For the most part, though, the assumption was that life would go on as before. The United Kingdom, of course, remained an important industrial power, just as the United States does today despite its trade deficit with China. Manufacturing exports comfortably exceeded imports. The balance of payments was in the black. The empire was massive; the Royal Navy patrolled the seven oceans. Weakness number four was the national mood of complacency, widespread across the nation despite the occasional soul-searching.

Finally, and here we return to the start of this chapter, the City was growing in weight and importance at the expense of industry. In only one period of the United Kingdom's economic history has finance been clearly subservient to manufacturing, and it is no coincidence that this was the era when Britain was rapidly industrializing. As now, the country had a regional divide in the first half of the nineteenth century, but it was the rural counties below the line from the Wash to the Severn estuary that were poor. By 1914, the centre of gravity of the economy had already shifted back to the capital, with an increasing reliance on the profits from foreign direct investment and speculation in overseas markets to bolster the balance of payments. For one brief period, the economy had been heading north. It was already starting to head south again.

Chapter 2

June 2014 in Lagos-on-Thames

> We were young, good looking and stupid. Now we're just stupid.
>
> Mick Jagger, speaking at the
> Cannes Film Festival, 19 May 2010

> The decadent international but individualistic capitalism in the hands of which we found ourselves after the war is not a success. It is not intelligent. It is not beautiful. It is not just. It is not virtuous. And it doesn't deliver the goods. In short, we dislike it, and we are beginning to despise it.
>
> John Maynard Keynes,
> *National Self-Sufficiency*, 1933

> Unreal City,
> Under the brown fog of a winter dawn,
> A crowd flowed over London Bridge, so many,
> I had not thought death had undone so many.
> Sighs, short and infrequent, were exhaled,
> And each man fixed his eyes before his feet.
> Flowed up the hill and down King William Street,
> To where Saint Mary Woolnoth kept the hours
> With a dead sound on the final stroke of nine.
>
> T. S. Eliot, *The Waste Land*, 1922

The crowd still flows over London Bridge and down King William Street to the corner of Lombard Street where St Mary Woolnoth stands. Were Eliot to stand on the steps of the Royal Exchange in August 2014, the vista would not be that different from a century earlier, and even though the horse-drawn omnibus has been replaced by the Routemaster double-decker, the traffic would not move much more quickly. The great poet, a fearful snob, would be thankful not to be able to see from his standpoint the former NatWest Tower, the Gherkin, the Shard or any of the other vulgar expressions of the City's self-confidence, but he might notice in front of the statue of the duke of Wellington at the foot of the Royal Exchange's steps the war memorial to those who died in the Great War. The only obvious sign that 100 years has come and gone is the postmodern building plonked at the end of Cheapside by the architect Sir James Stirling after a planning battle in the 1980s. Not a patch on Nicholas Hawksmoor's St Mary Woolnoth, Eliot might well think.

Physically, the heart of the Square Mile looks the same jumble of mighty thoroughfares and back alleys that it was in the days of Dickens and Trollope. Those who stream across London Bridge today would spot that the Pool of London is no longer choked with ships bringing cargo to the capital, but the Old Lady of Threadneedle Street still looms to the right, led by a new governor following the departure of Sir Mervyn (now Lord) King in the summer of 2013. The Mansion House is off to the left and Cheapside still rises gently up the hill towards St Paul's Cathedral. Closer inspection shows that the Royal Exchange is a high-class shopping mall, where City workers can browse at lunchtime for Hermès scarves, Gucci handbags, LK Bennett shoes and Agent Provocateur underwear.

Much, though, has changed. The Royal Exchange is no longer the hub of the City, let alone the beating heart of the most powerful nation on earth. London remains one of the globe's three financial centres, dominating that slice of the day after night falls in Tokyo and before day breaks in New York. But the City's centre of gravity has moved several miles east to Canary Wharf on the Isle of Dogs, where most of the investment banks have their European homes, and west to the cluster of hedge funds behind their discreet nameplates in Mayfair. Only a few of the biggest financial institutions are now British-owned, the so-called Wimbledon effect, in which London hosts the world's best but lacks domestic champions of its own.

It has been three-quarters of a century since Fred Perry was the last British man to capture the men's singles title on the grass courts of SW19, in the era when sterling could seriously be considered the world's premier reserve currency. Some would say the pound never recovered from the First World War, when Britain's assets were spent on more than four years of fighting on the Western Front. From the moment the United Kingdom finally came off the gold standard in 1931, the story has been one of devaluations of the currency once in every generation in an attempt to price uncompetitive exports back into global markets: officially in 1949, 1967 and 1992; as a result of market forces in 1976, and again in 2007, when the onset of the global financial crisis saw the pound depreciate by 30 per cent.

Lombard Street has changed too. Of the five big high-street banks, one is operated out of Hong Kong, one out of Madrid, and two out of the Treasury in Horse Guards Road. The financial crisis of 2007–08 resulted in two banks – Lloyds and the Royal Bank of Scotland (RBS) – being part-nationalized by the government, with all the others taking advantage of various Bank of England schemes that allowed them to trade in worthless 'assets' for gilt-backed securities and to fill their coffers with newly minted electronic money. David Cameron's government has for the past four years harboured the desire of returning Lloyds and RBS to the private sector, but has been unable to do so because the shares are still worth considerably less than Gordon Brown's government paid for them. Northern Rock, the bank that became a symbol of the financial crisis when it suffered the first run on a high-street clearer in more than 140 years, is now owned by Sir Richard Branson's Virgin group, but Sir Richard did better out of the deal than the UK taxpayer, picking up the Rock for little more than half the money pumped in by the then Labour government after it was nationalized in 2008.

The cotton and woollen mills are long gone, as are many of the companies in the electronics and motor vehicle sectors that flourished briefly in the 1930s and again after the Second World War. The decline of British manufacturing is symbolized by the fate of Longbridge in Birmingham. At the end of the 1960s it was the largest car plant in the world, employing 250,000 people, but after the collapse of MG Rover in 2005 most of the site was sold off for commercial and residential use. A few car workers are still employed at Longbridge, but they are employed by the Shanghai Automotive Industrial Corporation. The old Morris plant at Cowley, on the outskirts of Oxford, has survived, and is still successfully churning out the Minis that, along with Mary Quant dresses and the Beatles, were the symbols of the Swinging Sixties. The plant, though, is owned by BMW of Bavaria. It is a similar story for Jaguar and Land Rover, run by the Indian company Tata. In 2010, a comedy film (*Made in Dagenham*) was released about the attempts of women working in the upholstery shop at the Ford plant in Dagenham in the 1960s to secure equal pay. By the time it was screened, the factory had stopped assembling cars and needed just one-tenth of the workforce it had in the 1960s, when manufacturing employment peaked in the United Kingdom.

Industrial decline set in during the 1970s, but even when Margaret Thatcher became prime minister in 1979 there was still a large indigenous car industry, GEC was still expanding under the acquisitive stewardship of Arnold Weinstock, Raleigh bicycles were being made in Nottingham rather than Vietnam, and china was still being made in Stoke-on-Trent. Since the late 1970s deindustrialization has accelerated, and Britain's manufacturing base has been hollowed out by three deep recessions.

Gone too is the oil that briefly in the 1970s and 1980s offered the promise of a windfall to finance industrial regeneration. In 2014 the oil wells are all but dry, so Britain is no longer a beneficiary of high crude prices caused by strong demand from the emerging world and the gradual decline in production from fields where oil is cheap to extract. Oil and gas are imported from Russia and the Middle East, nuclear power stations are coming to their end of their lives, and Britain has only a handful of working coal mines. The words used by Sir Edward Grey in 1914 now have a more literal meaning: the lights are about to go out.

The United Kingdom is stuck in its deepest, longest and toughest recession since the Second World War. National output in 2014 is still below where it was when the downturn started in 2008, having fallen by more than 7 per cent during the first slump of 2008–09, then enduring a second, equally painful slide backwards. Ministers blame the second leg of the downturn on the slow-motion disintegration of the eurozone, but the legacy of debt, Britain's susceptibility to inflation, an intense squeeze on real incomes and the inability of the banking system to provide credit to small businesses are, if anything, more important factors.

The United Kingdom has been in an economic depression for seven years, a longer period of below-par growth even than that of the Great Slump in the 1930s. Three-quarters of the way through a lost decade, unemployment is well above 3 million and rising. Youth unemployment has reached the levels last seen in the 1980s; outbreaks of social unrest are regular occurrences. For the past five years, politicians of all parties have talked about the need to rebalance the economy, to wean the country off its dependence on private and public debt, so that growth can be led by exports, investment and what in happier times the increasingly beleaguered chancellor, George Osborne, called the 'march of the makers'. There is, in August 2014, not the remotest sign of this happening. Deprived of its traditional sources of growth – the speculative activities of the City of London, the money extracted from an overheating housing market to finance consumer spending on the never-never, construction, and public spending – the UK economy is dead in the water.

The postwar welfare state is under threat, as it becomes clear that a de-developing nation can no longer afford the generous public provision that befits an advanced economy. Over the years, policy makers have tried a variety of ways to make UK capitalism work. In the 1980s, they cut wages and removed the rights of trade unions. In the 1990s, they first joined and then left the European Exchange Rate Mechanism. In the 2000s, they persuaded the public to load up on debt. None of the remedies worked, at least not for long. Now, in 2014, free-market think-tanks are urging ministers to be bold, to shrink the state not to where it was in 1914 when Asquith was prime minister, but to the levels last seen when Neville Chamberlain returned from Munich with his 'piece of paper' in September 1938. The Britain of 2014 is a sombre, troubled country. The foreign journalists who flew into London to do their pieces about Swinging Britain in the 1960s and Cool Britannia in the 1990s now come to write long think pieces about what a de-developing country looks like.

What they find is a country that has been through its fourth – and toughest – recession since the Second World War. The depth of the slump, which saw activity drop by 5 per cent in one year alone, prompted hopes that the economy would bounce back quickly, as it had after the sharp slowdowns of the mid-1970s, the early 1980s and early 1990s. There have been times, in 2010 for example, when the pace of growth appeared to quicken, but these proved to be will o' the wisps.

On his arrival at the Treasury in May 2010, George Osborne said the reason the United Kingdom had the biggest budget deficit of any member of the Group of 20 leading economies was that it had the most unbalanced economy in the G20. That remains the case, because despite the government's claims that growth will be export-led, the UK manufacturing base is now so shrivelled at just 10 per cent of the nation's output that it cannot take advantage of a depreciating currency. The United Kingdom exports as much to Ireland, one of the few countries in Western Europe in a more parlous state, as it does to China, India, Brazil and Russia put together.

Around three-quarters of the growth in the boom years that preceded the financial crash came from financial services, the housing market, the construction sector, public spending and retail. All of them are struggling in an environment where household incomes are falling, banks are not lending, and the government is cutting spending. Policy makers are at their wits' end after trying all the conventional means of boosting the economy, and quite a few unconventional ones as well. Interest rates were reduced to 0.5 per cent in early 2009, a level not seen since the Bank of England was founded in 1694, and have been left there for five years. The Treasury has borrowed £700 billion since the start of the financial crisis. Cranking up the electronic printing presses has added a further £500 billion through the process known as quantitative easing, a programme under which the Old Lady of Threadneedle Street buys gilts from commercial banks in exchange for cash. Never has there been a monetary and fiscal stimulus like it.

And never has stimulus been so ineffective. Since the start of the crisis, the United Kingdom has borrowed more in seven years than in all its previous history. It has impoverished savers by pegging the bank rate well below the level of inflation, and indulged in the sort of money creation policies normally associated with Germany in 1923, Latin American banana republics in the 1970s, and more latterly, Robert Mugabe's Zimbabwe. Even so, the economy in 2014 is still only growing at 1.5 per cent a year, not nearly fast enough to find work for the young people entering the workforce and to soak up those losing their jobs in a shrunken public sector.

Historically, the United Kingdom has grown on average by about 2.5 per cent a year since the Second World War, so on that basis the level of gross domestic product (GDP) should be at least 15 per cent higher than it was when the recession began in 2008. Instead, it is still 1–2 per cent smaller, an underperformance of unprecedented proportions. As the hundredth anniversary of the outbreak of the Great War looms, policy makers talk of how they will eventually win their own war of attrition, and announce plans for the latest big push, involving the distribution of time-limited money – similar to those handed out by the John Lewis Partnership as loyalty rewards to its customers – in an attempt to get consumers spending.

It is at this point that the penny finally drops. The United Kingdom is the dead parrot in the famous *Monty Python* sketch, where the complaining customer demands to know why the Norwegian blue has been nailed to its perch and is told by the pet shop owner that had he not indulged in some rudimentary carpentry, the bird would have 'nuzzled up to those bars, bent 'em apart with its beak and Voom!' To which the customer replies, 'Voom? Mate, this bird wouldn't voom if you put four million volts through it! 'E's bleedin' demised!'[1]

The United Kingdom is, of course, a much richer country than it was in 1914, as is every other country on the planet. People enjoy creature comforts their forebears could barely imagine. They can freeze food to stop it going off, travel across the Atlantic in seven hours, read books on portable computer screens, take antibiotics when they are sick, and look forward to being active into their eighties. But there has been a century of relative decline. The empire on which the sun never set is no more, and the United Kingdom has slipped down almost every international league table: for manufacturing strength, for the size of its economy and for living standards. At first it was the other countries of the North that did the overtaking: the United States, Germany, Japan, the Nordic nations, but more latterly the rates of growth being clocked up in China and India suggest that it will only be two or three decades before the world's first and second most populous countries have caught up too.

These trends have been evident for decades, but the inability of the United Kingdom to pull itself out of its long economic depression has, for the first time since the semi-permanent state of emergency in the 1970s, left the sense that absolute rather than just relative decline has set in. As in many developing countries, there are parts of Britain where it is not advisable to walk the streets after dark. The rich have retreated into their gated communities while the public libraries close. Firefighters

refuse to use lifting gear to rescue members of the public
because health and safety regulations say it should only
be used for their own staff. Britain has become something
of a joke country where nothing seems to work properly.
The nation where Stephenson produced the first proper
railway now grinds to a halt when there is a dusting of
snow. Trains don't run; airports turn away passengers
because the managers skimp on snow ploughs.

To some, all this comes as no surprise. Down the
years, there have been repeated warnings about the
degeneracy of Britain's growth model, and the vulnerability
of the economy to a world where living on tick is no longer
an option.

A particularly perceptive account published only two
months before the financial crisis broke in the summer
of 2007 spoke of the United Kingdom's dependency on
the 'not-so-heavenly twins' of the City of London and the
housing market, warning that both were debt bubbles
waiting to burst. It warned, 'Either debt repayment will
depress the economy, or default-driven interest rate
rises will depress the economy. Either way, the economy
seems certain to be depressed.' Only a false modesty we
do not possess would prevent us from saying that this
warning was delivered in one of our previous books,
Fantasy Island, published at a time when the United
Kingdom had experienced 15 years of uninterrupted
growth and when the chancellor, Gordon Brown, was
fond of boasting that he had abolished 'Tory boom and
bust'.[2]

Then, as now, we expressed deep scepticism about
the fashionable view that Britain's native genius would
manifest itself in something called the 'knowledge
economy', a salvation to be found in the science labs of
Cambridge and the creative hubs of Hoxton. We viewed
such thinking as escapism on an epic scale, pointing

out that the United Kingdom was actually a country heaving with drinking factories, estate agencies, financial consultants and cut-price clothing chains. What's more, the escapism has gone on unabated. The Treasury and the Department for Business issued a joint report highlighting the growth potential of the British economy during 2011, in which they said one key advantage was that 'English remains the predominant language of business throughout the world.'

That may be the case, but it does not seem to have anything whatsoever to do with economic performance, because the UK share of global export markets continues to fall. German is spoken as a first language only in Germany itself, Austria and half of Switzerland (we don't count the Grand Duchy of Liechtenstein), but that has not prevented the Mittelstand companies of Bavaria and Baden Wurttemberg from showing British firms a clean pair of heels in the big emerging markets. The Germans, however, make an effort to understand the markets they are trying to enter, taking care not to offend cultural sensitivities while offering first-rate products and superb customer service. Faced with a client who doesn't speak English, the average monolingual Brit executive barks a bit louder and a bit more slowly.

Britain's great European rival from a century earlier has worked hard to break into the fast-growing markets of Asia and Latin America. Despite having high wages and a generous welfare system – factors trotted out to excuse the United Kingdom's retreat from whole swathes of industrial production – Germany's share of global trade rose from 8.9 per cent to 9.3 per cent in the first decade of the twenty-first century, while the UK share dropped from 5.3 per cent to 4.1 per cent. This performance looked even worse once demand for the financial and business services, one of the United

Kingdom's enduring sources of export strength, was stripped out. The United Kingdom accounts for just 3 per cent of the goods exported globally, down from 4.4 per cent at the turn of the millennium, and is a net importer of industrial products, food and energy.

Put simply, the United Kingdom used to be a great manufacturing nation but is one no longer. Making things required skills that were rewarded, and the fruits of that labour resulted in exports by and large matching imports, a reasonable division of the economic spoils between labour and capital, and a surplus that paid for increases in public spending. One of James Joyce's characters in *Ulysses* says that the proudest boast of an Englishman is that he paid his way, and for most of the twentieth century that was true. It is true no longer.

A brief summary of the state of the United Kingdom goes like this. The City has replaced manufacturing as the hub of the economy. Those in charge of the finance sector rook their customers and their shareholders to become filthy rich. Pay and rewards are skewed heavily towards the top 1 per cent of earners. Everybody else has to put up with wage restraint, but is able to consume more by virtue of the City's willingness to load everybody up on debt and the Bank of England's willingness to facilitate asset-price bubbles by keeping interest rates low. Most work is in low-skill jobs, with large dollops of public spending used to create white-collar jobs for graduates that would, in previous eras, have been held down by school leavers. Clearly, *Fantasy Island* was wrong: it was not nearly gloomy enough.

The economic audit of the Britain in 2014 contained in the rest of this chapter will seek to make good that error. Be warned: it does not make for comfortable reading.

What the thunder said

David Laws could scarcely believe his good fortune when he arrived at his new office at the Treasury in May 2010. In the carve-up of jobs that followed the formation of the United Kingdom's first coalition government since the 1930s, Mr Laws, a Liberal Democrat, had been given the post of chief secretary to the Treasury, second only in the ministerial hierarchy to the chancellor himself. The chief secretary is traditionally the Treasury's enforcer, the minister who tells Whitehall departments what they can and can't spend, and Mr Laws, a fiscally conservative Liberal Democrat in the tradition of Gladstone, was aware there were unpopular decisions to be made. To his surprise, he found on his desk a note from his predecessor, the outgoing Labour minister, Liam Byrne. It said: 'Dear Chief Secretary, I'm afraid to tell you there's no money left.'

The missive was duly read out when Mr Laws accompanied Mr Osborne to his first press conference, at which the chancellor announced that he was making £6 billion of spending cuts as the down payment on a programme designed to close Britain's biggest ever peacetime budget deficit. Labour, it was claimed, had come into power in 1997 proclaiming prudence but had left office the way it always did, having run out of money. This was only partly true, because when the financial crisis began in August 2007 the United Kingdom was running only a modest budget deficit, and more than a decade and a half of steady growth had left the national debt lower than that of Germany, France, the United States and Japan.

It could have been argued, quite correctly, that the public finances should have been in better shape after such a long period of uninterrupted growth, and that Labour should have been building up a surplus that it could draw upon if and when the good times came to an end. Such a course of action would have given Brown greater fiscal firepower to tackle the recession, and would have prevented the public finances from going so deeply into the red. But once the recession had started there was little alternative for the Brown government but to allow borrowing to rise, since raising taxes or cutting spending would have made things even worse. Ever since the 1930s, governments of both left and right have allowed what are known as the economic stabilizers to work: policy makers allow borrowing to take the strain during downturns.

The Byrne letter meant the coalition could describe a different narrative, in which Gordon Brown's profligacy had left the nation's finances in a parlous state, requiring rapid action to prevent the United Kingdom from going the way of Greece, a country that in May 2010 had turned to the European Union and the International Monetary Fund (IMF) for financial help. Byrne tried to claim his farewell note had been a light-hearted jest, but the damage was done. Messrs Osborne and Laws told voters that their measures, while painful, were unavoidable thanks to Labour's failure to 'mend the roof while the sun was shining'. Opinion polls showed that voters believed what the new government said, a view that became entrenched over the subsequent months as Labour's post-election leadership contest rendered it incapable of mounting any sort of fight back against the government.

Mr Laws was forced to resign as a result of a financial scandal after less than two weeks at the Treasury, but Mr Osborne and the new chief secretary, Danny Alexander, had a fair wind as they prepared what one commentator called the 'most far-reaching and precipitate attempt to achieve fundamental restructuring in an established welfare state in a larger Western economy in recent years'.[3]

Mr Osborne was keen to get a move on with his plan for two obvious reasons, although there were those who said he kept a darker purpose hidden. Politically, it made sense to get the bad news out of the way while the public still blamed Labour for the mess and while the next election was a long way off. Successful governments in the United Kingdom tend to be those that manage to align the economic and political cycles; raising taxes and cutting spending in the first half of a parliament so that they can be generous as polling day approaches. Economically, the argument was that the international financial markets needed to be reassured about Britain's creditworthiness: only immediate action would prevent a loss of confidence that would lead to higher interest rates on the money the government was borrowing, with knock-on effects for home owners and businesses. Mr Osborne's predecessor, Alistair Darling, had proposed measures that would have reversed the rise in public debt within nine years, while the Organisation for Economic Co-operation and Development, the Paris-based think-tank that advises the rich countries of the West, recommended that it be done in 14 years. Mr Osborne said that under his proposals the national debt would peak in four years, with the budget deficit virtually eliminated by the time of the next election. Only about 20 per cent of the improvement in the budget was to come from tax increases, primarily an increase in value added tax, with the remainder coming from spending cuts that were to fall on every local council, every Whitehall department bar Health and International Development, and on those claiming benefits.

The scale and severity of the spending cuts prompted some of Mr Osborne's critics to accuse him of an ideological attack on the state conducted under the cloak of expediency. They claimed the not-so-hidden agenda of the government was to dismantle the welfare state, moving closer to the US model where healthcare insurance is provided by either employers or individuals, and where the protection offered by the state during economic downturns is much weaker. Few expected the coalition government to opt for the Scandinavian model of government, where public spending accounts for at least 50 per cent of national output even during periods of robust economic growth; the fear was that Mr Osborne was intent on rolling back the state from the recent norm of 40 per cent of gross domestic output to between 25–35 per cent of GDP, levels that would require not just economy savings but the withdrawal of the state from whole areas of public service provision.

There was little evidence from Mr Osborne's published plans that this was what he had in mind. The cuts were certainly deep, but by the end of the parliamentary term the Treasury figures showed public spending as a share of the economy returning to its pre-recession level. Mr Osborne said his policy was the result of necessity rather than ideology: national output fell by 7 per cent in 2008–09 and public spending rose rapidly to 50 per cent of GDP. With tax revenues crumbling that level of spending could only be funded by borrowing, which neither the government nor the credit rating agencies were prepared to sanction. As the political analyst Andrew Gamble noted, it would require the government (or its successor) to continue to cut public spending at similar rate through the next parliament to see a substantial change in the size of the state and a shift to a new policy paradigm.[4] And as the months went by, it became clear that Mr Osborne had enough on his plate to deliver his spending plans for the 2010–15 Parliament without worrying too much about what he might do in a second term at the Treasury.

Historically, this was part of a trend. There had been numerous attempts by governments over the past 100 years, going back to the infamous Geddes axe of the early 1920s, to cut their coat according to their cloth. All had discovered that a gap opened up between what they planned and what they achieved, either because the machinations of Whitehall mandarins have proved to be just as devious in reality as those of Sir Humphrey Appleby in the television series *Yes Minister*, or because the economy has proved less strong than envisaged.

Mr Osborne's deficit-reduction strategy involved the economy growing by 2.4 per cent in 2011, rising to 3 per cent in 2012 and subsequent years. Eighteen months in, the chancellor told the House of Commons that he now expected growth to be 1 per cent in both 2011 and 2012, with borrowing sharply higher as a result. Like most of his predecessors, he found a way of blaming events beyond his control for the failure to meet the target. The crisis in the eurozone, Mr Osborne said, had blown him off course, forcing him to put back the time when as much money would be coming into the public coffers as was going out. In truth, the slowdown in the economy had predated the life-and-death struggle of European monetary union, and Britain had barely registered any growth from the end of 2010 onwards, underlining the warnings of those who had told Mr Osborne that the damage caused to the financial sector by the downturn of 2008–09 meant it was not the sort of recession from which Britain could easily or speedily recover.

In some respects, both the government and its critics missed the point. The failure of growth to match the expectations of the Office for Budget Responsibility, the fiscal watchdog set up by Mr Osborne to ensure that ministers were no longer able to manipulate forecasts for the public finances, was certainly an issue. But of rather more concern was that the real level of public indebtedness in the United Kingdom was much greater than the official figures suggested. There was, in addition, a mountain of off-balance-sheet liabilities from the live-now, pay-later private finance initiative, the future cost of public sector pensions and the need to provide care for an ageing population. The McKinsey Global Institute (MGI) looked at ten mature economies in 2010 and found that 'the UK experienced the largest increase in total debt relative to GDP from 2000 to 2009, with its ratio reaching 469 per cent'. Some of the increase, MGI accepted, was because of London's role as a global financial centre, but even so the United Kingdom had 'the second highest ratio of debt-to-GDP among major economies after Japan'.[5]

To service those debts and to meet the future needs of its population, the United Kingdom would need a vibrant economy capable of sustained and sustainable growth and delivering a perpetual budget surplus in excess of 6 per cent of GDP. What it actually had was an economic model excessively reliant on private sector debt. The public sector deficit was the symptom rather than the cause of Britain's economic weakness; the true explanation was a growth model excessively reliant on the indebtedness of private individuals and the banks that, in the alleged good times, lent them the money. It is to that we now turn.

The burial of the dead

'Neither a borrower nor a lender be.' The advice of Polonius to his son Laertes as he heads off to university would ring hollow for the current crop of undergraduates at English universities, burdened as they are with tuition fees of £9000 a year. In modern Britain, it is never too early to take the first tentative steps on the debt treadmill.

Yet in truth, Polonius's paternal talking-to was misguided. There is nothing wrong with extending credit, or receiving it, provided there is an assured stream of income to pay back what is borrowed. It is good business for an entrepreneur with a good idea to get a loan from the bank so they can buy machinery and hire the staff to operate it. Graduates with steady jobs and good prospects are making perfectly sensible decisions when they take out a home loan from a mortgage lender rather than wait until they have saved up enough to buy a property outright.

There is, however, a difference between credit acting as the lubricant of the economy and credit acting as a powerfully addictive drug, needed in even stronger quantities to get activity moving. To take a year at random, in 1964, when Harold Wilson was elected prime minister, before the era of credit cards and when a three-bedroom house in south-east England would change hands for around £3000, household debt was 14 per cent of the economy's annual output. Banks and building societies were careful to whom they lent money, and knew that the government would tighten credit controls in the event of any collective exuberance on the part of lenders. In 1964, the aggregate balance sheets of the UK banking system amounted to 46 per cent of the UK economy. Curbs on lending were first loosened in the early 1970s, and were abandoned altogether in the financial deregulation of the 1980s. The banks grew in size and influence, extending more and more loans with less and less capital in reserve if things went wrong. By

2009, the aggregate balance sheets of the UK banking system amounted to 497 per cent of GDP. Put another way, the paper value of the British banks was five times as big as all the goods and services produced by the economy in a year. Household debt by this stage had increased to 80 per cent of GDP. The private sector as a whole had debts worth more than 150 per cent of GDP.

One study found that in the years preceding the bubble, 70 per cent of UK growth was dependent – in one way or another – on the lending bubble.[6] Of the eight largest sectors of the economy, construction, real estate and financial services accounted for 39 per cent of national output. A further three – health, education and public administration – accounted for a further 19 per cent of GDP. These too were indirectly dependent on the private sector debt bubble, since the government assumed that higher levels of public spending were affordable due to the receipts coming in from the housing market and the financial sector. Ministers ignored warnings from the Institute for Fiscal Studies that the Treasury should not expect the receipts to keep rolling in.

Nor was that the end of the debt-fuelled growth. If the money spent by consumers in the high streets is added to the mix, debt was an important ingredient in seven-tenths of the value added to the economy by growth during the boom years. Consumers took advantage of rising house prices to remortgage their homes, taking the increase in capital value as income. Eyebrows were raised during this period at the activities of the UK private equity sector, which tended to buy companies with borrowed money, sweat the assets and take a quick profit. But as a study from the Centre for Research on Socio-Cultural Change (CRESC) at Manchester University noted in 2011, this was precisely what home-owners were doing with their properties:

Many doubted whether an expanding private equity sector was committed to production and job creation with social benefits as it claimed in its industry narrative; and instead feared that private equity was committed to redistribution and asset trading with private benefits, especially for the general partners of private equity firms who bought with borrowed money and could cash out on any increase in asset prices. The political classes and the media did not see that this was more or less what the whole country had been doing since the early 1980s, through housing equity withdrawal after remortgage, whose technical equivalent in private equity was the 'dividend recap' after debt refinancing.[7]

The numbers involved were impressive, if disturbing. During the five years leading up to the collapse of the bubble, the UK economy increased in size by £300 billion, which was slightly less than the equity withdrawal from bricks and mortar during the same half-decade. Put another way, if consumers had not been able to use their homes as cash machines there would have been no growth. This, though, was not genuine expansion; it was growth borrowed from the future, and when the bills started to roll in the sums were considerable. Mortgage debt was £1.2 trillion, with overdrafts and the money owed on credit cards worth a further £200 million. The government was in hock to the tune of around £1 trillion, while even the most optimistic estimate of unfunded public liabilities put the figure at £1.5 trillion. That made close to £4 trillion in total, making the United Kingdom a debt-addicted economy by any yardstick. Debt in increased by 11.2 per cent a year from 2003 to the end of the decade once public and private borrowing were taken together. But the downside to growth based on borrowing was that once the borrowing stopped, so did the growth.

The new coalition's answer to the riddle of how to get the economy moving again was to tackle public borrowing in order that both official and market interest rates could remain low enough to get people borrowing again. By 2009, however, the only individuals who get credit from the belatedly cautious banks were those who didn't want to borrow. Britain was caught in a high-debt, low-growth trap, which meant it was almost inevitable that the government would miss its ambitious targets for reducing the deficit inherited from Labour. Starved of the oxygen of debt, there was little prospect of Britain returning to the growth model of the past, in which the unsustainable booms in financial services and real estate paid for an expansion of public services. The message from all parties was that the economy had to be rebalanced away from consumer and government debt towards investment and exports, although this was easier said than done in a country where the productive base was too small and the City too big.

The agony in stony places

Every student of economic history knows the story of how the industrial revolution was born in the small workshops of Britain, with entrepreneurs labouring over their lathes and looms. What is less well known is that over the past quarter of a century, the UK manufacturing sector has returned to the womb. For the most part, the factories of Britain are no longer the dark satanic mills of the nineteenth century, let alone the Fordist behemoths that dominated the urban landscape in the middle decades of the twentieth century. There has been a doubling over the past 25 years in the number of manufacturing companies employing ten or fewer workers, and they now account for 75 per cent of all factories. By contrast, there are now estimated to be no more than 2000 factories dotted around the country employing more than 200 people, after a halving of their number since the early 1980s. Rolls-Royce, which is the second biggest maker of aero engines in the world, is very much the exception that proves the rule, employing 40,000 people in the United Kingdom. Most of the country's other large manufacturing companies are either involved in defence, as in the case of BAE, or foreign-owned, as with the Japanese car companies Nissan, Honda and Toyota. One-third of manufacturing production comes from the British offshoots of companies domiciled abroad.

If this were merely a matter of size it might not matter all that much. Smaller manufacturing firms might be leaner and meaner than their bigger, more cumbersome rivals. The new workshops might fulfil the same role as their forebears two and a half centuries ago, with small concerns producing big ideas. By this token, it doesn't matter that manufacturing's share of national output has fallen from 30 per cent to little more than 10 per cent since the late 1970s, or that the number of people employed in factories has more than halved from 7 million to less than 3 million. The national fantasy, peddled by politicians of all persuasions, is that British industry is what Drake's fleet was to the Spanish Armada, a nimble fighting force that could take on and beat a lumbering opponent. There is, predictably, little hard evidence to back this up.

More than 70 per cent of German firms are involved in technological innovation compared with just over 40 per cent in the United Kingdom. Britain's workers have fewer skills than those in the United States, Germany and France. Just 20 per cent of workers in Germany and 30 per cent of those in France are classified as low-skilled;

in Britain the figure is 60 per cent. Despite the extra money invested in schools, the United Kingdom has been falling rapidly down the OECD's league table of educational attainment, so that between 2000 and 2009 the ranking dropped from eighth to 28th in maths, seventh to 25th in literacy and from fourth to 16th in science.[8] It was true that 43 per cent of graduates in United Kingdom were in science, technology or mathematics-related courses, but precious few of them – less than 5 per cent – actually went into manufacturing. For those young people who didn't make it to university, the chance of getting on-the-job training as an apprentice was much lower than for their contemporaries in continental Europe, despite repeated attempts by the government to persuade employers to train a new generation of skilled workers. Half the research and development in the United Kingdom is accounted for by just two sectors – pharmaceuticals and aerospace – while the use of robots is far more widespread in Sweden and Germany than it is in Britain.

There are success stories, highlighted repeatedly in official reports that talk about Britain's great manufacturing legacy and the potential to build on the nation's strengths. These, though, tend to be rather like the punk rock records of the 1970s: a riff based on a limited number of chords (Rolls-Royce, GlaxoSmithKline, Dyson), with the occasional JCB thrown in by way of variation.

Britain does not have a lengthy roster of world-class companies, and even those that tend to be cited as world class increasingly source their production overseas. In 1979, the United Kingdom was responsible for sourcing 96 per cent of a JCB digger; by 2010 that share had fallen to 36 per cent. James Dyson, who produced a report for David Cameron on how to make Britain the high-tech capital of Europe, now makes his vacuum cleaners in Malaysia, having outsourced everything apart from the design of his products and the company's HQ functions. In the past, manufacturing output tended to pick up when the economy was growing, with spurts of activity following the recessions of the early 1980s and the early 1990s. After the UK exit from the European Exchange-Rate Mechanism, the combination of higher taxes, a weak housing market and a 15 per cent devaluation in sterling resulted in manufacturing acting as the driving force for recovery. Since the turn of the millennium, the performance has been dismal. Manufacturing production did not pick up in the five-year period leading up to the financial crisis in 2007, while the subsequent 25 per cent devaluation in sterling did nothing to improve the growth rate of exports.

This was not entirely surprising because the steady hollowing-out of Britain's manufacturing base meant there was no longer the capacity to take advantage of a cheaper currency. Somewhat belatedly, the Confederation of British Industry (CBI), the country's biggest employers' organization, announced in 2011 that there was a desperate need to nurture Britain's 'forgotten middle', the medium-sized companies that employ between 50 and 500 people. John Cridland, the CBI's director-general, said the United Kingdom had nothing to compare with the Mittelstand, the deep seam of companies, many of them family run, that explained Germany's industrial and export success:

> Medium-sized businesses are truly a forgotten army, and now is the time to unlock their potential. We should be championing, nurturing and encouraging our mid-sized firms so that more of them grow and create jobs. For too long these companies, which could inject tens of billions of pounds into our economy, have fallen under the radar of policymakers.[9]

What Mr Cridland said was true, although the problem started higher up the industrial food chain with Britain's lack of large manufacturing concerns that were home-grown and home-owned. In other Western countries – Japan, the United States, France and Germany – the companies employing 50,000 or more employees were at the top of supply chains that supported the medium-sized companies beneath them. Where Britain had seen its big concerns wiped out as a result of inept management, economic policy blunders or a slavish adherence to hands-off industrial strategies, its rivals had taken direct and often decisive action to ensure that they retained a broad range of manufacturing capability. The United States used aggressive government procurement to favour American manufacturing; Germany encouraged the development of a green technology sector through a generous feed-in tariff which rewarded households that installed solar panels; France would not have dreamed of handing a contract for new railway rolling stock to a foreign supplier, as happened in the United Kingdom.

In the United Kingdom, apart from a brief period in the dog days of Gordon Brown's government, there was a paranoia about 'picking winners'. The focus was on short-term shareholder value rather than allowing companies to invest for the future. When ministers privatized companies they paid little heed to the needs of the domestic companies that were supplying them. All too often there was a belief that a group of 'entrepreneurs' would ensure a bright future for manufacturing, despite evidence that British venture capitalists were deeply unimaginative and tended to live by the simple mantra of 'buy it, sweat it, flip it'. Governments of both left and right pledged that they would strain every sinew to help, exemplified by the Department for Business Innovation and Skills (BIS) when it said 'The Government is committed to doing everything possible to ensure that the world is open to our trade and open to our investment.'[10] This statement of intent provided no clue to how ministers intended to prise open these markets, or what they would do when the bigger emerging countries decided that they wanted to develop their own high-tech industries and knowledge-intensive services, sectors in which Britain is alleged to have a global competitive edge. Chris Benjamin, a retired civil servant who worked in BIS in one of its many previous incarnations, was deeply unimpressed with what he considered to be recycled nostrums and gimmicks from ministers with no strategy for arresting industrial decline:

> These are declarations that would have carried some weight during the Opium War, when steam-powered warships like *Narcissus* could smash China's junks and coastal forts, with a few battalions of sepoys in support. But today, when Britain has negligible authority in the world, such rhetoric is so much quixotic nonsense.[11]

It might have been a different story had the windfall from North Sea oil and gas been used to reshape the manufacturing base in the quarter century from the mid-1970s, when energy secretary Tony Benn in 1975 officially opened the pipeline that brought the first crude ashore. What the Germans or the French might have achieved with the windfall can only be envisaged; they almost certainly would not have blown the lot funding tax cuts and unemployment benefits. On the other side of the North Sea, the Norwegians have shown how to husband the proceeds of an unexpected boon: they have salted the royalties and revenues from their oil fields to establish a sovereign wealth fund that has been invested sagely to pay for the cost of an ageing population.

A study from PricewaterhouseCoopers found that the United Kingdom could have built up its own nest egg – bigger than the sovereign wealth funds of Kuwait, Russia and Qatar combined – had it put tax receipts from oil and gas fields into a long-term fund.[12] The first half of the 1980s was the period of maximum opportunity, since oil prices were high just at the moment the volume of oil coming ashore was building towards its peak. At that point oil revenues were worth around 3 per cent of national output, the equivalent of almost £50 billion a year in today's money. Sadly, however, this was also the period when North Sea oil revenues allowed Margaret Thatcher's government to cut taxes and pay benefits to the more than 3 million people who were on the dole. Instead of paying for the retirement of the baby boomer generation, the government provided the wherewithal for that generation to spend more than it earned, and in many cases to speculate in the housing and stock markets. In the mid-1980s the government took the opportunity to bestow favour on a key sector of the economy; unfortunately, the sector it chose was not manufacturing but the City of London.

Sweet Thames, run softly, till I end my song

Sir Mervyn King hails from Britain's manufacturing heartland. His father worked on the railways, and the London School of Economics professor who became governor of the Bank of England was educated at Wolverhampton Grammar School before going on to Cambridge. A lifelong Aston Villa supporter, it is said of Sir Mervyn, 'You can take the boy out of the Black Country but you can't take the Black Country out of the boy.'

Under Sir Mervyn's stewardship, the Bank earned

a reputation for being strongly critical of the activities of the City of London. Sir Mervyn said he felt intense sympathy for those manufacturing companies that went to the wall without the government lifting a finger to help them, while the bankers who were responsible for bringing the country to edge of financial and economic disaster were bailed out by the taxpayer. Speaking to Charles Moore of the *Daily Telegraph*, Sir Mervyn looked backed nostalgically to the days when banks were run by the sort of martinet Arthur Lowe portrayed in *Dad's Army*: 'There isn't that sense of longer-term relationships [hence the demise of the local bank manager]. There's a different attitude towards customers. Small and medium firms really notice this: they miss the people they know.'[13] In the same interview, Sir Mervyn went on to say that since the Big Bang of 1986, banks had increasingly taken bets with other people's money, while too many in the financial services industry thought 'if it's possible to make money out of gullible or unsuspecting customers, particularly institutional customers, that is perfectly acceptable'.

For two decades and more, the policy establishment – including Sir Mervyn, it has to be said – turned a blind eye to what was going on in the City, and facilitated its wild speculation by monetary policies that ensured there was a copious amount of easy credit. The financial sector grew like Topsy, and when anybody had the temerity to question whether it needed to be cut down in size, the arguments deployed were the same as those used to justify Britain's arms industry: this was a sector that employed a lot of people and generated a lot of wealth. There were precious few centres of excellence in the United Kingdom, so why not help the City to become a world beater rather than hinder it by getting in the way of the risk takers? Ministers bought this logic. They ensured that regulation was light touch in order to promote 'innovation'; they went in to bat for the City in Brussels and Luxembourg to ensure that dirigiste European regulations were not imported; they had no problems with traders making a mint provided they could cream off some of the proceeds to recycle as higher public spending. It did not register that the only ways City traders could be making such high returns were by ripping off their employers and shareholders, or taking monumental risks. The City never actually created as many jobs as its supporters claimed, but it certainly increased in power and influence in the 21 years between Big Bang and the crash of 2007.

Only then did the pennies fall from the eyes of those whose job it had been to police the City and ensure that its activities did not cause systemic risk to the economy. Adair Turner, the former head of the Confederation of British Industry (CBI), who in 2008 became chairman of the Financial Services Authority, the body that made a hash of policing the City, said it was necessary to challenge the idea that financial innovation was 'axiomatically beneficial in a social as well as private opportunity sense'.[14] In an earlier interview with *Prospect* magazine, Lord Turner had gone further, calling some of the activities of the City 'socially useless', and expressing support for a financial transaction tax, a *cause célèbre* on the left since it had first been proposed by the American economist James Tobin in the early 1970s as a way of throwing sand in the wheels of the foreign exchange markets.[15]

These comments came as the Bank of England sought to quantify the cost to the economy of allowing the City of London to take ever-bigger bets with ever-smaller reserves of capital and liquidity, so that they were exposed when the market turned against them. At one level, the damage caused by the collapse of the City's Ponzi schemes was modest: the direct transfer of wealth from the taxpayer to pay for the bail-outs of RBS and Lloyds amounted to a little less than £20 billion, or just over 1 per cent of national output. The Bank of England felt, however, that this was an underestimate of the real damage caused to the wider economy by the banks, since their activities led to a global recession. The losses caused were estimated at between $60 trillion and $200 trillion for the global economy, and between £1.8 trillion and £7.4 trillion for the UK economy. In Britain's case, the upper estimate was five times the economy's annual output, prompting the author of the report[16] to note that calling the numbers 'astronomical' was to do astronomy a disservice, since there were only hundreds of billions of stars in the galaxy.

In two respects what happened in Britain after the Big Bang would have been familiar to those living in the developing world. First, the United Kingdom suffered from what economists call Dutch disease, a phenomenon that normally involves the discovery of a natural resource such as oil, which produces a balance of payments surplus, a higher exchange rate and the loss of competitiveness for manufacturing exports. In the UK case, the Dutch disease was not caused by oil but by the excessive size of the financial sector, which not only attracted hot money into London, thus driving up the value of sterling, but also gobbled up the cream from Britain's universities.

Second, the City conducted its equivalent of a military coup, a silent affair that required no tanks on the street and no disappearances in the middle of the night, but which saw an elite take control of the country and a disproportionate share of its wealth. The numbers were mind-boggling. In 1980 the chief executive of Barclays Bank earned a little over £87,000 a year, 13 times the pay of the average worker in the United Kingdom. In 2010 he was paid £4,365,636, or 169 times the average wage. At Lloyds Bank, remuneration policy was slightly more restrained: the chief executive of a bank almost half-owned by the taxpayer had to rub along on a mere £2,572,000. That represented a 3141.6 per cent increase over the past three decades, and meant he earned 75 times as much as the average Lloyds cashier. As with Barclays, in 1980 the ratio had been 13 to 1.

Sir Mervyn King privately railed against the institutional capture of the government machine by the financial sector, and it was indeed impressive – if disconcerting – to watch the way in which the banks mobilized resistance to the tougher controls on them demanded by Lord Turner and others. It was admitted that regulation of the banks had been too lax in the bubble years, leading directly to the crash. It was admitted also that a failure to put in place suitably onerous curbs on the financial sector risked a second and perhaps more serious crisis. Finally, there was widespread disgust at the way in which the fruits of growth had been captured by a small minority, and in many cases salted away in offshore accounts to avoid paying tax. One estimate of the money lost to the Exchequer through tax evasion put the figure at £70 billion, not far short of the £85 billion in spending cuts Mr Osborne announced would be needed to fill the black hole in the Government finances.[17]

The waste land

Yet nothing happened, at least not as a result of the first recession.

By the summer of 2014 it was a different story, as the economy started to claw its way, inch by inch, out of the second downturn in five years. The crisis this time started not in the trailer parks of Florida and Nevada but in the capitals of Europe, where governments found that they could only finance their debts at exorbitant rates of interest, and tired of trying to force rebellious populations to swallow ever-stronger doses of austerity. In the end, they did what states have done down the ages: they defaulted on their debts, leaving banks nursing colossal losses. As in 2008 and 2009, the financial institutions that professed to love capitalism red in tooth and claw came running to their governments to help. Once again they got it, but this time with much stronger conditions attached. Finally it was accepted that there had been a profound intellectual failure to understand the threat posed to economic and financial stability by too much credit and over-leveraged banks, and that something needed to be done about it.

But the cost of inaction was heavy. The landscape in the summer of 2014 was as bleak as that of the Western Front on Armistice Day in 1918. With the exception of those on the highest incomes, average living standards had not grown in well over ten years, the bleakest period since before the Second World War. There were no longer sniggers when the depression was compared to Japan's lost decade of the 1990s. Unemployment in Britain was above 10 per cent of the workforce, while a million men and women on incapacity benefits had lost their entitlements as part of the government's welfare reforms. Around 600,000 had been pushed out of the benefits system altogether, most of them in the most disadvantaged parts of Britain: towns like Merthyr Tydfil in South Wales and Easington in County Durham. The proportion of the unemployed out of work for more than a year was well above 30 per cent – more than three times the level in the 1950s, when wages as a share of national output tended to average around 60 per cent. In those days workers were able to buy the goods they produced, while those owning the factories made decent profits, and the taxes paid by both labour and capital provided the state with the revenue to expand the welfare state. The boom of the 1950s and 1960s came to an end in the early 1970s, when the wage share rose sharply and profits collapsed.

Capitalism entered a period of crisis. The share of wages was reduced by mass unemployment and stricter trade union legislation. When the squeeze on wages resulted in deficient demand, that issue was solved by increasing the hours worked per household, either through higher levels of participation or by double (or treble) jobbing. When that avenue was exhausted, the answer was ultra-cheap monetary policy, which created the conditions in which individuals would take on more debt, bid up the cost of property, and then remortgage so that they could extract income from rising capital values.

In the period up until the early 1980s, wage earners could rely on their unions to secure for them a decent share of an expanding economy. As productivity increased so did earnings in almost a one-to-one ratio. Indeed this trend lasted well into the 1990s, when a 1 per cent increase in gross domestic product resulted in a 0.89 per cent increase in pay. But in the 2000s this relationship broke down, so that in the first seven years of the new millennium the average UK worker saw their pay go up by just 0.43 per cent for every 1 per cent increase in national output.

This dampening of wage growth had deflationary implications. If productivity rises more quickly than real wages, the supply of goods in the economy exceeds demand, leading to unsold products and services, and unemployment. The debt bubble was one manifestation of this phenomenon: a widening trade gap was another, such was the uncontrolled nature of the credit expansion.

In 1950 the United Kingdom had a trade surplus in manufactured goods worth 10 per cent of GDP, and was a net exporter of energy as a result of coal production, an impressive surplus even accounting for the problems faced by those countries that had seen their industrial capacity crippled by the Second World War. By 2014 the United Kingdom had not run a surplus in manufactured goods for more than three decades. Despite the dampening effect of the recession on imports, the trade deficit was running at around £120 billion a year, around 8 per cent of national output. Trade in services helped plug the gap, as did the interest, profits and dividends from international investment, but these were not sufficient to quell fears about food and energy security in an increasingly unstable world.

This is the way Britain looks a century after the guns of August 1914. It is a country where the economy is hobbled by the government's attempts to control the budget deficit, by the efforts of consumers to wean themselves off debt and by the slow-motion break-up of the eurozone. The City has contracted in the two downturns after 2007, manufacturing is too small to take advantage of a depreciating currency; crashing global commodity prices mean the Russian oligarchs and the oil sheikhs are no longer artificially boosting the London property market. It is a country that cannot live with debt yet cannot live without it. It is a country where the trend in the balance of payments is getting steadily worse, and which has the income inequality of the United States without any of America's economic dynamism. It is a country where the oil wells are drying up and all the state assets worth anything have already been flogged off. It is a country where long-term unemployment is having a scarring impact on the young for the second time in 30 years, leading to outbreaks of unrest each summer.

It is a country where the trend rate of growth has fallen to around 1 per cent a year, yet the United Kingdom is curiously prone to higher inflation than other nations. It is a country deep in crisis.

Chapter 3

Welcome to the beautiful south

[T]here is no movement forward; nothing is being resolved. The nation appears to be playing a game with itself.
V. S. Naipaul, *The Return of Eva Peron*, 1980

No country has yet made the journey from developed to underdeveloped. Britain could be the first to embark upon that route.
Peter Jenkins, *The Guardian*, 27 September 1978

Come down from your swell co-ops, you general partners and merger lawyers! It's the Third World down there!
Tom Wolfe, *The Bonfire of the Vanities*, 1987

The summer and autumn of 2011 was a strange and troubling time in British life, not least the because of the famously erratic weather, which displayed many of the features of autumn in the summer and bursts of near-Saharan sunshine in the autumn. The disturbing nature of public affairs gathered force into the first six months of 2012, as did the topsy-turvy nature of the climate, with a mild New Year followed by a cold February, a balmy March and the wettest April on record.

On the surface, the bare bones of public affairs seemed straightforward enough. The coalition government grappled with the fourth and perhaps most serious year of the global financial and economic crisis, as the British people entered a second consecutive year of falling real living standards.

On 30 June 2011, hundreds of thousands of civil and public servants, teachers and lecturers walked out on strike in protest at public spending cuts.

On five days from 6 to 10 August, London and other cities suffered major rioting and other disorder, the worst such disturbances since the dole-queue era of the early and mid-1980s. Some blamed the sharp rise in unemployment, especially among young people.

For those disillusioned with the coalition, there was little inspiration to be had elsewhere on the political scene. One year into his leadership of the Labour Party, the youthful Ed Miliband had yet to persuade the public to see him as a future prime minister.

Nor did 2012 seem to promise anything other than more of the same on a magnified scale. The 'mad March' saw, in rapid succession, an enormous row over a Budget, which cut the top rate of tax from 50 to 45p while phasing out the preferential tax regime long enjoyed by pensioners, the training of soldiers to drive petrol tankers in the event of a threatened strike by the Unite union, and the resignation of the co-treasurer of the Conservative Party, Peter Cruddas, after undercover journalists recorded him offering access to David Cameron and to Downing Street policy staff in return for very large donations to party funds.

Then there was the furore when it became clear the Budget had also slapped VAT on the sale by shops of still-warm pastries such as sausage rolls and Cornish pasties. 'Pastygate' descended into farce as photographs appeared of David Cameron and George Osborne eating said foodstuffs while it was unclear at what temperature the new tax would kick in.

Meanwhile, remarks by the Cabinet Office Minister Francis Maude that motorists would be advised to prepare for the threatened tanker drivers' strike by topping up their tanks and keeping a spare jerry can of fuel triggered an entirely predictable wave of panic buying, with many petrol stations drained dry. All this before a single driver had walked off the job.

Meanwhile, a government that once prided itself on its love of liberty found time to announce two highly illiberal measures. The first was the 'snooper's charter' under which police and security services would be granted sweeping access to details of conversations over e-mail and social networks. The second was a proposed minimum price for alcohol, guaranteed to make drink less affordable for anyone less wealthy than Messrs Cameron and Osborne (that is, almost everyone).

Commenting on the latter proposal in *City AM* newspaper, Chris Snowdon wrote:

> Does anyone now remember the [Coalition's] YourFreedom website which asked the public to nominate 'unnecessary laws and regulations' for the scrapheap? ... [It] now exists only in the National Archives, so future historians can marvel at the golden summer of 2010 when deregulation briefly seemed possible.[1]

Without doubt, 2011 and early 2012 was a serious and difficult time for the British. But so it was for the people of many other countries. Around the world, a private sector credit crunch had been transformed, with the transfer of liabilities from the financial sector to the public sector, into a sovereign debt crisis. In one capital after another, harassed politicians had been working round the clock and round the calendar to hold national and international financial systems together while police battled enraged demonstrators and sometimes rioters. What was so different – and so strange – about Britain?

To look more closely at this period is, as Sherlock

Holmes may have said, to discover that the British case presented certain features of particular interest. There was, for example, the curious affair of the government's attitude to household debt.

On 4 October, early drafts of David Cameron's speech to the Conservative Party conference the following day suggested he would claim that solving the debt crisis would require 'households – all of us – paying off the credit card and store card bills'. Alarm as to what such a course of action would do to an economy already suffering from weak consumer demand forced a hasty rewrite. In the new version, Mr Cameron merely observed that the country had been suffering from a debt crisis and 'that's why households are paying down their credit card and store card bills'.

A routine political gaffe? Possibly not. The forecasts of the government's independent fiscal watchdog, the Office for Budget Responsibility, actually required British households to borrow more money if the government's deficit-reduction plans were to be achieved. Was the prime minister in ignorance of his own economic policy? If so, it was a gaffe on a major scale.

Nor was this an isolated example of policy contradiction. Over at the Department for Business, Innovation and Skills (BIS), firms and individual traders were being invited to rip up those rules they disliked. Here is how the BIS website put it:

> Business is a vital partner for BIS in the fight against red tape. We need business to tell us which legislation and policies are too burdensome, too bureaucratic and too unwieldy – those which sound like a good idea but simply don't work out in the real world.[2]

One such well-meaning but impractical regulation may well have been that suggested by a consultation on:

changes to employment law to encourage a more fair and flexible approach at work. The consultation seeks views on a new system of flexible parental leave which will allow mothers and fathers to share leave, and give parents and employers greater choice about how leave is taken; on how to extend the right to flexible working to all employees.[3]

This consultation exercise, completed on 8 August, was being carried out by the very same department, BIS.

One final piece of wildly self-contradictory official activity lay at the heart of economic policy making. On 3 October, Mr Osborne told the party conference of a new scheme called 'credit easing'. This would involve the government spending billions of pounds buying bonds issued by businesses, including small and medium-sized businesses. He said:

[A]s part of my determination to get the economy moving I have set the Treasury to work on ways to inject money directly into parts of the economy that need it such as small businesses. It's known as credit easing. It's another form of monetary activism.[4]

It is not. In fact, it is a form of fiscal activism of the sort against which the government was supposed to have set its face. The Treasury was planning to exchange its own high-quality bonds, or 'gilts', for lower-quality business bonds. In short, this was a fiscal stimulus dressed up as a quasi-monetary measure. In this parallel universe it was, apparently, quite all right to do what you had insisted you would not do, provided you said you were doing something else.

Elsewhere, developments regarding the relationship between the state and the citizen were taking an alarming turn. Conventional wisdom on all sides of politics had it that Britain was increasingly a tolerant, easy-going, relaxed sort of place. Taking the reins of power from Gordon Brown on 11 May 2010, David Cameron paid tribute to his predecessor, saying that, after more than a decade of Labour rule, Britain was 'more open at home and more compassionate abroad'. This was the official version. Indeed, it had been so for a very long time, stretching all the way back to John Major's stated desire, on becoming prime minister in 1990, to see 'a country at ease with itself'. The reality told a rather different story. Indeed, in a number of bizarre and unpleasant ways, the relationship between state officials and the individual was becoming increasingly disadvantageous to the latter and increasingly intrusive on the part of the former.

We begin in Mr Osborne's area of responsibility, with the nation's tax service, HM Revenue & Customs. On 7 July 2011, it issued for consultation a document with the innocuous title 'Bringing HMRC's information powers into line with international standards'.[5] In effect, this proposed giving the Revenue new powers to demand that people and companies tell them about a piece of economic activity that might or might not be taking place. One example is a belief by the Revenue that a wealthy person does not take care of their own garden, when there appears to be no tax record of a gardener. Another example is a furniture-making workshop of whose wood supplier there is no tax record. In other words, the Revenue believes a piece of economic activity may be taking place, but can find no record of it. The new power could be summed up as: 'We don't know if anything taxable is going on, but you had better tell us what it is – or else.'

As the title of the consultation document makes clear, the Revenue claimed this new power was necessary in order to bring its powers into line with those of similar tax authorities abroad, with which the United Kingdom has mutual assistance arrangements. This claim was treated with some scepticism in accountancy circles. But a feature of British officialdom was a constant demand for 'tough new powers', a demand pressed regardless of circumstances. So when a branch of the state fell down on the job, this was cited as evidence of the need for more powers, and when a branch of the state was performing reasonably well, this showed the officials concerned could be trusted with such powers. Examples of the former include cases where social work departments failed to spot life-threatening cases of child abuse until it was too late, while examples of the latter include the 'pressing need' to give the police and security services beefed-up powers to deal with terrorism. (Even when terrorist attacks succeed, we are assured that many more were foiled but that alas, for security reasons no details can be made available.)

While tax officials prepared to involve themselves more deeply in the affairs of members of the public, a sizeable proportion of the nation's nurses appeared to be disengaging from their patients. In August, it emerged that a number of hospital trusts had issued nurses with red tabards bearing the words 'Do not disturb: Drug round in progress.'[6] This was apparently a response to the danger that, were nurses to be interrupted by patients, it could lead to their dispensing the wrong medicines. Widespread criticism of this novel addition to the nurses' uniform, in which it was pointed out that the drug round was sometimes the only occasion on which patients had the chance to speak to a nurse, underlined how far the public image of the one-time 'angels' had declined during the previous 20 years. Yes, there was something of a furore. But many did not seem particularly surprised. One trust, at least, later amended the wording to make it less forbidding.[7]

Meanwhile, on 14 July it was reported that a London judge, Recorder Caroline English, 'made legal history'. That was certainly one way of putting it. She discharged the jury in a case of benefit fraud – believing that some jurors had been interfered with – and continued the case alone, convicting four defendants and jailing three of them. This extraordinary event in a country that had long prided itself (somewhat inaccurately) as the birthplace of trial by jury had been made possible by 'tough new powers' in the 2003 Criminal Justice Act.

While judges were empowered to dispense with the services of mere lay people in the jury box, VIP visitors to the 2012 London Olympics – as we mentioned earlier – would be able to dispense with the tedium of routine highway regulations.[8] Furthermore, as Simon Jenkins, writing in the *Evening Standard* on 28 September, added:

> While the transport authorities are thus plotting inconvenience, the police are plotting fear.
>
> Regular press conferences raise threats of terrorist incidents and dark conspiracies. There are to be practice runs of terror attacks on Hyde Park. There are reports that the transport police will be issued with Heckler and Koch machine guns to tote on the Underground.[9]

Elsewhere, the Olympics were being held up as a great success. On 27 July an item on the Radio 4 programme *Today* began, 'A year to go to the London Olympics and everything has been built on time and on budget. Cue for much rejoicing and not a little amazement. That's not usually the way we do things in this country, is it?'

No indeed, and as the item progressed it became clear that it still was not. John Humphrys, the *Today* presenter, pointed out that the Olympic Delivery Authority's definition of 'on budget' applied only once it was taken into account that the budget had been increased from its original estimate of £2.4 billion to £9.3 billion.

On 19 October, the Human Fertilisation and Embryology Authority (HEFA) decided to treble the compensation paid to women who donate eggs to help infertile couples to have a child. To criticism that this would act as a financial inducement to donate eggs, the HFEA retorted that the criticism was factually inaccurate. The money could not be an inducement, because European law forbade the payment of inducements. It allowed only the payment of compensation, so this was being classed as compensation.

Our nine vignettes may seem to suggest an official class mired in contradiction (the first three), intrusiveness (the next four) and delusion (the last two). It could be argued that this is nothing very new. Posturing during the Second World War about the United Kingdom as a member of the 'Big Three', alongside the United States and the Soviet Union, was surely the grand-daddy of delusions? The highly intrusive 'little Hitlers' of officialdom made up a long-running focus of public resentment in the late 1940s and early 1950s. Judges sat without juries in some trials during the long-running emergency in Northern Ireland. As for contradiction in high places, post-war *voltes-face* on defence, immigration, foreign policy and transport are the stuff of Whitehall legend. What makes the position today any different?

We would argue there are two major factors. First, the bizarre and often inexplicable behaviour of modern British officialdom and quasi-officialdom is incoherent and directionless. There is no objective – whether laudable or reprehensible or somewhere in-between – to which this behaviour is being directed, no war of national survival being prosecuted, no ration-book economy being policed, no public order crisis being addressed, no existential world role to work out. True, there is, as we shall see later, a vague official ideology, bound up with 'what sort of country we want to be' and assorted definitions of 'Britishness'. But this ideology is, we suggest, merely another aspect of the weird ways of officialdom, not their objective.

Second, this behaviour is wildly inconsistent, not merely from one police area to the next, one bank to the next, one civil service department to the next, but even within the same organization and sometimes even the same branch or office. Demands on one day for photo-identification, denial on one day of access to a road or street for no apparent reason, a ban on photographing one's own children in a public place on one day, the refusal of welfare benefits on one day on the ground that the applicant has not diligently sought work – all these impositions can melt away the next day without a word of explanation.

In the same way, apparent goodies on offer from the state can be withdrawn with little notice, whether they are tax breaks for favoured industries, subsidies for approved activities or something as humdrum as promises of more frequent dustbin collections. Sometimes one part of the official machine counteracts another, thus David Cameron's call for nationwide street parties to celebrate the wedding of Prince William and Catherine Middleton on 29 April 2011 was flatly contradicted by the many local authorities that placed huge bureaucratic hurdles in the way of such celebrations.

Britons' experience of officialdom and quasi-officialdom does not resemble the endless bureaucratic arctic winter of the immediate postwar years or, far worse, of the pre-1989 Iron Curtain countries. Rather, it is a garish and bewildering midsummer scene, populated by abnormal and extraordinary creatures and spirits, some friendly, some not, some helpful (although often at untangling problems that they themselves have created), some mischievous, some downright malevolent, appearing, vanishing, flitting hither and thither without any apparent reason or purpose.

All this is, of course, enormously wasteful and inefficient, whether one favours a social-democratic mixed economy on Continental European lines or the more freebooting full-blooded private enterprise model associated with the United States (however much of a caricature this association may involve).

Not only did the public sector payroll expand by more than 600,000 between 1997 and 2010 (it has since been reined back by spending cuts), in the private sector there has been an explosion in the numbers of what can best be described as the functionaries of the British economic order: legal professionals, human resources managers, training staff and security guards. As with their public sector counterparts, much of what they do appears to have little purpose. Nor, as a rule, are their duties discharged consistently.

The answer makes no sense? Then change the question

All this is deeply disturbing to those of us with an interest in Britain's economic prospects. Huge numbers of employees appear engaged in a carnival of inexplicable activity. Larger numbers still are either paying for this activity or being inconvenienced (or worse) by it – or both. Those who see Britain's economic and social future on well-ordered European lines, and those hoping for a small-state laissez-faire future, will be equally alarmed. As will anyone looking for a judicious blend of the two, or for something quite different: an alternative 'green' economy, perhaps. Getting from where we are to where they want to be seems a near-impossible task.

But perhaps they are committing what is known as a 'category error'. They see a developed nation with well-established public institutions thrashing about in a bewildering manner, all the proposed solutions to its problems having no effect, apparently, other than to make things worse. What, however, if they are simply looking for the wrong thing in the wrong place, rather like cricket fans who have unwittingly taken their seats at a hockey venue and are puzzled beyond measure by the antics on the pitch?

What if it is simply no longer very useful to regard Britain as a developed nation?

Various frightening contemporary phenomena can seem less scary with a shift through time or space of the perspective from which they are being viewed. Thus violent football crowd behaviour in the 1970s and 1980s was horrifying when compared with the dignified demeanour of inter-war soccer supporters, those archetypal working-class men with flat caps and mufflers. It was less so when set against the game's rowdy medieval past.

Outbreaks of indiscipline in the field during the US involvement in Vietnam in the 1960s, and widespread evasion of military service at home, seemed shocking when compared with the cheerful stoicism with which US servicemen set out to fight Germany and Japan from 1941 to 1945. It would have been less shocking had the comparison been made not with the attitude of the soldiers of the Second World War but with those engaged in ill-defined and apparently pointless conflicts across history, whether in pre-Enlightenment Europe or post-colonial Africa and Asia.

Widespread power blackouts and bomb explosions in Britain in the early 1970s stood in stark relief against the 'rising expectations' of the affluent society of the late 1950s and 1960s. They appeared, however, as minor irritants when compared to the zero expectations of wartime, then just 30 years in the past.

And the contemporary United Kingdom may seem more comprehensible, may make more sense, if it is viewed not as a first-world industrialized nation, a member of the Group of Seven leading economies, permanent member of the United Nations Security Council and founder member of the International Monetary Fund (IMF) but as something quite different: a third world country in the making.

Most of the human race lives in the developing world. Some of the countries concerned are on the verge of joining the developed world. Why should some other countries not be heading in the opposite direction? After all, had the Group of Seven rich nations existed in 1945, Argentina would have been a member. Relegation is not unheard of. And just as for individuals, so 'social mobility' must apply to states. This is especially so given the parallels between the personal and the national, in terms of the ending of a period in which all could get better off at the same time. Within the United Kingdom, the enormous expansion of white-collar, middle-class employment in the postwar years has long ended, and with it has ended a painless method of adding more people to the ranks of the salaried classes without their needing to displace any of those already enrolled. Now, for some to win, others must lose.

Similarly, mounting pressure on the world's resources

– as seen in the enormous rise in commodity prices in recent years – is bringing to an end the happy state of affairs in which more and more countries could be welcomed into the first-world club without any of the existing members being asked to resign.

The pending relegation of the United Kingdom is not simply a question of earnings or wealth, although real living standards have been declining. It is about a way of seeing the economic and social system in a manner that hangs together. Insist on the United Kingdom's developed-world status, and the sheer incoherence of public and commercial life – the laughable inconsistencies, the corporate rapacity, the simultaneously intrusive and ineffective security apparatus – appears enraging and inexplicable. Look at Britain as one would a developing nation, and these features appear unremarkable, even natural.

Take some broad-brush aspects of life in the third world, observable as such in varying degrees from Indonesia and the Philippines through parts of the former Soviet Union and Middle East, on through Africa to South America and beyond. There is the fragile national identity and disagreement over what that identity ought to consist of, and indeed on the proper boundaries of the nation or nations in question. There is the utter disregard for consistency and objectivity in public discourse involving either public or private sector organizations. There is the disconnection between the stated and the real functions of various organizations and pieces of law or regulation. 'Sterile areas' and 'exclusion zones' round public buildings and party conferences are often viewed as having less to do with protecting politicians than with controlling the public. Health and safety announcements on public transport are sometimes delivered at volumes that breach health and safety regulations, leading one to suspect that their real purpose is to cow the passenger. Burdensome regulations supposedly designed to stop money laundering are widely believed to have more to do with stopping tax evasion than their stated purpose of choking off funds destined for the Real IRA or Al-Qaeda. Similarly, measures to 'tackle binge drinking' have the happy side-effect of raising more tax to fill various holes in Britain's shaky fiscal foundations. The lifting in October 2011 of restrictions on the ownership of legal practices was suspected of having rather less to do with promoting 'choice' and 'competition' and rather more to do with the destruction of an independent profession and the transforming of lawyers from partners or aspiring partners into corporate wage slaves.

Trust in public officials and corporate executives is low, to put it mildly. Yet to describe the atmosphere as one of cynicism would be misleading. All the signs are that British people place a high value on family life, friendships and other forms of personal relationships. The cynicism starts on the other side of the garden gate, when the citizen enters the supposedly much-cherished public realm. It is here where, despite all the talk of 'civil society', public space', 'the Big Society' and so forth, there is so little 'society' to be found.

The common occurrence of the ignored wailing of the car alarm in its small way encapsulates much of this. The alarm is ignored partly because it is assumed it is sounding in error; partly because, even if the car in question is actually being stolen, no call to the police is thought likely to produce much by way of response; and partly because any attempt to confront the suspected car thief immediately puts the citizen in danger, from the alleged wrongdoer, the authorities (for 'taking the law into his own hands'), or both. Ignoring the car alarm is an entirely rational response to the way the world works. So, in a thousand ways small and large, is opting-out of any civic and public activities likely to bring the citizen into contact with the dysfunctional, costly and intrusive state, with its vetting, barring, form filling and codes of conduct.

In true banana republic style, however, the state itself is only too happy to march into the resulting no man's land, touting its 'listening exercises', its propaganda campaigns and general flurry of expensive activity as evidence of a robust civic culture, dispensing 'play leaders' to encourage children to do what they used to do anyway, arranging marathons and other sporting events, joining forces with supposedly independent charities and other bodies frequently in receipt of public funds to jolly along the citizenry with campaigns for 'responsible' drinking, healthy eating, cycling to work and the rest.

And of course political activity is, in the eyes of the nation's leaders, a self-evidently worthwhile form of social engagement. So much so, in fact, that the parties involved are deserving recipients of what they believe ought to be generous amounts of taxpayers' money. On 29 October 2011, the Press Association news agency reported a plan for a huge increase in public subsidies: 'Political parties should receive state funding worth up to £100 million over a five-year parliament, a Government-commissioned inquiry is expected to propose.'

The dirty dozen: the evidence in the case

Our argument is that some years before the 2014 anniversary, it had become clear that the succession of failed quick fixes for the United Kingdom's economic and social problems had left a hollowed-out country ripe for membership of what had once been known as the third world, but is better known today as the developing world or simply 'the South'. This is not meant as an insult, nor as a lament for past glories. Rather, it is, we believe, a realistic description of the nation's position. At the very least, we believe it provides a useful perspective from which to view Britain's difficulties.

The 'third world country' tag is used routinely in pub and kitchen-table conversation in response to railway strikes, to political sleaze, to the council's failure to empty the dustbins, to the use by dog owners of the pavements as an animal lavatory. We are not using the expression in that way. Nor, in fact, are we simply saying that it is instructive to imagine, when pondering the economic and public life of the nation, that our major public figures are dressed in bemedalled military uniforms that they have no right to wear, funny/sinister clowns inventing a makeshift ideology as they go along. (But actually this could be instructive – the curious-minded citizen ought to try it some time.)

A developing economy – or strictly, in the case of the United Kingdom, a de-developing economy – exhibits certain features. It has a chronic and apparently insoluble balance of payments problem. It cannot find work for all its young people, and contains a large number of unemployed graduates, traditionally a major source of social tension. Despite this, it imports workers from abroad to fill the gaps left by its own dysfunctional education system, and it supplies beer money, in the form of cash benefits, to its hard-to-employ native workers. Its economic policies lack clarity: on tax, on inflation, on public expenditure. It is particularly vulnerable to price movements in major world commodities. Above all, and perhaps in summary of these symptoms, it is weak, dependent on outsiders for finance, skilled workers and energy supplies.

Going South

There is no accepted definition of a developing nation, The United Nations Development Programme (UNDP) uses a 'human development index' to separate developed from developing nations, an index that measures life expectancy, education and income. Those in the top quartile are 'developed'; the remaining three-quarters are 'developing'.

The World Bank divides the world into high, middle and low-income countries on the basis of income per head. The IMF separates nations into two categories, advanced and emerging/developing, based on income and other factors. In an IMF working paper published in 2011, 'Classifications of countries based on their level of development: how it is done and how it could be done', Lynge Nielsen noted:

> [W]hen it comes to classifying countries according to their level of development, there is no criterion (either grounded in theory or based on an objective benchmark) that is generally accepted. There are undoubtedly those who would argue that development is not a concept that can provide a basis upon which countries can be classified .... While many economists would readily agree that Burkina Faso is a developing country and Japan is a developed country, they would be more hesitant to classify Malaysia or Russia. Where exactly to draw the line between developing and developed countries is not obvious, and this may explain the absence of a generally agreed criterion.[10]

Later Nielsen gave an example of the sort of muddle that can result. In 2007–08, he wrote, the UNDP replaced its 'industrial country' grouping with two criteria for advanced status – membership of the rich nations' club, the OECD, or being a country in either central or eastern

Europe or a member of the ex-Soviet bloc grouping, the Commonwealth of Independent States:

> [T]he developing countries group was retained. This presentation, however, had partially overlapping memberships; for example, OECD members Mexico and Turkey were also designated as developing countries and the Central/Eastern European countries of Czech Republic, Hungary, Poland, and Slovakia were also members of the OECD ... these overlapping classifications were resolved by introducing the new category 'developed countries' consisting of countries that have achieved very high human development; other countries were designated as developing. The distinction between developing and developed countries was recognised as 'somewhat arbitrary'.[11]

That is certainly one way of putting it.

We respectfully prefer not to base our case on the many and varied definitions (to call them standards would be to overstate the case somewhat) on offer from international bodies such as these, but instead to offer evidence in support of our argument that are rooted, we hope, in common sense. Thus it would be absurd to compare the United Kingdom today with poverty-stricken Somalia, but equally absurd, we believe, to set it alongside Singapore in the 1980s, an officially developing country hurtling at tremendous speed towards the first world status that it has now achieved. Challenged to state our case in a few words, we could base the United Kingdom's pending third world status on the fact that public and commercial services work badly, that the average person is becoming poorer rather than richer, that the economy has been pulled horribly out of shape and that government in the widest sense is hopelessly dysfunctional, with different branches of the state frequently at loggerheads with one another.

We prefer, however, to beg the reader's indulgence while we lay out our case more expansively, with the following twelve points of, we hope, compelling forensic evidence.

First, and perhaps most telling, there is the constant search for charismatic political leadership, at least among the political classes, opinion formers and others inside the 'Westminster village'. In the past two decades Tony Blair, David Cameron and Nick Clegg have been, on occasions, hailed as destined to play this part. They may subsequently have disappointed, but they had their time in the sun. By contrast, those felt lacking in this department have faced denigration beyond all reason. Just look at the vitriol heaped by the media and others on Gordon Brown and Sir Menzies Campbell, with Ed Miliband now possibly being measured for the drop. True, Mr Brown enjoyed a brief reputation as what the *Economist* described as 'a plain blunt man and ecumenical father of the nation'.[12] But that this image proved fleeting is rather less alarming than the fact that it was ever even partly accepted in the first place. Third world countries may need 'fathers'; modern, properly functioning developed nations do not.

Mr Brown is just one of those believed at one point to have star quality and then to have been judged after all to be deficient in this regard. The rivals in the 1992 General Election, Neil Kinnock and John Major, also come to mind. Rarely is the fact itself of the demand for such a leader ever subjected to much scrutiny, even when inevitably the leader figure fails to live up to expectations. These expectations are great indeed, albeit vaporous and hard to define. It is taken as read that the country is in urgent need of radical, even revolutionary, change, and that things cannot, in some ill-defined way, go on as they are. The leader figure will supply this change. Those few senior people in public affairs who appear to find life pretty amenable as it is, such as the lord chancellor, Kenneth Clarke, are treated as curiosities, as 'cards' who add to the gaiety of the nation but who are not to be taken seriously.

On 19 February 2011, the coalition responded to criticism of its planned upheaval in the National Health Service (NHS) by accusing Ed Miliband of having 'no vision' for the NHS. In modern Britain, leaving well alone does not qualify as a 'vision'. Or, in a phrase beloved of ministers, company directors, bureaucrats and others, 'The status quo is not an option.' Oddly enough, this radical rethink of the country's present and future never proves especially radical. The true, decayed state of the economy is not mentioned.

It could be argued that the apparently preordained failure of the leader figure is nothing new. Back in 1967, David Frost and Antony Jay argued that British elections, far from representing the sophisticated measurement of public opinion in a modern democracy, were better seen as a 'tribal ritual of self-denial and purification' in which the 'joke-king' of anthropological study is deposed and a new one chosen. 'It enables the English to pretend that their own faults are, in fact, the faults of the ritual figure.'[13]

However, we believe a new and more disturbing tone has crept in since the 1960s or even since the early part of the 1979–90 premiership of Margaret Thatcher, someone routinely described as having 'charisma' to spare. Far from simply building people up in order to knock them down, those demanding 'dynamism' and inspiring leadership seem quite genuine – indeed, almost desperately so. But given the inchoate nature of what it is that is being demanded of the leader figure, their failure is almost pre-programmed.

V. S. Naipaul, in the book quoted at the head of this chapter, wrote of Juan Peron, Argentina's president from 1946 to 1955 and again from 1973 to 1974, '[H]e hadn't begun badly. He had wanted to make his country great. But he wasn't himself a great man; and perhaps the country couldn't be made great'.[14]

Second is the apparent requirement for a supposedly all-encompassing political philosophy to be espoused by the charismatic leader. In recent years, these 'visions' have included the 'third way' of Tony Blair, the 'work of change' espoused by Gordon Brown and David Cameron's 'Big Society'. Intriguingly, this last, with its emphasis on people taking charge of public services in an endearingly do-it-yourself sort of way, echoes the 'self-management' and 'power to the people' doctrines seen in the past in such diverse developing countries as Libya, Tanzania and China. The application of these credos to everyday government is not merely problematic (one would expect no less when attempting to put philosophy into practice) but nigh on impossible, which suggests something lacking in the theoretical structure. Tony Blair piled Downing Street high with 'delivery' and 'strategy' units, yet delivery proved elusive. Gordon Brown declared the era of spin to be over, and later hired a top public relations expert apparently to craft 'a compelling narrative' of his achievements in office. It did not compel.

Nor are these philosophies easy to explain in simple language. In this regard they bear little resemblance to fascism, communism, Islamism or any other international ideology. Rather, they are idiosyncratic and subject to repeated reinterpretation. In this they resemble more the ever-shifting doctrines of Mexico's Institutional Revolutionary Party, Ireland's once-dominant Fianna Fail party, or to make a last mention of Argentina, President Peron's *justicialismo* movement.

Given the cloudiness of the ideology – or 'big idea', to use the modern media terminology – it is perhaps unsurprising that the would-be charismatic leaders seem to steer clear of too definite a position on the major issues that once divided British politicians: public ownership, nuclear weapons, the Atlantic alliance, Europe or trade union law. Instead, in the style of Big Man leaders in the third world, our own top dogs are wont to issue rambling and random proclamations unconnected to any discernible philosophy or to any normal conception of the proper functions of government. Mr Cameron's obiter dicta have included the importance of fathers being present at the birth of their children and the wrongfulness of WH Smith in promoting the sale of chocolate in its stores. Again in common with the big-boss leaders of the developing world, Mr Cameron (and Messrs Brown and Blair before him) has given his own officials a public tongue-lashing, in his case for being the 'enemies of enterprise', a rebuke delivered at the Conservative Party's spring forum in Cardiff on 5 March 2011.

The said officials probably keep their heads down, knowing it will soon blow over. After all, it has done before. There is never much follow-through. The Big Man's various abandoned initiatives litter the landscape like the rusting machinery and half-built skyscrapers of so many post-colonial states.

Third, the state itself has an overarching ideology, unnamed in the case of the United Kingdom, that stresses the harmonious nature of the national society and the enormous strength that it draws from its diverse parts. The official philosophy of *pancasila*, under which Indonesia was governed during the long reign of President Suharto, is a classic example of this sort of compulsory feel-good doctrine. Were society really as harmonious as claimed by the official version, it would presumably not be necessary to keep saying so. This ideology contains much specific propaganda about the national character ('Britishness') and national 'values', prompted no doubt by porous frontiers, uncertainty over who is entitled to live in the country, and anxiety over the intentions of those entering the national territory. In true post-colonial style, the authorities stress simultaneously their commitment to international brotherhood and the 'fact' that our own nationals are somehow special, superior to those dwelling in less happy lands.

Fourth, there are extensive tax and regulatory inducements to banks and multinational corporations to locate in the country concerned. Corporation tax, the one levy paid exclusively by limited-liability entities, seems in danger of dwindling away. It was reduced to 50 per cent on Budget day in March 1984. By the end of 2011 it stood at just 28 per cent, and was due to be reduced over the next three years to 24 per cent.

Since the turn of the century, shipping companies too have been lured to the United Kingdom by favourable tax treatment. The tonnage on the British shipping register has nearly quadrupled between 1990 and 2011, according to 2011 figures from the United Nations Conference on Trade and Development.

In the wake of banks, companies and other corporate arrivals come, of course, wealthy individuals, those for whom London is a desirable base for tax and regulatory reasons. Indeed, their insulation from Britain's economic woes helps make parts of London seem at times like a foreign city. On 12 December 2010, the *Mail on Sunday* reported thus:

> The City elite may live in the UK and run businesses from here, but they are immune to tiresome little issues – such as the Budget deficit or staying

employed – that so preoccupy the rest of us. 'Since the market recovery in 2009, 92 per cent of our clients have been non-resident and/or non domiciled,' says Naomi Heaton, CEO of London Central Portfolio [a residential property investment company].[15]

Political leaders are divided in their attitude to these wealthy incomers. Sometimes individual politicians swing between welcome and hostility. The public too is divided. But the official view is that only hotheads and opportunistic populists stir up ill-feeling towards foreign banks, non-domiciled taxpayers and the rest. Responsible politicians, the 'serious' people, know the City souk is essential to our national prosperity. Ministers' infatuation with the casino industry in the mid-2000s was another worrying echo of attitudes in much of the developing world, where gambling appears as just another aspect of financial deregulation, alongside tax haven status. Examples include the Bahamas, the Seychelles and Mauritius.

Fifth, the public sector resembles an archipelago of self-contained and unaccountable baronies. Across police, education and health, the workforces concerned refuse to perform their duties without large additional payments on top of their salaries, either in cash or kind: police overtime, 'teacher workload reduction', the notorious general practitioner (GP) contracts. This last referred to a 2003 agreement with GPs that was later described by the National Audit Office, the spending watchdog, as giving family doctors a windfall, given that their productivity subsequently fell, at a cost to the taxpayer of £1.76 billion more than the Department of Health had expected. The report, in February 2008, said GPs who ran their own practices had been given large pay rises while giving up responsibility for the 24-hour care of their patients.[16] Not that the public employees concerned are remotely abashed by this. On the contrary, they – or at least, their representatives – are hugely sensitive to any criticism and consider themselves to be martyrs to their vocations, if not actually saints.

After the August 2011 riots, the police were widely criticized for having stood by and allowed shops and other businesses to be looted and burned. But for Sir Hugh Orde, president of the senior police officers' club, the Association of Chief Police Officers, such criticism was in large part 'totally unjustified'. He mocked the idea that the United Kingdom may be able to learn anything from the American approach, stating that 'the British model is probably the top'.[17]

In education and policing, hostility by practitioners to public choice and involvement is explicit. In other areas, it is camouflaged more effectively. Town hall bureaucrats and local councillors pay themselves huge salaries and allowances. No one is surprised when local authorities react to spending cuts by axing services to the poor, rather than reducing payrolls. For years, the ministerial response to filthy hospitals and patient deaths from 'superbugs' has been to draw up beautiful diagrams of 'organizational restructuring'.

Sixth, a vast pseudo-private sector, controlling railways, water, gas and electricity, seems permanently engaged, apparently in cahoots with ministers, in conspiracies against the public. Energy prices head ever upwards, and rail companies have even levied huge 'fines' on people who have alighted from trains before the end of the journeys for which they have paid.[18] Occasionally ministers promise reviews or changes in the law to bring these monopolistic bodies to heel, but little results. After the winter of 2010–11 brought Britain's banana-republic transport system to a halt, for the second winter running, the government proposed giving itself the power to fine airports that close because of poor snow precautions. After 13 years of Messrs Blair and Brown, the airport operators probably had a shrewd idea of what they had to fear from such a 'tough crackdown'. Nothing.

It was a similar tale in October 2011, when David Cameron summoned Britain's big six energy companies for a 'summit' at Downing Street. There had been suggestions that the prime minister would read the riot act to British Gas, Scottish Power, Scottish & Southern Energy, EDF, E.ON and Npower. In the event, they agreed to write to their customers advising them of how to switch to a cheaper tariff. Somehow, it seems likely that the power companies could probably live with this, given that the tariffs themselves remained dense and impenetrable to anyone other than the most dedicated bargain-hunting consumer. The same is true of a range of tariffs in other sectors, from general insurance to telecoms and mobile telephone services. In 2011, the official watchdog Consumer Focus criticized high-pressure doorstep selling by some energy companies which pushed people into signing up for deals that were not necessarily the best for that household.

Seventh, the real private sector contains a dense undergrowth of businesses engaged in dubious or downright worthless activities, such as helping people avoid their debts on a legal technicality, cold-calling individuals to sell them flaky 'investments', managing insurance claims in the interests of one party against the other, and supplying various 'opportunities' to go into business as a franchisee or similar. Some such opportunities prove to be highly misleading.

At the shady end of the accounting profession, routine tax avoidance – taking advantage of loopholes that Parliament itself has created – is old hat. Bizarre schemes have been hatched to exploit so-called sideways relief, in which losses made in one enterprise can be offset against profits made in another. Artificial 'businesses', complete with their own 'losses', have been set up to shield profits. More extraordinary still, non-existent 'jobs' have been created to take advantage of tax relief for losses occurred during the course of employment. In light of this clearly abusive activity, the abovementioned attempt by Revenue & Customs to arm itself with ever-more intrusive powers is not entirely incomprehensible, albeit two wrongs famously do not make a right.

All this before we examine the City, and its endless 'churning' of corporate assets through mergers and acquisitions that, overall, have been proved to subtract rather than add to shareholder value, quite apart from the damage they might do to the wider community. During quiet periods, financiers bemoan the lack of 'deal flow', and their concern is reported faithfully in the media. Once activity picks up, the 'good news' is also broadcast.

Britain's fund-management industry routinely involves so many different 'charging points' – where someone takes a piece of the client's money – that it is not unusual for the actual fund to grow very slowly indeed. In one case reported in *The Guardian* on 3 October 2009, a reader had made monthly contributions totalling £70,000 over a 15-year period between 1994 and 2009. When he asked for a valuation, he found the fund manager had turned his contributions into just under £70,000. Over the 15-year life of the investment the FTSE 100 index had increased by 66 per cent, but transaction costs meant the fund management industry took 3.2 per cent a year in costs.

Furthermore, the large numbers of people employed to stand on pavements handing out leaflets, cheap telephone-call cards and free newspapers, or attempting to sign up customers for various services, is a sure sign of incipient third world status. The pavements are clear in well-ordered first world cities. Street hassle is commonplace in developing countries.

Eighth is a fondness for dubious statistics and 'science'. 23 March 2012 saw David Cameron propose a minimum unit price for alcohol on the ground that: 'Binge drinking isn't some fringe issue, it accounts for half of all alcohol consumed in this country'.[19] This meaningless statistic (as it is such a vague concept, the definition of binge drinking can be made to fit the statistic) presumably came from the same official fiction factory as the original government 'safe drinking' guidelines in the mid-1980s. In an interview with *The Guardian* on 20 July 1996, Richard Smith, one of the expert team from the Royal College of Surgeons that drew up the 'safe limits', said the committee had no real idea how much drinking was 'safe', so 'we plucked a figure out of the air'.

More recently, official guidance suggested that for parents to allow their youngsters to get used to wine and beer with a small glass now and again in the approved middle-class fashion was actually a very bad idea, and likely to lead to drink problems in their children's later life. The BBC, for once, actually scrutinized state anti-alcohol propaganda rather than simply broadcasting it, and the results, on Radio Four's statistics programme *More or Less*, broadcast on 18 December 2009, cast some doubt on this claim, to put it politely.[20]

Thirty-odd years ago, the state's health education apparatus began to popularize the notion that those items previously among the first to be axed by anyone trying to lose weight – such as bread, potatoes, pasta and rice – were actually very healthy. Since that time obesity has become a national 'crisis', according to the same health educators, while diets that explicitly reject this official advice (such as the Atkins and Montignac diets) have experienced enormous popularity.

We have no idea whether decades of 'healthy eating' advice have contributed to the rise in the numbers of people who are overweight; we note merely that officialdom clearly finds the thought too much to bear, thus it resolutely does not think it.

Meanwhile, David Cameron was trying, in the manner of Big Men leaders across the developing world, to make his people 'happy'. In April 2011, the Office for National Statistics began research to ask people to rate their own well-being as part of a groundbreaking scheme to measure the nation's 'happiness'. An official 'happiness index' was expected to be launched in 2012. This, remember, is in a country whose leaders, despite spending half of national income, were unable to protect life and property in the August 2011 riots.

Ninth, as with many emerging nations and sub-nations, there are legal and practical doubts as to the extent of Britain's self-government and national independence. Submissions to the European Union in many key areas, and to the European Court of Human Rights, echo the limited self-government awarded many British and French territories in the immediate post-war period and still obtaining in those remaining European possessions. In true third world fashion, British politicians' attitudes to external authority alternate between truculence and subservience. In 2011, David Cameron vacillated between insisting that the eurozone's woes marked a wonderful opportunity to reclaim powers long since ceded to the European Union, and insisting with equal vigour that the crisis marked the worst possible time to adopt such a negotiating stance. His December 2011 veto of a new EU treaty was swiftly followed early the next year in a climbdown over the key reason for the veto, the use by an inner group of EU members of the union's institutions.

The United Kingdom has long prided itself on an ancient constitution and time-hallowed public bodies, but some British institutions, such as the Supreme Court, are very new. The court has already been at loggerheads with ministers on a number of cases, one of which – that relating to government policy on forced marriages – appeared to involve the court overturning policy on the sole ground that it was unlikely to be effective.

The country's proposed elected upper house, or senate, does not yet even exist. The potential for clashes on the key issue of power over taxation – cause of both the 1909 Budget crisis and the subsequent 1911 Parliament Act – was obvious. The 1911 Act codified a long-standing convention that peers, being unelected, could not block 'money bills'. But an elected senate would have every right to be involved, morally if not legally. Nick Clegg, the deputy prime minister overseeing Lords reform, has said he hopes the basic relationship between the two houses will remain as it is now, with the upper house having no say over budgets. But will it be that easy once the upper house is elected?

The same is true of the suggestion in 2011 that plans by the Treasury to allow the Scottish government to issue bonds would not impact on the United Kingdom's overall public borrowing because there would be limits laid to the amount that could be issued. But the Scottish administration considers itself to be a government, not a county council. For how long would these limits hold? All this is without considering the impact of Scottish independence, should its electorate choose that path.

Tenth, the state's own enforcers are increasingly treated with the greatest suspicion, from the police through council officials and social workers to 'community support officers' and even the pseudo-official 'traffic marshals' in evidence near large construction sites. Their rules of engagement with the public whom they are supposed to serve are highly uncertain. The police kill people and are then exonerated at 'independent' hearings. Other uniformed officials, such as 'penalty fares' inspectors on the railways and RSPCA officers, have on occasions tried to bluff the public into believing they have powers that they do not in fact possess. Unsurprisingly, many prefer to give officialdom in general a wide berth.

In the new climate, an enormous increase in police numbers has not produced the sort of unalloyed public approval that could have been expected in years gone by. In evidence to the Home Affairs Committee of backbench MPs in March 2010, the Labour government noted:

> Between April 2000 and September 2009 police officer strength has increased by 20,155 to 142,688. At the same time police staff numbers have increased by 26,258 to 82,340, freeing police officers for frontline duties. We introduced Police Community Support Officers (PCSOs) in 2002 and by September 2009 their number was 16,632.[21]

(These numbers refer to England and Wales only.)

At a conference hosted by the centre-right think-tank Reform on 29 June 2011, Theresa May MP, the home secretary, said policing 'should start with the knowledge of what the public actually want'.[22] This may seem an extraordinary statement to the visitor from overseas. But after years in which police chiefs have appeared to pursue their own notions and priorities, regardless of public opinion, it sounded unexceptional.

There has been a sea change in the authorities' handling of incidents. Once, the police and other agencies prided themselves on minimizing the public disruption in such cases; the police officer's stolid injunction to people to 'Move along' as there was 'Nothing to see' was almost as much of a cliché as 'Evening all'. No longer. At the drop of a hat roads are sealed off with plastic tape, road blocks are set up and the authorities exercise without delay the full panoply of 'tough powers' that they have been granted over the past two decades. On the day of the 7 July 2005 bombings in London, pubs across the capital closed at the request of the police. Nobody knew why, or under what authority, these closures had been requested.

Nor are the police alone in this. On 1 September 2011, a single trespasser on the railway line at Thornton Heath in South London caused the shutdown, during rush hour, of almost all services out of Victoria Station to Kent, Surrey and Sussex. The incident barely made the news. Nobody was surprised. In Third World Britain, the ability to disrupt other people's lives is a sort of badge of status among society's minor authority figures. The fluorescent bib is the mark of petty officialdom, the twenty-first-century version of the air raid warden's helmet, albeit the wardens performed, on the whole, a rather more vital task than many of those undertaken by their successors.

Eleventh, political leaders routinely invoke a 'real' citizenry that is being held down by a parasitical middle class, and they promise a great upheaval in the distribution of jobs, opportunity and property to remedy this ancient wrong. The supposedly put-upon are to be the elite's great allies against the independent bourgeoisie. This is quite routine across the third world, from the 'Africanization' of civil service and other public sector jobs in the post-colonial era (currently known as 'nationalizing' posts in Nigeria) to Malaysia's *'bumiputra'* system of discrimination in favour of ethnic Malays – the word translates as 'sons of the soil' – and against the urban Chinese population in particular in matters of education, business formation and civil service jobs.

In Britain, the 'real citizenry' is a somewhat vague entity, but it comes into clearest focus in discussions about university places, work traineeships or work-experience opportunities, and representation in the higher professions, such as the law. Thus Mr Clegg took the lead for the coalition in demanding that universities do more to 'widen access', and in February 2011 accused them of practising 'social segregation'. By April, he had moved on to unpaid 'internships', another device, apparently, for keeping the sons of the soil from their rightful place in the sun.

Not to be outdone, perhaps, Mr Miliband told his party conference on 27 September 2011 that he was 'the guy who is determined to break the closed circles of Britain'. The narrative is always the same, in that the halting or even reversing of the process of social mobility in the last 25 years is entirely the fault of a self-serving clique that is running a seraglio of closed shops in higher education, law, medicine, the media and so forth. That these appalling, grasping snobs, or their predecessors, must presumably have been so much more broad-minded in the 1950s, 1960s and 1970s is never mentioned, because to do so might lay the blame where it more probably belongs, on the many inadequacies of the state as a provider of school education.

Furthermore, as is the case in many developing countries, the leaders are or have been themselves members of precisely the educated, privileged group against which they now inveigh. After all, Mr Cameron's son of the soil credentials (Eton and Oxford) are not obvious. Neither are those of Mr Clegg (Westminster and

Cambridge), or even Mr Miliband, who at least preceded his time at Oxford, the London School of Economics and Harvard with a state education, albeit at the well-regarded Haverstock School in north London. But then, as we have seen again and again, glaring contradictions of the sort that would torpedo first world politicians matter very little in the undeveloping world.

Twelfth, the economy – and society as a whole – is increasingly becoming less a community of law and increasingly a community of trust. In other words, more and more business and personal activity is taking place 'off the radar'. The 'nudge and the wink' economy is booming, not solely for reasons of tax evasion. In a world of apparently burgeoning and illogical regulation and capricious court judgments, people are ever less willing to put anything down in writing. Increasing numbers of businesses have no employees – they subcontract to the self-employed instead. Nor is this entirely a matter of straightforward business activity. More and more semi-commercial relationships, such as the making and sale of home-made produce, are moving into the shadows.

The 'trust' economy may sound agreeably bucolic, but sustained economic growth depends on a willingness to do business at long distance with people one has never met, all within an intelligible framework of law. We return to this topic in Chapter 8.

We could have added other points. There is the third world notion that high officials possess a secret knowledge denied the rest of us that not only informs policy but renders objections from ordinary people worthless. Thus the hazy concept of 'harm' is used to justify making alcohol more expensive; banning prostitution, we are told, is 'all about' stopping a quite different phenomenon, human trafficking, about which state agencies such as SOCA and Scotland Yard have information that the public does not; people 'known' to be contemplating terrorist outrages are detained or otherwise restricted after secret hearings. And the vast state propaganda machine – 'spin', in the misleadingly flip catchphrase – is surely a candidate for Exhibit A.

Then there are the buffoonish policy inconsistencies and contradictions, the huge public contracts for computer systems, defence equipment and infrastructure projects that go spectacularly haywire and run billions of pounds over budget, the grandiose military adventures for which there is not enough money.

Leaders show a child-like fascination with technology. On 4 March 2012, it was reported that an 'iPad app' had been designed for David Cameron to give him a 'management dashboard':

> [T]he PM will then be able to see real-time data on government performance, polling, the markets, inflation statistics, what's trending on Twitter, search patterns on Google – anything, in other words.[23]

In third world style, the authorities alternately conflict with religious organizations and cosy up to them.

But we hope our 12 points on their own make our case for Britain's imminent relegation to the developing world. Put it another way, with all identifying names removed, they would certainly not be read for the first time as the description of a functioning first world country.

Chapter 4

A century of failure: the big fixes and why they went wrong

Croker: 'Hang on a minute lads, I've got a great idea.'
The Italian Job, 1969

Easy live and quiet die.
Sir Walter Scott, *The Bride of Lammermoor*, 1819

Plain living and high thinking are no more:
The homely beauty of the good old cause
Is gone.
William Wordsworth, *England, 1802*, 1807

In Britain Budget Day has its own special ritual. Even the apolitical take an interest, in the way that those with no love for horse racing often have a flutter on the Epsom Derby, when the chancellor of the Exchequer stands on the doorstep of 11 Downing Street on a spring afternoon holding the red box containing his speech aloft for the cameras, kisses his wife (if he has one), then sets off for the Palace of Westminster to present an account of the nation's finances and its economic prospects. Once upon a time, the pageantry involved the second lord of the Treasury taking a stroll in St James's Park to feed the ducks, although this is now seen as too much of a security risk. It was also the case in more innocent times that chancellors jealously guarded their budget secrets, retreating with their civil

servants into what was known as 'purdah' for weeks
before the big day, before revealing all to a crowded
House of Commons. Indeed, one of the subjects of this
chapter lost his job for telling a journalist what was
in his speech minutes before announcing his measures
at the despatch box. That, though, was a long time
ago when standards in public life were stricter. More
recently, Treasury officials and special advisers drip-feed
the contents of the budget speech into the media in the
days leading up to Budget Day, perhaps leaving one
big announcement in reserve for the speech itself.

The modern trend is for budgets to be shorter and
snappier than the three or four-hour monsters of the
nineteenth century, but few linger long in the memory.
Gordon Brown was chancellor for more than a decade
between 1997 and 2007, yet his two biggest decisions
– to grant the Bank of England independence and to
keep the United Kingdom out of the euro – were not
announced on Budget Day. The last truly memorable
budget was that of Nigel Lawson, who in 1988 cut the
top rate of income tax from 60 per cent to 40 per cent
and trimmed the standard rate from 27 per cent to
25 per cent. There was such uproar that the chamber
had to be cleared twice before the chancellor could
complete his speech. For the most part, though, even
the most avid observers of UK politics would struggle to
remember the details of any one of the budgets of Mr
Brown or his Conservative predecessor Kenneth Clarke,
who – in a brief break with tradition – used to deliver
his financial packages in the autumn. As for Kingsley
Wood, John Anderson, David Heathcoat-Amory, Peter
Thorneycroft: these long-forgotten chancellors are
the bit players of British twentieth-century political
history. Nor do the better known occupants of the
always go on to clamber to the top of the greasy pole:

Mr Clarke, like Denis Healey and R. A. Butler before him, vied for the title of the best politician never to be prime minister. Of the ones who did make it, only Sir Winston Churchill could honestly claim to have had a more successful time when he moved next door to 10 Downing Street. Mr Brown, like James Callaghan before him, became prime minister half way through a Parliament, presided over a period of economic crisis, and was defeated at the subsequent election. John Major followed Margaret Thatcher into 10 Downing Street after barely a year as chancellor, but after a honeymoon period that saw him win a fourth term for the Conservatives against the odds in 1992, spent a miserable five years coping with financial humiliation, scandal and rebellions over Europe.

George Osborne was 38 in early May 2010 when he became the youngest politician to become chancellor of the Exchequer since Randolph Churchill 120 years earlier. After being handed the job in the new coalition government by David Cameron in May 2010, Mr Osborne hastily worked up an emergency budget within six weeks, but his first full package of measures was announced on 23 March 2011. For the occasion, the chancellor was sporting a new smart-looking attaché case, the National Archive having decided that the leather red box first used by Gladstone in the 1860s had become so frail that it might fall apart if used again. But if the box was new, the same could not be said of the speech, which contained echoes – frequently strong, often distant – of those delivered by the previous 31 holders of the office since the end of the First World War. The budget was a homage to the fiscal rectitude of the inter-war years, so much so that Mr Osborne's critics said it was a return to the 'Treasury view' of the 1920s and early 1930s, the idea that spending by the government should equal the revenue it collected in tax, no matter what the state of the economy. Yet Mr Osborne's hour-long speech promised more than mere bean counting: it also offered a plan for growth, a pledge to harness science and technology, to broaden the economy out from its narrow base in financial services, to surf the green wave of the future, to redistribute prosperity to the regions.

'Yes, we want the City of London to remain the world's leading centre for financial services,' the chancellor said, 'but we should resolve that the rest of the country becomes a world leader in advanced manufacturing, life sciences, creative industries, business services, green energy and so much more. This is our vision for growth.'[1]

As was ever the case over the previous 100 years, there were 'difficult decisions' to be taken and 'major reforms' that had to be pushed through. The alternative, as no doubt Phillip Snowden, Harold Macmillan, Roy Jenkins or Sir Geoffrey Howe would have said, was to accept economic decline and a continuing fall in living standards. By the end of his speech, Mr Osborne was in full flow:

> We are only going to raise the living standards of families if we have an economy that can compete in the modern age. So this is our plan for growth. We want the words: 'Made in Britain', 'Created in Britain', 'Designed in Britain' 'Invented in Britain' to drive our nation forward. A Britain carried aloft by the march of the makers.

Most if not all of the economic themes of the past century were encapsulated in Mr Osborne's speech: modernization, reversing decline, and cutting coats according to the availability of cloth. Above all, there was the sense, familiar since 1918, that there was a way of unlocking Britain's innate talent and thereby rewinding the historical clock to the days when Gladstone's budget box was pristine. Chancellors since the heyday of Lloyd George at the Treasury have been like rabbit golfers convinced that all they need to do is find the magic ingredient that will turn them into contenders for the Open. And when after a couple of rounds on the course they have not been able to whack the ball 300 yards straight down the fairway, they have tried something else. After being bunkered a couple of times, they do something else again. As Alec Cairncross once said, there have been 'plenty of crises, false starts, failures and reversals of policy, misconceived ideas and matters that might have been better managed'.[2]

Like the struggling golfer with pretensions to lift the claret jug on the eighteenth green at St Andrews, the United Kingdom has failed to understand that winning the Open is about having a good plan and sticking to it, practising day after day to fine-tune a swing on the driving range. Such single-mindedness has rarely been in evidence in this country, which has never quite been able to work out for long enough exactly what the objectives of economic policy should be.

There are four main goals that governments tend to pursue: strong growth, full employment, price stability and trade balance. Some countries, such as the United States, have preferred a combination of the first two objectives; the visceral cultural legacy of the 1930s means that Washington has an aversion to high levels of joblessness. For Germany, the folk memories of 1923, when homeowners tossed worthless piles of Reichmarks into furnaces to keep warm and trundled wheelbarrows full of cash through the streets in search of a loaf of bread, are more powerful reference points than the unemployment in the early 1930s that helped bring Hitler to power. German economic policy remains biased towards low inflation and a trade surplus to this day. The United Kingdom has never been quite sure what its priorities should be, especially in the period since the Second World War.

Some governments have favoured growth and full employment; others have leaned towards price stability and external balance. Despite the structural weakness of the UK economy, many governments have added a fifth policy objective – to make Britain less unequal. The result has been that governments – even if for perhaps understandable reasons of history – have tended to bite off far more than they can chew. The United Kingdom has not experienced the trauma of being invaded for almost 950 years and has not seen its economic infrastructure destroyed by total war. Empire, the industrial dominance of the nineteenth century, victory (even at enormous cost) in two world wars: all these factors created the sense that for the United Kingdom it was not enough to opt for the limited horizons of the French or the Germans.

The administrations of the 1950s broadly supported a policy of expansion, but occasionally stamped on the brakes when strong growth led to a trade deficit or rising prices. The government of Ted Heath between 1970 and 1974 perhaps exemplified the confused nature of policy making: it began as a party dedicated to sound money, deregulation and trade union reform, but subsequently embarked on an ill-judged dash for growth when austerity pushed unemployment above 1 million. For the past 94 years, UK economic policy has either been the story of quick fixes adopted with the zeal of a convert only to be abandoned when there is no miracle cure, or the gathering together of a bundle of incompatible policy objectives pursued after the fashion of Mr Micawber in the hope that something will turn up. In that respect, Mr Osborne's speech – even down to its use of the clunky phrase 'the march of the makers' – was totally unexceptional. As we shall show in the rest of this chapter, there have been no shortage of ideas, no dearth of initiatives or creative thinking. Some of these ideas have emanated from the Treasury, some that were not have been thwarted by the Treasury. All have failed to find the key to permanent economic success. In one respect only has the United Kingdom been transformed into the equivalent of Tiger Woods: it shares his tendency to be caught with his trousers down.

Geddes: the axe man cometh

When the guns fell silent at 11 am on 11 November 1918, the United Kingdom was in a parlous economic state. The wealth accumulated during the previous century had been spent – and more – in four years of total war on the Western Front. There was pent-up inflationary pressure which had been suppressed by rationing, the national debt had soared and there was an army in khaki that had to be demobilized. To make matters worse, Britain was heavily reliant on the sunset industries of the nineteenth century – coal, shipbuilding, cotton. It was struggling to keep pace in the growth sectors that had been thrown up by the second industrial revolution at the beginning of the twentieth century.

What happened next was the biggest boom–bust the country has ever experienced, more violent even than the Lawson boom of the late 1980s or the housing bubble that preceded the crash of 2007. Much of the productive base of the economy had either been converted to military use or been destroyed, while consumer spending had been artificially restrained by rationing and high taxation. The coalition government of Lloyd George believed it had a duty to the servicemen returning home from the war, and so while providing almost unlimited quantities of cheap credit it also boosted real incomes by reducing the working week without changing wage rates. The result was a classic case of too much money chasing too few goods: the money supply exploded, consumer spending soared, and prices rose by 25 per cent between the spring of 1919 and the summer of 1920, a record not to be broken until the mid-1970s. Speculation was rife, leading to a bubble in asset prices, which eventually collapsed, partly because of its own unsustainability and partly because the Bank of England made borrowing more expensive by pushing the bank rate to 7 per cent.

The collapse was brutal: the drop in output in 1921 was sharper than that suffered at the depths of the Great Depression a decade later, and it took 16 years for UK production to return to the levels seen in 1918. Higher wage costs for industry resulted in mass layoffs, and the unemployment rate rose from 2.5 per cent to 20 per cent. Prices fell by 25 per cent as inflation was replaced by deflation.

There was widespread unhappiness about what was seen as public spending profligacy, leading to the rise of an anti-waste party that scored significant successes in by-elections. In addition, it was felt that a return to pre-war normalcy required the government to balance the budget, thereby freeing resources for private investment. Enter Sir Eric Geddes, with a background in business, who had been brought into Lloyd George's wartime cabinet as one of the men of 'push and go' who would bring some private-sector expertise to the cabinet table (a constant refrain over the past 100 years). Geddes was made first lord of the Admiralty at a time when the German U-boat menace was at its height, became better known by the public when he said the Germans would be squeezed at the Versailles peace talks until the pips squeaked, became the first minister of transport in Lloyd George's peacetime government, and was then give the task of pruning public spending, which by the early 1920s was running at three times the prewar level of 9 per cent of national output. The budget Geddes was told to trim was one thousand times smaller than that which troubled Mr Osborne on his elevation to the Treasury in 2010: public expenditure by Whitehall departments was estimated to be £603 million in 1921, and ministries were told to cut this by 20 per cent to just under £500 million. They came up with £75 million of savings and Geddes was instructed to come up with recommendations for saving a further £100 million – a 30 per cent cut in all.

This he did, in three reports published in the first few months of 1922. The largest cuts fell on the armed services, with education – to the disgust of what was then the *Manchester Guardian* – being the next biggest casualty. As if to show that nothing much changes from generation to generation, smaller sums were to be saved by a war on Whitehall waste and by selling off council houses. The response of the Cabinet also set a pattern for future years: ministers chipped away at the Geddes recommendations so that the £100 million of projected savings became £54 million. Despite strong support from the prime minister and from the public, the Geddes axe did not – and could not in the changed circumstances of the 1920s – return Britain to the night watchman state that existed pre-1914. The cost of coping with economic failure, high unemployment in particular, and the demands for higher social spending that had been generated by the war, meant the ambition of cutting public spending by 8 per cent of GDP was frustrated. There was instead a 5 per cent reduction by 1925, which allowed income tax to be lowered from 22.5 per cent to 20 per cent, but by the end of the decade the cuts had been more than recouped, as they were in later decades when a blunter axe was wielded.

Winston and the barbarous relic

There are plenty of candidates for the prize of the worst economic policy blunder of the past 100 years, all of them involving misguided attempts to maintain or manipulate the level of the pound. In bronze medal position is the decision by Harold Wilson's government to maintain the level of the pound for three years after the 1964 election rather than devaluing immediately. The silver medal goes to the Conservative Party in 1990 for its decision to join the European Exchange Rate Mechanism (ERM) at an over-valued rate just as the economy was hurtling into recession. But pride of place goes to Sir Winston Churchill for his decision to take Britain back on the gold standard in 1925, an error that hobbled an already weak economy, pushed up unemployment and was the primary cause of the General Strike the following year. Unlike most of those responsible for Britain's 'fixes', Churchill is revered rather than loathed. Had his political career ended when he left the Treasury in 1929, as for many years looked likely, that would not have been the case, and in the 1930s when he opposed both Hitler and the abdication of Edward VIII he was seen as a broken reed.

Churchill's mistake was, in one sense, inevitable. He was no economist and was faced with a policy establishment that was as united its support for gold, as were the Confederation of British Industry, the Trades Union Congress (TUC), the Liberal Democratic party and the bulk of both the Conservative and Labour parties for membership of the ERM. What's more, the gold standard had been such a symbol of Britain's nineteenth-century global mastery that it was only to be expected that there would be a hankering for the good old days. The problematic economic conditions of the 1920s meant that after trying fiscal rectitude, the next fix for Britain's postwar ills was a dose of Victorian monetary policy, a return to the gold standard at its prewar parity of $4.86.

This had been a priority for the Bank of England and the Treasury since it had been recommended by the Cunliffe committee in 1919, and for the three years after the slump of 1921 the Bank's governor, Montagu Norman, paid more concern to the external value of the pound than he did to the need to stimulate a sluggish domestic economy. The result was that the pound gradually rose in value against the dollar – and against European currencies – making Britain's exports less competitive. Keynes argued that the three years of price stability between 1922 and 1925 showed that a floating exchange rate need not result in inflation, but Norman insisted that it had been the credibility gained by the commitment to return to gold that had resulted in the benign outcome. 'These three years of "managed finance" have been possible only because they have been made up of steps – deliberate steps – towards a golden summer'.[3]

Eventually the traditionalists had their way. A rearguard action by Keynes and the wartime chancellor, Reginald McKenna, failed to embolden Churchill, who was instinctively against a return to gold but allowed himself to be swayed by the Bank and the Treasury. Here,

too, there are strong hints of policy debates and policy
mistakes to come in almost every subsequent decade.
Too much attention was paid to the interests of the City,
to those who believed that a strong currency led to a
strong economy rather than vice versa, and insisted that
the interests of financiers and industry were the same,
even though they were not in 1925 and rarely have been.
Critics of the decision said that an over-valued exchange
rate would cause higher unemployment, while supporters
argued that the problems of the UK economy could not
be resolved simply by changing the value of the pound
on the foreign exchanges. Both sides had a point.

Keynes was withering in his condemnation of Churchill,
warning that there would be higher unemployment as
workers resisted the downward pressure on wages needed
to price UK goods back into export markets. Modern
historians tend to take a less critical view, arguing that it
was the structural problems of British industry, which as
we noted in a previous chapter were evident before 1914,
that caused the sluggish performance of the economy in
the inter-war years. The return to gold did not help, but
it was the reliance on struggling sunset industries such
as cotton, coal and shipbuilding, and the failure until
the 1930s to make advances in the newer technologically
based sectors, that caused the real damage. Structural
change was slow, the contrast between Britain and the
United States in the 1920s stark:

> The economic difficulties of the late 1920s cannot be
> attributed to gold paranoia alone; there were other,
> more deep-seated problems involved (chief among
> them, perhaps being the supply shock of 1919–20). A
> more realistic exchange rate might have alleviated the
> situation, and provided opportunities to escape the
> doldrums, but it was not a panacea.[4]

Keynes foresaw the economic pain and the industrial strife that would be caused by a return to gold. What he did not envisage was that little more than six years later Britain would be forced off the gold standard for good, the first country to make that momentous and – as it turned out – beneficial decision.

Neville before Munich

Justifiably, the 1930s have a terrible reputation. It was the era of mass unemployment and extreme poverty, of Jarrow marches and street battles, all set against the drift towards war. Yet the 1930s were also one of the occasions in the past century when the United Kingdom came close to getting the economy right. The downturn triggered by the Wall Street Crash of 1929 was not as severe as in other countries, largely because the economy started from a low base, and there was a first-mover advantage from being the first country to devalue. Ramsay MacDonald's minority Labour government had in the summer of 1931 faced the same dilemma as confronted John Major in the summer of 1992 – should it tighten policy in order to defend the currency at a time when the economy was in recession?

As in 1992, policy makers insisted that the fixed exchange rate would be defended to the utmost, but showed a reluctance to back the rhetoric with action. Many Labour MPs refused to support cuts in the dole designed to enhance credibility in the financial markets at a time when unemployment was already running at 20 per cent, and the government was replaced by a national government in which MacDonald remained as premier. The decision to come off gold prompted the comment from Tom Johnson, former Labour Scottish secretary and lord privy seal: 'Nobody told us we could do that', while Jackson Reynolds, president of the First National Bank of New York, spoke for many international observers when he said that 'it felt like the end of the world'.

But as in 1992, abandoning the fixed exchange rate allowed the government to focus on building up the domestic economy. A lower pound meant lower interest rates, and a cheap money policy helped create the house-building boom in the suburbs. The long-delayed switch away from the old nineteenth-century staples at last got under way, and a light engineering sector began to flourish along the arterial roads of London and the other major cities. By 1935, the manufacturing company that employed the most people in Britain was Unilever, followed by Guest Keen & Nettlefold, ICI and Vickers. An increasing slice of investment took place in the growth industries such as cars, chemicals and electrical goods. The economy became less export-dependent, but a combination of a weaker currency and the tariff wall built around the empire shielded domestic producers from foreign competition. The system of imperial preference meant the United Kingdom had a source of cheap raw materials and ready-made markets, albeit soft ones that tended to grow more slowly than the global average.

Between 1931 and 1937 industrial production rose by 70 per cent, and there were signs that UK firms were learning lessons from both the United States and Germany. Companies became larger, mass production techniques became more widespread, science became more important and spending on research and development was increased. Throughout this six-year period the chancellor of the Exchequer was Neville Chamberlain, reviled since 1940 for his policy of appeasing Hitler, but a quietly effective finance minister under first MacDonald and later Stanley Baldwin.

Indeed, Chamberlain's career was the mirror image of Churchill's: he would have been deemed a success had he retired from politics when he left the Treasury in 1937 rather than becoming prime minister.

Chamberlain's macroeconomic strategy was similar to that of another chancellor from the Midlands, Kenneth Clarke, 60 years later. Both kept fiscal policy tight and relied on cheap money and a competitive pound to deliver the growth that would allow them to cut taxes and increase public spending. By 1934 Chamberlain was able to announce to the Commons, 'We have now finished the story of Bleak House and are sitting down this afternoon to enjoy the first chapter of Great Expectations.'

Chamberlain's approach was, by today's standards, dangerously interventionist. He had first-hand experience of running a manufacturing business in the Midlands, which led to him being snobbishly called a 'provincial manufacturer of iron bedsteads' by Lloyd George (a provincial solicitor), and as the younger son of the avidly protectionist Joseph Chamberlain was neither a free trader nor a believer in market forces. On the contrary, he forced through a series of measures that in the heyday of Margaret Thatcher (a provincial grocer's daughter) would have been decried as 'picking winners'. Chamberlain handed a state subsidy to Cunard to ensure that the transatlantic liner *Queen Mary* was built; he encouraged the formation of a cartel in the iron and steel industry that boosted output; he took steps to protect domestic agriculture, which led to an increase of almost 50 per cent in the acreage devoted to wheat; and he invested £35 million to create the publicly owned monopoly of the London Passenger Transport Board, which one of his biographers said 'gave Britain for a time the most efficient and the most design-conscious underground system in the world'.[5]

It has to be said that many during the 1930s considered *Bleak House* a better description of Britain than *Great Expectations*, and the post gold standard recovery needs to be put into perspective. The main reason for economic recovery was the housing boom, which accounted for one-sixth of the increase in activity between 1932 and 1934 even though it only accounted for 3 per cent of the economy. Manufacturing performance improved but failed to close the big productivity gap that had opened up with the United States in the years immediately before and after the Second World War. The motor industry was growing, but exports of cars accounted for only 12 per cent of the UK total in 1935, compared with 41 per cent for cotton.

The inter-war period as a whole saw a continuation of the trend evident before 1914. The UK share of global trade in manufactured goods fell in the 1920s when trade volumes were rising, and fell even more sharply in the 1930s when they were declining. In 1937, the last year before rearmament started to affect the shape of the economy, UK exports were at little more than 70 per cent of their pre-war level, and it took until 1950 for them to exceed the volumes seen in 1913. The percentage of exports going to the empire increased as UK firms found the going tough in the faster-growing markets of the United States and the bigger European markets – Germany, France, Belgium and the Netherlands. In short, the industrial renaissance of the 1930s was similar to those seen after depreciations of sterling in the 1980s and 1990s; vigorous for a time but incomplete. There was talk of bright futures and corners being turned, but by the time Chamberlain finally gave up on appeasement and took the United Kingdom to war in 1939, there was a lot more to be done.

War and its aftermath: two men from King's

The age of mass unemployment came to an end with the Second World War. The jobless total had halved during the 1930s, but still remained at 8 per cent in 1938. But first rearmament and then mobilization brought down the jobless total from 2 million at the start of 1939 to below 1 million when Hitler invaded the Low Countries and France in the spring of 1940, and 500,000 in early 1941, when the United Kingdom was fighting alone.

Until capacity constraints emerged in 1943, growth grew rapidly by more than 6 per cent a year on average, mopping up the last pockets of unemployment in the depressed regions, prompting a surge in the number of women in the workforce and transforming what had been, despite the cosy cartels and monopolies, a free-market economy into a planned regime dominated by the state.

Two postwar developments had their origins in this period. One was the socialization of the means of production, with a command and control approach to industrial production for the war effort and the direction of labour. The second development was the result of Keynes's success in persuading the Treasury to turn the rules of prewar public finance on their head: rather than start from the principle of balancing the books, Kingsley Wood accepted for the first time in his 1941 budget that fiscal policy should be governed by what was needed to win the war. Using more modern statistical tools, the government would decide what the potential of the economy was, then use direct controls such as rationing, and to a lesser extent tax, to ensure that resources were transferred from consumers to the state, thereby keeping inflation in check.

Spending on the war effort rose from 7 per cent of

national income in 1938 to 55 per cent in 1943, while over the same period consumption dropped from 87 per cent of GDP to 55 per cent. The strategy succeeded by allowing the United Kingdom to remain undefeated until the arrival of the United States and the Soviet Union in the war, while high taxes and shortages meant inflationary pressures were suppressed. But as in the 1914–18 conflict there was a high price to pay for victory. The United Kingdom liquidated overseas assets, borrowed money, and investment fell by two-thirds in the first four years of the war. The economy's net wealth by 1951 was lower in 1945 than it had been in 1913, while the struggle for national survival meant exports at the end of the Second World War were barely more than a third of their level in 1939.

It would be wrong to exaggerate what was considered in 1945 a 'financial Dunkirk', because other European countries – France, Germany and Russia – had suffered even greater damage to their economic fabric, and in the cases of Germany and Russia a far higher loss of life. Over the years it has been the received wisdom that other European countries used Marshall Aid from the United States to rebuild their industrial capacity from scratch, while the United Kingdom had to make do with scraps in order to patch up its aged factories. This is a myth: the United Kingdom received more Marshall Aid than any other country, and by the end of the first phase of postwar reconstruction the average age of its non-residential capital stock was the lowest of any of the G7 countries.

As one account puts it:

Thus there appears little in Britain's immediate postwar circumstances that was particularly disadvantageous: it is partly this which has given such force to the popular notion that Britain won the war but – in terms of subsequent economic performance – lost the peace. Britain's problem needs a different specification: less one of objective material circumstance than of attitudes and expectations.[6]

So what were the attitudes and expectations that held Britain back in the postwar era? First, there was the pride of the victor: for the second time in little more than a quarter of a century the United Kingdom had galvanized herself, mobilized for total war, and triumphed. Little needed to be done to nationalize industries that had effectively been run from Whitehall during the war, or so it was thought. There was, moreover, none of the national introspection seen in Germany, and to a lesser extent France, in 1945. Second, while rationing had meant there was little for consumers to spend their money on during the war, the return to full employment and higher levels of production saw real incomes rise. Once the war in the East ended in August 1945 there was pressure to unleash this pent-up demand, even though the greater need was to channel resources into modern investment. Third, consumers also wanted higher spending on the welfare state, their demands stimulated originally by the deprivation of the 1920s and 1930s, then spurred by the Beveridge Report of 1942 and the election of the Attlee government. Finally, the United Kingdom still felt it deserved the trappings of a great power: the empire, military bases around the world, the sterling area, a nuclear bomb.

The scale of Britain's ambition is that even the United States, which accounted for half of world output in 1945, did not promise voters higher living standards, vastly expanded social provision and heavy military spending overseas. Indeed, when Lyndon Johnson did try to combine his Great Society programme with a scaling-up of America's involvement in Vietnam it led to higher inflation, balance of payments problems, and eventually the break-up of the postwar Bretton Woods fixed exchange rate system. The United Kingdom, while not quite flat broke in 1945, was in a far weaker economic state than the United States two decades later, yet voters believed – or were led to believe – that the transition from the command and control wartime economy to the New Jerusalem would not just be swift, but be possible without making sacrifices at home or abroad.

Towards the end of the war Keynes had written the Cabinet a memorandum about the way to finesse postwar reconstruction in which he warned:

> Our own habits are the greatest obstacle in the way of carrying out almost every one of the above recommendations. All our reflex actions are those of a rich man, so that we promise others too much. Our longings for relaxation from the war are so intense that we promise ourselves too much.[7]

This was a perceptive assessment.

Keynes was, of course, one of the dominant figures of the postwar era, even though he died within a year of the war's end. The other dominant British economist, Hugh Dalton, shared the same background of Eton and King's College Cambridge, but was a man of different temperamental stamp. Keynes's mission, as a liberal capitalist, was to save the free-market system from itself; Dalton, viewed as a traitor to his class by the right, believed in planning, nationalization and redistribution, took delight in outraging his political opponents, and has justifiably earned the reputation as the most socialist chancellor in Labour's history. Keynes was Dalton's tutor at Cambridge, and perhaps for that reason, the relationship between the two men was not always warm: Keynes did not have a high regard for Dalton, whom he referred to in private as 'the dirty doctor', and made sure the chancellor's officials knew it. Dalton, according to one account, 'found himself in the strange position of needing his chief economic adviser's good opinion rather than the other way round. A non-economic Chancellor might have felt less upstaged.'[8]

Even so, for the last months of his life Keynes was in the subservient role as he conducted long negotiations in Washington about the terms of an American loan needed to finance Dalton's plans for a socialist economy. The US Treasury was less willing to bankroll what it considered a dangerous anti-capitalist experiment in the United Kingdom than Keynes had envisaged, and so rejected calls for a generous $6 billion grant and instead insisted on a smaller $4.4 billion loan with strings attached. The loan allowed the Attlee government to enact the measures to tackle the five giants identified by Beveridge as blocking the road to progress – Want, Ignorance, Squalor, Disease and Idleness – and to bring the Bank of England, coal, the railways, civil aviation and electricity into public ownership in its first two years in power. Dalton also prepared unashamedly redistributive budgets and sought, with mixed results, to keep the cost of borrowing low.

But one of the strings attached by Washington to the loan – a commitment by the United Kingdom to make sterling convertible into dollars by July 1947 – caused a financial crisis that marked the point in the United Kingdom's postwar history where socialism gave way to demand management and fine-tuning of the economy, based (not always faithfully) on the doctrines espoused by Keynes in the *General Theory*. Dalton's November 1947 Budget is remembered for the indiscretion to a lobby journalist on his way into the chamber that led to his resignation. The leak overshadowed the deflationary nature of the emergency package, deemed necessary to rebuild UK reserves of dollars after the run on sterling earlier in the year.

Of all the big fixes, that pushed through by Dalton in the first two years of the Attlee administration was the most ambitious and profound until Margaret Thatcher's counter-revolution in the 1980s. The aim was to make Britain fairer, more efficient, less scarred by unemployment and pockets of regional poverty, and the success of the Labour government was that – unlike in 1918 – there was no attempt to turn the clock back to an imagined prewar Elysium. Even so, it was still a fix that failed. The Attlee government did not realize that the controls needed to crank up production of Spitfires and Hurricanes were too crude for peacetime. Nor did it fully comprehend that the support for socialist measures was, for the most part, based on pragmatism rather than ideology: the command and control model had ensured the nation's survival and the public was willing to give it a chance after 1945. Labour's core support remained solid for the entirety of the Attlee government, which in six and a half years never lost a by-election and recorded its highest ever share of the vote when narrowly losing the 1951 election, but support among floating voters dwindled as the financial crisis and attempts to pursue too many goals at once forced a tightening of controls and even tougher rationing. The 1984 film *A Private Function* captures the mood of 1947, with the citizens of a Yorkshire town seeking to outwit a food inspector by raising a pig illegally for a dinner to celebrate the royal wedding.

If the Attlee government overestimated the strength of socialist fervour, it underestimated the weakness of free-market capitalism, which as the historian David Kynaston notes, was at a low ebb in 1945:

> High taxation, Victorian-style private enterprise stigmatised by its inter-war association with mass unemployment; large-scale concerns (public like the BBC or the Bank of England, private like ICI or Shell or the clearing banks offering jobs for life and career paths predetermined to almost the smallest detail; the state fresh from its finest hour and now offering the opportunity to transform society – altogether, it is instinctively plausible that the '1945' moment represented a nadir of capitalism's animal spirits.[9]

Another chronicler of this period, Correlli Barnett, is withering in his criticism of postwar governments' failure to recognize that the United Kingdom could not afford both a world-player role, increased spending on welfare and the recasting of the economy in the brief period of opportunity that existed while rivals such as Germany and Japan rebuilt their factories from the rubble. It was never really likely that the United Kingdom would settle in 1945 for the role on the global stage of Sweden or the Netherlands, having faced invasion in the summer of 1940 only to emerge victorious five years later. Nor was the Attlee government minded to delay building work on the New Jerusalem. As a result, resources were diverted away from infrastructure projects and manufacturing investment to pay for military bases in Germany, family allowances and – later – the cost of fighting the Korean War.

The newly created British Rail was starved of investment, in contrast to France where the engineer Louis Armand was given the resources by the government to create the best railway system in Europe. Not until

13 years after the end of the Second World War did Britain start to unveil its answer to Hitler's autobahns – an eight-mile stretch of motorway around Preston in Lancashire. The underinvestment was important in two respects: it limited the ability of the economy to grow and it undermined public support for the nationalized industries.

But if socialism failed to embed itself in Britain, the same could be said of Keynesianism. There was certainly greater intellectual support among the policy establishment for what was seen as a more modern approach to economic management, based around expansion, full employment and a great role for market forces. It is also the case that the heyday of Keynesianism, the quarter-century between 1948 and 1973, saw rapid growth, low unemployment, a decrease in inequality and an expansion of the welfare state. But Britain's growth was less impressive than that of its rivals, and the period was littered with periods of stop–go in which balance of payments constraints (although modest by recent standards) and the need to defend the pound forced chancellors to stamp on the brake.

For a while, problems were disguised by the postwar boom, which in the words of John F. Kennedy was a rising tide that lifted all boats. By 1950, exports were 50 per cent up on their prewar levels and more than half of global car exports came with a made-in-Britain stamp. Yet the strength was illusory: although global competition was as yet weak, there was a tendency for UK firms to respond only slowly to changing patterns of demand and to rely heavily on the captive, or semi-captive, markets of the Empire. The fundamental problem was the same as it had been for half a century or more; a failure to recognize that the right macroeconomic policies were a necessary but not sufficient condition for success. That required changes to design, industrial organization, education, labour relations, and none of these were adequately addressed during the Golden Age.

Other factors were also at work. It is by no means certain that Keynes, primarily a believer in the use of monetary policy to manage the economy, would have agreed with the fiscal fine-tuning of his disciples in the 1950s and 1960s, and to the extent that he would have given his backing to use of the budget as a regulator of demand, he would have insisted that surpluses be run in the good times to balance deficits in the bad times. More importantly, Keynesian demand management in the postwar period was never properly embedded in an institutional structure that would deliver full employment without inflation or industrial strife. Some countries, such as Austria, did develop a corporatist structure in which government, industry and unions could reach consensus on how to divide the fruits of the full-employment society. In Britain the system remained adversarial, with policy makers using credit controls, import restrictions, higher taxes and pay policies – both voluntary and statutory – in an attempt to prevent an economy running at or above full capacity leading to upward pressure on the cost of living.

Jean, Tony and Ted: hate figures of the modern age

The 1950s and 1960s were a 'wilderness of budget nightmares, cancelled projects and general embarrassment', according to Simon Winder in *The Man Who Saved Britain*.[10] The man in question was Ian Fleming's James Bond, who was a literary sensation in the 1950s before becoming a celluloid smash in the 1960s. Bond was competent, technologically savvy, brutally efficient, and successful at a time when the economy had a Licence to Fail. Whether he was about to be sliced in two by Goldfinger or needed to find a way of exposing Hugo Drax as a cheat at cards in *Moonraker,* Bond could always find a way out of a tight spot. When 007 tried something it worked, something that could not be said of the economy, which remained stubbornly resistant to the many attempts at making it as resourceful and quick on its feet as Bond had been when faced with the Spectre thug Red Grant in the scene on the Orient Express in *From Russia with Love.*

It was not for the want of trying. The search continued throughout the 1950s, 1960s and 1970s for the strategy that would modernize Britain, symbolized by two white elephants: nuclear power and Concorde. Governments tried nationalization and a bonfire of controls; they increased and cut public spending; they had policies to incentivize industry to invest, relocate and merge; they proposed reform of trade unions, expanded higher education, pledged to improve training, encouraged higher spending on research and development. The era ended in the winter of 1973–4 when sharply rising oil prices killed off the long postwar boom, pushed inflation above 25 per cent, prompted a run on the pound that required the intervention of the International Monetary Fund, and created the conditions for an entirely different approach under Mrs Thatcher in the 1980s.

Jean Monnet features twice in our story, since he was put in charge of French postwar reconstruction by Charles de Gaulle at the end of the Second World War before becoming one of the architects of the European Common Market in the 1950s. Both projects attracted envious glances from the British side of the English Channel, as it became clear that a decade or more of underperformance was not a temporary phenomenon. The Conservatives had tinkered with Labour's postwar settlement, returning iron and steel to the private sector and removing the last vestiges of rationing, but accepted the case for full employment and higher welfare spending. As housing minister, Harold Macmillan had a better record for building council homes than Nye Bevan.

Even so, by late 1950s, both the German and French economies were growing more rapidly than the United Kingdom's. Higher public spending failed to boost the growth rate in the late 1950s, leading instead to the familiar problems of overheating and stop–go, and creating the conditions for the next three fixes: Europe, planning and technology, all of them intertwined. The United Kingdom, it was said, needed to unshackle itself from the past; to recognize that the Age of Empire had ended and the Age of Europe had begun. Lessons should be learned from France, where Monnet's system of 'indicative planning' resulted in annual growth of 4.5 per cent a year in the three decades after 1945, compared with just under 3 per cent for Britain. Finally, as Harold Wilson stressed in his famous 'White heat' speech to the Labour Party conference in 1963, there were the lessons to be learned from the jet age and the exploration of space: the country needed fewer men in tweed jackets on grouse moors, more men in white coats beavering away in laboratories.

After failing to join the Common Market at its launch in 1957, the United Kingdom applied for membership for the first time in 1961, only to be rebuffed by de Gaulle. At the same time, the government had looked at France's use of indicative planning since 1946 and liked what it saw. This led to the setting up of the National Economic Development Council, which in turn prepared the ground for the Wilson government's National Plan and the creation of a Ministry of Technology (Mintech).

Indicative planning originated in France, and was carried out by the Commissariat Général du Plan, headed by Monnet. The intention was to boost growth by identifying bottlenecks and shortages at an early stage, and a cadre of technocrats set objectives, directed investment towards national champions and sought to use precious resources in as efficient a way as possible. Very much a rationalist project in the tradition of the Enlightenment, the French plan was intended to show business that there were opportunities to make money, hence leading to higher private investment to match the increase in public spending.

Predictably, importing indicative planning from France proved more difficult than importing cases of Chateau Lafite or bottles of Chanel No. 5. It was not just that Monnet was a rather more talented administrator than John Selwyn Lloyd, a mediocre politician out of his depth in the Treasury of the 1960s. After liberation, France was in all respects a shattered nation. It had been invaded twice in a generation, had had the worst performing economy of all the great powers in the 1930s, and was ready for the shock treatment Monnet was urged to deliver. Unlike in Britain, there was no question of a trade-off between social spending and resources for infrastructure and industrial investment; the building of new homes and the provision of pensions had to wait as money was spent on railways, coal, shipping, hydro-electric power plants and petroleum refineries. Profits rose as a share of national income while the share taken by salaries and wages fell. When Selwyn Lloyd got round to sketching out his idea of using a tripartite National Economic Development Council as the centrepiece for raising the growth rate to 4 per cent a year, he hoped to secure support from both unions and employers for wage moderation. He hoped in vain.

Wilson considered these early attempts at planning to be amateurish, and decided that what Britain needed was a new Department of Economic Affairs (DEA), which would be separate from the Treasury and responsible for a National Plan, a White Heat department that would make Britain a 'cutting-edge' economy, and a 'big is beautiful' Industrial Reconstruction Company dedicated to achieving economies of scale and seen as an alternative to nationalization.

The idea of the National Plan was that by setting a target of an annual 5.5 per cent increase in exports necessary to achieve 4 per cent growth, industry would have the incentive to expand, as it had in France. What appeared to be lost on Wilson was that the unspoken motto of French governments in the 1950s and 1960s was 'devalue early and devalue often'. From the outset, the National Plan was made impossible by the doomed attempts to avoid a sterling devaluation, and the only variable that increased in line with the blueprint was government spending. The DEA lost the Whitehall turf war with the Treasury, and although not formally abandoned until 1969, was effectively dead from the time of the deflationary July measures in 1966.

'White heat' has been criticized ever since as a piece of empty rhetoric, an early example of sound-bite politics, but this is a harsh judgement when set against the plethora of initiatives from chancellors up to and including Mr Osborne for harnessing Britain's science base. As with many of the fixes contained in this chapter, there was little wrong with the concept: from the start, the problem has been implementation.

Wilson made Frank Cousins, general secretary of the Transport and General Workers Union, the first minister of technology in 1964. It was a typical piece of Wilson political cleverness, because he thought Cousins could secure union support for the shift to high-tech production, which the prime minister assumed would have knock-on consequences for jobs. It was not one of Wilson's better appointments, as he recognized when he replaced Cousins with the far more suitable Anthony Wedgwood Benn within two years. Like Monnet, Mr Benn had a part to play in two of the postwar fixes. He was viciously attacked in the 1970s as a left-wing firebrand, and more gently lampooned in his earlier incarnation as the slightly geekish techno man, obsessed with everything from answering machines to supersonic air travel. Despite being considered a political lightweight ('Wedgy ... refuses to face the real difficulties because he has a second-rate intellect', his then Cabinet colleague, Richard Crossman sniffily observed), few would now quibble with Mr Benn's analysis of Britain's predicament in the mid-1960s (and thereafter):

> Britain had become the workshop of the world, he would say, between 1750 and 1850, when national efforts had been directed towards industrial development. In the century to 1950, however, Britain had gained an empire, and the highest respect went not to the engineers or producers of wealth but to the conquerors and administrators of wealth overseas. Britain had captured the markets, quite literally, with her troops. Now there were no more colonies and Britain must return to the development of industry, which had made the country powerful in the first place.[11]

White heat was a classic case of trying to do many

things at once. The idea of sponsoring four 'key' industries – computers, electronics, telecommunications and machine tools – showed foresight, while the major reorganizations in computing, engineering and cars to form International Computers Limited (ICL), General Electrical Company and British Leyland were a worthy stab at creating national champions of the sort successfully created in France and Japan. Yet time, energy and vast amounts of public money were also spent on Britain's civil nuclear power industry, on the financial black hole that was Concorde, and on lame ducks like Upper Clyde Shipbuilders.

Mintech absorbed the Ministry of Aviation in February 1967, a time of financial stringency in the period between the July measures and the devaluation of sterling in November 1967. Mr Benn quickly realized how much public money was being wasted on prestige aviation projects, and at the annual dinner of the Society of British Aerospace Companies in June 1967 he said that previous aviation ministers financing the industry from taxpayers' money had 'run off with sums of money that made the Great Train Robbers look like schoolboys pinching pennies from a blind man's drum'. That said, Mr Benn was prone himself to a bit of the hype regularly trotted out by those who warned that failure to support projects like Concorde would leave Britain without a first-class aviation industry. As the Anglo-French jet was wheeled out in Toulouse in 1969, Mr Benn said: 'It'll change the shape of the world, it'll shrink the globe by half. We're trying to build the Model T Ford of the supersonics for the 1970s and 1980s. It replaces in one step the entire progress made in aviation since the Wright Brothers in 1903.'

Robert Millward notes that at the time Wilson was making his 'white heat' speech in 1963, Britain's commitment to science – whether measured by scientists, engineers, or spending on R&D – compared reasonably well with the United States, Germany and France. By the late 1970s the United Kingdom was lagging well behind West Germany and Japan, and been caught up by France in civil R&D. Even in 1962, however, R&D was heavily weighted towards:

> activities which reflected its vain ambitions to remain a major world political power. Britain devoted a larger share of its R&D expenditure to military and space expenditure than did any other country except the USA, and the result was a crowding out of investment in other parts of the economy that had a higher potential for long-term growth.
>
> UK spending in 1962 on industrial research and development included virtually the same proportion on the aircraft industry (35 per cent) as the US (36 per cent) but significantly less than Germany in electrical machinery, instruments, vehicles, other machinery and chemicals. The predominance of UK activity in military and aircraft development was especially unfortunate. This was not a big area, and it was impossible for Britain effectively to compete with the USA; in addition, it fostered the ideal of 'pure engineering', led to big commercial mistakes like Concorde and creamed off the best scientists and engineers. In stark contrast, parts of mechanical engineering had hardly any graduate engineers at all before 1960.[12]

But if the Wilson government could justifiably be accused of pursuing goals that were mutually incompatible, it was nothing on the short-lived and unlamented administration of Edward Heath, a government that piled as many quick fixes into three and a half years as had been seen in the previous quarter-century. First, there was proto-Thatcherite Heath, promising to roll back the state, clean up industrial relations and allow market incentives to flourish. Then there was 'U-turn Ted', panicked by the impact of his tough new approach when two 'lame ducks' – Upper Clyde Shipbuilders and Rolls-Royce – ran into financial problems. Subsequently there was go for growth Ted, boosting public spending and abandoning direct rationing of credit, a disastrous policy that saw the money supply increase by 62 per cent in two years and prompted the first, though not the last, of Britain's postwar housing bubbles. Heath inherited a belief in big government, had plans to build the Channel Tunnel and a third London airport; he reorganized local government and the National Health Service; he began by jailing trade unionists under the Industrial Relations Act and ended by bringing in threshold agreements, which guaranteed wage bargainers above-inflation settlements as prices went up. Throughout, Heath was driven by a belief that the United Kingdom's destiny was to be part of Europe, and he succeeded where Macmillan and Wilson had failed by securing UK entry into the European Economic Community at the third time of asking in 1973. He left office with Britain on a three-day week and inflation on course for the postwar record of 26 per cent achieved 18 months later.

The coda to this period was Mr Benn's second incarnation, as the short-lived industry secretary in the Labour government of 1974–9, in which he proposed tripartite planning agreements with each sector of the economy in which financial support from the government would be contingent on industry's compliance. For the top 100 companies planning agreements were to be mandatory, while a National Enterprise Board (NEB) would hold shares in a score of leading firms, providing

Whitehall with a say in how they were run. There was never any real sign that Wilson would have favoured such an approach even had the economic climate of the mid-1970s been less harsh. As it was, only two planning agreements were ever signed and Mr Benn was quickly shunted off to become energy secretary.

The NEB was set up, and performed a twin role. It provided support for companies in trouble, most notably British Leyland and Rolls-Royce, which between them accounted for three-quarters of the £780 million invested by the NEB by 1979. In the case of Rolls-Royce, today one of the United Kingdom's few world-class manufacturing companies, support for the 'lame duck' proved remarkably successful. The NEB, excoriated at the time (and for many years afterwards) for attempting to 'pick winners', also built shareholdings in companies making semiconductors, electronic office equipment and computer software. Today, particularly seen against the vastly larger sums spent bailing out the banks, these look like rather smart investments.

Maggie, Maggie, Maggie

When the Labour Party met in Blackpool for its annual conference in September 1976, the financial crisis precipitated by the first oil shock had reached its climax. Sterling was falling fast on the foreign exchanges and help had been sought from the IMF. Inflation was coming down from its postwar peak but was still well above 10 per cent; the balance of payments was deeply in the red and the budget deficit was expected to hit a peacetime record of 12 per cent of GDP. The prime minister, James Callaghan, decided it was time for a few home truths, and used his speech to inform the nation that the party was over. There would be no attempt by the government to spend its way out of recession, since that policy would merely lead to higher inflation.

This was the moment, rather than the subsequent arrival of Margaret Thatcher in Downing Street in 1979, that marked the shift to an entirely new approach to economic management. The foundations for the next big fix – monetarism – were dug in the dog days of the 1974–9 Labour government, when far more attention was paid than hitherto to the growth in the money supply and the public sector borrowing requirement. The difference between the Callaghan administration and that of Mrs Thatcher was that the former embraced monetarist tools out of necessity, the latter out of conviction. When she came to power in May 1979, Mrs Thatcher and her closest advisers believed that the aim of macroeconomic policy was low and stable inflation, and that the way to achieve this goal was by control of the money supply.

The thesis was quite simple: the government would keep the money supply in check, and if workers chose to price themselves out of a job then so be it. Fiscal policy, the mainstay of demand management during the 1950s, 1960s and 1970s, would have a subordinate role; instead of fine-tuning, public borrowing would be reduced to free up resources for private investment and to help keep interest rates low. There was no explicit target for the exchange rate, which like all other prices would be allowed to find its own level. Unlike Heath, Mrs Thatcher stuck to the path of deregulation even when the economy fell into deep recession, and indeed accelerated the rolling-back of the state through privatization, a policy barely mentioned in the 1979 manifesto and which did not really get under way until 1984.

Eventually the Thatcher big fix of 1979 would lead to the two big fixes of the past two decades – inflation targeting and an industrial policy based on the financial services industry. There were, however, many twists and turns along the way as the limitations of monetarism were exposed. It proved impossible for the Treasury and the Bank of England to control the broader measure of the money supply, including bank deposits, particularly after the abolition of exchange controls and domestic curbs on credit growth. Sterling M3, the target adopted for the money supply by Mrs Thatcher in 1979, grew by 16 per cent on average throughout the 1980s, and was quietly dropped by Nigel Lawson in 1987.

Fix number two was to target a narrower measure of the money supply based on notes and coins, but when basing policy on loose change also proved problematic, Mr Lawson turned to the exchange rate. Having come to power committed to a freely floating pound, the chancellor first tried shadowing the German mark, in the hope that Britain could import low inflation from the continent, then stepped up pressure for the United Kingdom to join the ERM, which it eventually did in October 1990. The ignominious exit of the country from the ERM less than two years later led to a new big idea. Instead of targeting proxies for inflation – the money supply or the German mark – the government would henceforth target inflation itself.

Far from providing economic stability, Mrs Thatcher was responsible for a raging boom sandwiched between two recessions. Inflation was suppressed but not killed off, with wage demands held down by high levels of unemployment. The promised reductions in government spending did not materialize, with the original aim watered down, first to a reduction in inflation-adjusted terms, and when that was not possible either, to a plan to reduce public spending as a proportion of national output. Manufacturing productivity did grow more rapidly in Britain than in rival nations during the 1980s (a reversal of the postwar trend), and this was in small part due to the government's policy of attracting inward investment. More important factors were the destruction of industrial capacity in the early 1980s, the strength of the boom in the late 1980s and the scope for catch-up with other countries. There was no industrial renaissance, as shown by the trade deficit in manufacturing, which in 1982 went into the red for the first time since the dawn of the industrial revolution and grew steadily wider as the decade wore on. Consumers took advantage of financial deregulation to borrow more money, which they spent on homes, holidays abroad and durable goods. The banks expanded their activities as manufacturing struggled; the increase in imports of goods was disguised by exports of oil from the North Sea, where production peaked in the mid-1980s.

Only for a brief interlude, between 1992 and 1997, was there any deviation from this model. In the period after Black Wednesday, exports became cheaper as a result of a falling pound, while falling house prices and rising taxes kept consumer spending in check. There was a rebalancing of the economy towards manufacturing and exports, and by the time the Major government was removed from office the balance of payments was briefly close to balance. Tony Blair came to power convinced that it was possible to extend market forces into new sectors of the economy – the public realm, in particular – and harness them for social ends. This was the 'third way', a big fix that in reality was a patch-up job on the big fix of the 1980s. Inflation targeting was made more formal through independence for the Bank of England; a minimum wage was introduced alongside some modest easing of constraints on trade unions; resources were channelled into regional development agencies; and the fruits of growth were spent on higher public spending and tax credits. But there was a continuum from the 1980s in that control of inflation remained the cornerstone of macroeconomic policy, supply-side reforms were seen as the way to improve the growth rate, and booms in house prices, financial services and consumer spending disguised weaknesses that manifested themselves in a deteriorating trade balance.

Labour's real big fix came under Mr Brown, when he was forced to adopt the sort of interventionist strategy advocated by Mr Benn in the 1970s. The government nationalized Northern Rock and took large stakes in Lloyds and Royal Bank of Scotland. There was an industrial strategy based around picking winners; macroeconomic policy was geared to boosting growth and reducing inflation. The experiment was, like many of the others detailed in this chapter, short-lived, and under Mr Osborne a different course has again been charted.

Mr Osborne's message – a familiar one, it has to be said – is that there will be calm seas ahead once the current storm has been negotiated, even though the history of a hundred years of big fixes is that battening down the hatches has been rather more common than splicing the mainbrace. The success of economic policy has traditionally been judged by the interplay of the four big variables mentioned earlier – growth, unemployment, inflation and the balance of payments. To these can be added two new performance indicators: fairness and environmental sustainability. A successful economy would, over time, have more growth, lower inflation, lower unemployment, a stronger trade performance, and be both less unequal and have a smaller ecological footprint. In this respect, the most successful period in the past 100 years was the 1950s, when there were strong growth, full employment, low inflation, only intermittent problems with the balance of payments, decreasing levels of inequality and the first attempts – through the Clean Air Act – to tackle pollution. Since then, all the trade-offs have worsened, as they have in fairness across the developed world, even if not as spectacularly as in the United Kingdom. A century of fixes has left Britain in the position where lower levels of activity are accompanied not just by higher unemployment, but by bigger trade deficits, stronger inflationary pressure, greater inequality and more intense pressure on resources. That is a measure of their failure.

Chapter 5

Into free-fall: the no-strategy strategy

You can't have luck when someone else has skill. So a long time ago
we decided to invest in the stock market. There's no skill in that.
Amy Tan, The Joy Luck Club, 1989

The ship was cheer'd, the harbour clear'd
Merrily did we drop.
Samuel Taylor Coleridge,
The Rime of the Ancient Mariner, 1798

Go with the flow.
Advertising slogan for London Docklands, c. 1990

For those who like to seek connections beneath the
surface of events, the dying months of 2011 would have
proved fertile ground. Apparently disparate happenings
proved, on closer examination, to have intriguing links
with each other.

For example, 6 October saw the publication of a new
code of conduct for solicitors in England and Wales, a first
step towards a wholesale shake-up of the legal profession
scheduled for the following year. The code, published by
the self-explanatory Solicitors Regulation Authority, had
been rendered necessary because the reforms would allow
outside investors for the first time to own part or all of
a law firm. Hitherto, practices had been structured as
partnerships, with each partner required to be a qualified
solicitor.

The legislation behind this change, the Legal Services

Act, 'is set to liberalise Britain's £23 billion legal market', the *Financial Times* reported on 6 October. If there were any solicitors of a traditional bent on whose ears the phrase 'legal market' grated, there was no mention of them in this or similar reports. In a separate article in the same newspaper on the same day, the justice secretary, Kenneth Clarke, was quoted indirectly as suggesting these changes could prove to be to the legal profession what the 'Big Bang' reforms of 1986 had been to the City's financial services industry.

That was a funny thing. Because not only had the Big Bang taken place 25 years earlier to the very month, the explosion of rewards and influence that had followed, quite apart from the enormous scale of the subsequent risk taking, widely blamed for having played a key role in the post-2007 financial crisis, had prompted the Occupy movement to park its tents outside St Paul's Cathedral in perhaps the most widely reported and controversial protest in Britain since the poll tax riot of March 1990.

Far from the City, in terms of geography, China's activities in Africa were prompting concern round the world. So-called 'infrastructure for minerals' deals had seen China build railways, roads, hospitals, airports and other facilities in return for lucrative mining concessions in countries including the Democratic Republic of Congo and Zambia. Given the dilapidated state of much of the infrastructure in sub-Saharan Africa, international opinion had been muted for some years. After all, if Chinese know-how could give these countries, ravaged as some were by years of civil war, something approaching twenty-first-century facilities, why would anyone object? Furthermore, there were suggestions that the same deals had been on offer to western nations, but that the Chinese had moved first. The early bird had caught the worm, as was only right and proper.

But by late 2011, concern was mounting, Critics accused China of failing to create skilled local jobs and ignoring human rights abuses in countries such as Sudan, rich in oil, and Zimbabwe, with its diamond resources. In October 2010, two Chinese mine employers in Zambia were charged with attempted murder after shooting miners during a pay dispute.

In November 2011 Damian Thompson, a senior commentator with *The Daily Telegraph*, drew together many of the strands of western anxiety, accusing China of a latter-day colonial 'scramble for Africa'. In an article for the paper on 26 November, he wrote:

> There's a school of thought which says that China's *modus operandi*, however brutal, at least gets things built. In contrast, Western aid is tipped into dictators' pockets without anything to show for it. But the benefits of Beijing's 'investment' are elusive, because the Chinese don't usually employ Africans to perform anything but menial tasks. Chinese construction engineers build motorways and hospitals without passing on the skills to maintain them. The result: everything falls into disrepair within a decade, by which time the copper is safely out of the ground.[1]

Just two days later, the *Financial Times* led its front page with a story headed 'Chinese boost for Osborne strategy', which reported:

> George Osborne's hopes of persuading the private sector and foreign investors to help rebuild Britain's ageing infrastructure receive a boost today, as China Investment Corporation, the country's $410 billion sovereign wealth fund, announces plans for new investment in the UK.[2]

Time was when British adventurers such as Cecil Rhodes persuaded chieftains such as Matabele leader Lobengula to sign away their people's birthright in return for dubious benefits conferred by a supposedly more advanced civilization. But in 2011, Britain seemed to be on the same side of the fence as today's still-benighted African states. What was good enough for the Congo was good for the United Kingdom.

The link between China's African ventures and its proposed investment in Britain is clear enough, although many in Britain and perhaps China would hotly deny any such comparison. What are less obvious are the connections between all the above events: law-services 'reform', Big Bang, China in Africa and China in Britain. All are events quintessentially of the last quarter-century. They tell a story of the path that the United Kingdom has followed during those 25 years. They underline the unspoken but absolutely fundamental economic attitude of that period, that yesterday's problems are problems no more, that to have regarded them as such was 'primitive' and that everything will be all right on the night.

Put another way, this was economics as described by not Maynard Keynes or Milton Friedman but Freddie Mercury, who famously declared at the end of Queen's 'Bohemian rhapsody' that 'nothing really matters to me'.[3]

In this weirdly nihilistic world, why should stockbrokers and law firms not be sold to the highest bidder, regardless of the consequences? Why should we not let the Chinese invest their savings – savings that we are too feckless and spendthrift to have built up for ourselves – in our critical infrastructure projects, regardless of China's record elsewhere in the world?

This no-strategy strategy, neither a full-blooded free-market approach nor a European-style commitment to social democracy, has created an economic vista that amounts to little more than an archipelago of stoutly defended island fortresses occupied by powerful interest groups that have managed to stake a claim to money and power. No connecting principles link these islands. This principle-free economic structure is, on examination, shocking to those accustomed to the arrangements of the first world. It would be rather less so to those who are familiar with many of the economies of the developing world.

That Britain's economic status was bound to decline after the First World War seems obvious, as does the further sharp decline after the 1939–45 conflict. But the last quarter-century of grievous policy errors has greatly aggravated the position. The United Kingdom's loss of world-power status may have begun with the outbreak of war in 1914; its descent to third world status began with the end of another conflict, the cold war, in the mid-1980s. Freed of its chief external security commitment, and entranced by the potential offered by the globalization of finance, the United Kingdom abandoned not only any pretence to be a productive, manufacturing economy but any attempt to sort out the difficulties that, since the First World War, had frustrated the creation and sustenance of such an economy. Until 1985, the 'quick fixes' may have been ill thought-out and badly executed, but they were at least designed to build an export-orientated economy with strong positions in precision engineering, manufacturing, science, chemicals, computers, aerospace and the rest. After 1985, the negatives against which the fixers had applied their remedies in vain were found, after all, to be positives: the balance of payments did not matter, the tidal wave of imports was a sign not of sickness but rude economic health, easy credit was good, not bad, and property speculation and asset stripping were, in a phrase much used at the time, part of the solution, not part of the problem.

Back to the start: the ides of March

There is a natural reluctance to believe in retrospect that great events can have occurred as closely together as was indeed the case. For example, did the Soviet Communist Party really vote to give up its monopoly on power just five days before Nelson Mandela was released from prison? Yes, indeed – the relevant dates are 7 February and 11 February 1990. Just to round off an extraordinary few days, 11 February also saw the reigning world heavyweight boxing champion Mike Tyson defeated by the relatively unknown Buster Douglas.

Rewind five years, to March 1985. On the third of the month, the extraordinarily bitter year-long British miners' strike ended in defeat for the miners. On 11 March Mikhael Gorbachev was elected by the Soviet politburo as general secretary. And on 28 March, US president Ronald Reagan addressed the New York Stock Exchange thus: 'That's our economic programme for the next four years – we're going to turn the bull loose.'

This was the beginning of a new era, one in which western organized labour would be considerably weaker than it had been for decades, in which the great experiment of Soviet communism would unravel and disappear, and in which finance would break the bounds of custom, practice and the nation state, and appear to offer a perpetual new prosperity.

One nation after another in the western world drank of this heady brew. US unions were weakened and its once-strict banking regulations effectively scrapped. Japan privatized its railways and its telephone service. France lifted exchange controls and ended national military service as the threat from the east disappeared. A 'peace dividend' was declared in one country after another as military commitments were scaled down. Trade union bosses found themselves in a chilly new world, especially those whose members worked in the private sector and whose jobs could be 'outsourced' in a newly liberalized world labour market.

But no country drank as deeply as the United Kingdom. A unique mixture of circumstances – a costly financial and emotional commitment to the cold war, a persistent record of economic underachievement since 1945, the clout of the City of London lobby, which was diminished in the postwar years but never disappeared – made the United Kingdom especially susceptible to the most excessive expressions of what US president George H. W. Bush called a 'new world order'.

The transformation wrought by this potent cocktail was often described as one in which market forces and general liberalization howled through British life at hurricane force, upending traditions and institutions and allowing the country both to live more freely and to amass an enormous and unsustainable pile of debt. There is much in this analysis, applied to all aspects of life. It is perhaps extraordinary to recall that until 1988 pubs in England closed by law every afternoon, that until the early 1980s mortgage rates were set by a cartel of building societies and applicants had to demonstrate an ability to save before they could borrow, that before 1986 the job of government bond broker was inherited by whoever was senior partner of the firm Mullens, that until the late 1990s the casino industry existed in a barely tolerated state of official disapproval, that until the turn of the century gay people in England and Wales were required to conform to a legal regime quite different from that governing relations among heterosexual people, and that until the Police and Criminal Evidence Act 1984 the rights of the suspect in criminal cases were, to modern eyes, shockingly vague.

Indeed, for some years after 1985 it did seem that a new 'post-postwar settlement' was taking shape, one in which lessened job security and a more conditional and stringent welfare system would be counterbalanced by a much greater degree of personal autonomy, not merely in terms of personal behaviour and, to use the hackneyed expression, activities 'between consenting adults in private', but across a much broader range of personal choices. If the cradle to the grave welfare state was no more, with 'jobs for life' a similarly extinct notion, then the modern yeomanry would make its own arrangements, with 'portable' pensions, lifetime telephone numbers, easy-to-switch banks and mortgage accounts and a 'portfolio' working life.

Furthermore, it would go where the work was and make its own domestic arrangements, whether cohabitation, single parenthood, serial monogamy or whatever else seemed to offer personal happiness.

Not everyone welcomed this new ethos, not least the party most identified with the old order, Labour, which was out of office from 1979 to 1997. But even here, the pleasures of this essentially private new life were becoming plainer to see.

Ron Todd [then leader of the Transport & General Workers Union] made the point with deadly accuracy just a couple of months ago when he asked: 'What do you say to a docker who earns £400 a week, owns his house, a new car, a microwave and a video, as well as a small place near Marbella? You do not say,' said Ron, 'let me take you out of your misery, brother.'[4]

Away from its traditional industrial heartland, the left was increasingly coming to believe – with some, but far from total, justification – that the postwar settlement had itself been built around the needs not of 'the people' as a whole but of special interest groups, chiefly male manual workers and a privileged white-collar class of bureaucrats, technicians and educators, and that anyway, this particular party was now well and truly over.

Fiction writers took up the theme:

> Through all this, Alan [a car-plant worker standing for election as shop steward] began to think that history was at work rather than individuals, governments, countries; that history had its own momentum and was swinging the organisation of life in Britain, probably the entire west, away from labour intensive industry.[5]

Complaints of an 'atomized society' were heard frequently but were somewhat beside the point. Even were the close-knit communities of yesteryear still to be available for habitation, a dubious proposition in perhaps a majority of cases, how many actually wished to live there? Even the renowned champion of the nation's pit villages, miners' leader Arthur Scargill, had a flat in the famously anonymous Barbican development in central London. And as the German socialist George Lichtheim had put it many years earlier, those calling for the abolition of the consumer society were usually those who did not have to work for a living.

The new maisonettes, semi-detached houses and 'executive' homes of the 1980s and beyond may been described as shoeboxes, rabbit hutches and the rest by their critics, but to their occupants they may well have seemed a concrete expression of a more personal, more bespoke way of life. Former Labour MP Phillip Whitehead saw signs of this development from the late 1970s:

> Nine out of ten households had a fridge, a television set, three quarters a telephone, more than half a car and central heating. The home became a leisure centre, a retreat for DIY and gardening. So great were its comforts, in fact, that some studies showed it acting as an insulation against despair or political action if personal circumstances were drastically changed through redundancy.[6]

This sometimes intense sense of privacy in relation to the outside world applied also within households, as couples, thrown together by long-distance pursuit of short-term employment contracts, adopted an admirably discreet approach.

> Both Sandra and Oliver are reticent about other times. Sandra is divorced, but Oliver knows little of why or when. 'Nuff said,' says Sandra, crisply. 'Over and done with.'[7]

And work was indeed moving further afield. New operations in the car industry shunned the one-time 'British Detroit' – the corridor stretching from the Morris plant at Cowley near Oxford to the motor hub of the Midlands – in preference for Swindon (Honda), Derby (Toyota) and Sunderland (Nissan). For the printing business, the future now lay in Peterborough or Portsmouth, or the new home of many newspaper production plants, in London's docklands. City high-flyers and their support staff might have moved to Canary Wharf (itself the dark side of the moon to traditional eyes) but lowlier banking and insurance personnel found their jobs decanted far beyond London's boundaries.

This was the age of the 'greenfield site'. In such circumstances, it is perhaps unsurprising that many chose to lead 'greenfield lives', far from their roots. Increasingly, they worked for themselves – the number of self-employed rose from just over 2.7 million in 1985 to more than 3.5 million in 2003. It had reached more than 3.9 million by 2011 (all figures from the Office for National Statistics).

As the 1980s progressed, it would have been easy to see all this as a rebirth of a classic liberal economy and society, with all the disadvantages, in terms of insecurity of employment and social life, coupled with all the advantages in terms of personal freedom and a lack of intrusion by the powers that be. Anyone attending a lord mayor's dinner at the Mansion House in the heyday of Nigel Lawson's chancellorship would have had little trouble in believing that a new Victorian age was being born, one of vigorous industry and sturdy self-reliance. Amid the white tie and tails, as the chancellor and other honoured guests were clapped in to the strains of the march from Handel's *Scipio*, as the loving cup was passed round, the atmosphere of bullish individualism would have been heady indeed.

And quite misleading.

The end of the cold war, the defeat of the trade unions and the new era of turbo-charged global finance had quite genuinely brought about a new era. But it was not to be one of unbridled personal freedom. Quite the opposite. It was not even, as the post-2007 bank bailouts were to show, an era of renewed economic liberalism.

True, Britain's elite, in Westminster, Whitehall, the City, the media, the law and so forth, had collectively seemed, consciously or not, to have abandoned various wearying economic and social struggles, under way since the end of the First World War, aimed at maintaining a first-rank international economy and its precondition, a sober and industrious society. True, the new doctrine had it that many of the problems of yesteryear were in fact not problems at all, whether excessive consumer credit or all-day drinking.

But this had little or nothing to do with bringing into being some sort of liberal utopia. Lord Randolph Churchill's dictum – 'trust the people' – was little in evidence. In many ways, 'the people' had never been less trusted. In the 15 years between 1985 and the end of the century, numerous assaults were made on the liberty of the person, such as spot testing for drink and drugs, surveillance by security cameras, the planting of government-approved 'messages' in television drama by scriptwriters who seemed to prefer 'tackling issues' to telling stories, demands for employers to adopt 'alcohol policies', official campaigns to 'change attitudes' on various matters, and endless 'advice' and 'guidelines' on diet, safety and health, with 'drinkwise' campaigns and 'national no-smoking day' to generate some official communal good feeling about these 'messages'.

Meanwhile, routine state intrusiveness was at a level that would have horrified the citizens of earlier years, as Ross Clark's experience showed:

I have a little ticket from the Sussex Constabulary. It is a small memento from the day in 2004 when I was stopped and searched at Gatwick Airport by a policewoman carrying a very large and frightening machine gun. One doesn't argue with such weapons. Yes, of course she could have a peek inside my bags (which, incidentally, had been through an X-ray machine not half an hour beforehand). Satisfied I was carrying nothing of interest she then offered me a little certificate saying where and when I was searched – and the reason why. I am still fascinated by the reason she gave for searching me: she ticked a little box marked 'Going near equipment'. What kind of exciting equipment do they have at Sock Shop, where I had been idly browsing? ... Towards the end of my brief conversation with the policewoman at Gatwick I had a good idea why she was really stopping me. What, she wanted to know, did she consider my ethnic group to be? She proffered me a list: White British, British Asian ... and so on. I declined to say, even when her eyes opened wide with disappointment. Sorry, I said, but she would have to put me down as REFU – that is the category for refuseniks who, as is our right, decline to co-operate with this bureaucratic nonsense.[8]

Clark concludes:

And off she went in search of someone else of the right skin colour, to make up her ethnic quotas for the day.

One wonders how many of the 32,062 people stopped and searched by the police last year were searched for this same reason: to make up the numbers.[9]

Nor did officialdom seem to trust business any more than it trusted the individual. Periodic exhortations emanated from Whitehall urging the nation's 'wealth creators' (the description used when business was back in favour) to treat customers better, to employ more female executives, to export more, to invest more, and so on.

Ultimately perhaps the governing elite did not trust itself, and like Caliban in *The Tempest*, saw its own failings reflected in the mirror of British households and companies. Exhausted and frustrated by the effort to fix the economy in a way that would enable it to be productive and capable of trading with the world on equal terms, and freed of the onerous constraints of being a major

participant in the cold war, the British establishment
gleefully embarked on a rake's progress dressed up as
a return to the nation's salty, pre-industrial merchant-
venturing roots.

As it quaffed freely of the heady 1985 vintage, a quarter-
century journey to the third world had begun.

Letting go: the UK economy and the world

The 40 years after 1945 were a story of repeated attempts
to 'solve' the United Kingdom's multiple economic
problems. Politicians of both parties shared two
fundamental views about the economy. The first was that
its performance since the war had been unsatisfactory,
in comparison not only with the country's neighbours
and competitors across the Channel and with other
economies overseas, but also with its full potential. In
true public-school style, it stood accused of having failed
to compete against its most important rival – itself. The
second was that this potential, this ideal economy, was a
realizable entity; that there was a level of performance to
which the United Kingdom ought not only to aspire but
towards which it ought to make swift certain strides. As
Douglas Hurd put it:

> I, and I believe others, thought there was a real chance
> after 1970 that Mr Heath and his colleagues would
> break out of inherited attitudes and make possible
> a sharply higher level of achievement by the British
> people. In short, there was a chance that they could do
> for Britain what Adenauer and Erhard had done for
> Germany, and De Gaulle for France.[10]

Illustrating the remarkable continuity of analysis across

the decades and between the parties, here was Labour's Aneurin Bevan, in his penultimate speech in the House of Commons, on 3 November 1959:

> [H]ow to persuade the people to forego immediate satisfactions in order to build up the economic resources of the country [?] ... that is the problem and it has not been solved yet.

He went on:

> We failed to solve it. We frankly admit that. In the years immediately after the war we made very great efforts to build up fixed capital equipment and sacrificed our Parliamentary majority .... So the problem for us today ... is to try to reconcile popular representative government with setting aside sufficient of the national income in order to expand productive resource.

This fear in official circles that elected governments would be unable to persuade voters to 'forgo immediate satisfactions' stretched right back to the war. Popular histories and nostalgic television programmes and films suggest the hitherto-austere British suddenly embarked on a love affair with fripperies and consumer trinkets sometime round the mid-1950s, coincidental with the first stirrings of rock'n'roll and the birth of 'the teenager'. In fact, as the UK submission for aid from the Marshall Plan made clear in September 1948, rationing of essentials had, perhaps paradoxically, bred a taste for those things that money could buy:

> The difficulties of the present economic position do not present themselves in an obvious form to the British public. Unemployment is barely noticeable; jobs are

apparently secure; industry is finding it easy to earn profits; wages are relatively high; the necessities of life are fairly distributed; and because they cannot buy many necessaries, many people have money which they can spend on things which they would otherwise regard almost as luxuries.[11]

We examine in a separate chapter the various 'fixes' in terms of strategic economic and industrial policy with which British governments before 1985 sought to restore the nation's economy to what was seen as its rightful place. Here, we look briefly at what were seen as the indicators of success: the 'exams', if you like, that the economy was expected to pass. Or perhaps it is more useful to think of economic management, in a much-used postwar simile, as like juggling various balls in the air indefinitely. To drop one was to risk being booed off stage.

In the immediate postwar period, the most important of these balls were, in no particular order, the maintenance of sterling's exchange rate, principally against the dollar; the maintenance of full employment; the suppression of inflation; the promotion of exports and the consequent improvement of the balance of payments; the upgrading and expansion of the housing stock, with special reference to social housing; the expansion of industry, in particular the building up of Britain's presence in newer industries, ranging from chemicals and medicines through computers to aircraft manufacture and nuclear power; and the steady improvement of the standard of living of the people.

In later years, this lengthy list was boiled down to what amounted to a pithy soundbite: the pursuit of an export-led, high-wage, high-growth, high-tech, low-inflation economy.

The political class had certainly set itself a bewildering, not to say overwhelming, set of objectives which, while not necessarily contradictory (although maintenance of a fixed exchange rate is liable frequently to frustrate the pursuit of other goals), could almost have been designed to make life difficult. Indeed, once rationing was abolished in the early 1950s and various other controls were lifted thereafter, the juggling act became still more nerve-shredding.

Nor did the demotion of the importance of one of these juggler's balls necessarily make life any easier for those in high office. For example, the devaluation of sterling in November 1967 and the decision to let it float on foreign exchanges in June 1972 ought to have relieved the pressure. But by then a new ball was in the air: prices and incomes policy, with ministers tying themselves to pledges to cut 'at a stroke' the rate at which prices were rising (Heath in 1970) or to reduce the 26 per cent annual inflation in August 1975 to 10 per cent a year later and single figures by the end of 1976 (Heath's successor Harold Wilson in 1975).

In keeping with this, the incoming Conservative government in 1979, led by Margaret Thatcher, deliberately dropped the prices and incomes policy ball only to begin juggling with a new and very tricky replacement: targets for the growth of the money supply.

Indeed, the ethos of the 1945–85 years was that there was something unsporting about an administration that, to vary the analogy, seemed to be trying to shrug off some of these burdens. Harold Wilson commented:

Faced with a major sterling crisis, Britain went on to a regime of floating exchange rates.... The US-dominated International Monetary Fund had relaxed its strict regime. The Conservative Government was therefore able to meet a crisis by devaluing without having to face all the misery which the Labour Government had known in the mid-1960s until – and indeed after – the cataclysm of the 1967 devaluation. The Conservatives devalued at will, and not a dog barked.[12]

The incoming Conservative government of 1979 sounded little different from its predecessors in its promise of a strenuous pursuit of a wide range of objectives that would lead to the restoration of the United Kingdom's rightful place as a top-echelon world economy. Thus:

> The Government was given the job of creating a New Britain – a Britain that is paying her way in the world ... a modern Britain in tune with the spirit of the present and not of the past.[13]

> [Our] approach entails living within our means, paying our way in the world, mastering inflation, reviving the wealth-creating part of the economy.[14]

The first of these quotes is taken from *The Go-Ahead Year,* a sympathetic account of the early part of Wilson's 1964–70 period in office written under the pseudonym Demos, not to be confused with the contemporary think-tank of that name. The second is from *The Right Approach: A statement of Conservative aims*, published in 1976 by Conservative Central Office.

True, both full employment and, as we saw earlier, prices and incomes policy had been abandoned as short-term objectives by the incoming Tory government, although to be fair full employment had effectively been dropped by its Labour predecessors. But the Conservatives promptly saddled themselves with two replacements, the abovementioned money-supply targets and targets for deficit reduction. Both were enshrined in a 1980 document, *The Medium Term Financial Strategy (MTFS)*.

In many ways, the 1979 government marked a sharp

break with postwar practice. But not in the sense that we are exploring here, that of publicly targeting a set of variables in the belief that success in doing so would transform Britain's economic prospects and restore its grandeur and eminence. Nor did the unhappy record of such pursuits, whether in repeated sterling devaluations or pay policies that buckled in the third year, end in 1979. As Nigel (now Lord) Lawson, architect of the MTFS in his job as financial secretary to the Treasury, recalled:

> The MTFS was not fulfilled in any literal sense, at least not on the monetary side. The liberalisation of financial markets which we had ourselves launched changed the meaning of the monetary aggregates and made them much more difficult to predict and control .... The fiscal side of the MTFS wore better than the monetary side.[15]

Funnily enough, a very different type of 'Tory radical' had long expressed the view that all this activity, all this juggling of balls, all these self-imposed burdens, all these attempts to restore the United Kingdom to some preordained rightful place in the economic league table, were entirely pointless, the product of wilful delusion in high places and – to use an expression that he would never have employed – an all-round waste of good drinking time.

John Enoch Powell (1912–1998) was minister of health (what would be now called health secretary) from 1960 to 1963, a role in which he was highly regarded by many in the medical profession. Nicholas Timmins, in his 'biography of the welfare state' *Five Giants*,[16] ranked him as 'one of the few great Ministers of Health', below Aneurin Bevan but alongside Barbara Castle, Sir Kenneth Robinson and Kenneth Clarke. That, however, is not why he is remembered today.

Powell's views on race (routinely described as

'incendiary', which is fair enough) are perhaps unfortunately his major legacy, and effectively ended his mainstream political career. His staunch opposition to British membership of the European Union is still recalled by many, and has perhaps worn better than his views on immigration, although the latter topic is once again high on the public's agenda. He represented Wolverhampton South West as a Conservative MP from 1950 to 1974, and South Down as an Ulster Unionist MP from 1974 to 1987. An early devotion to the British Empire had, by the 1960s, been transformed into almost its opposite, a determination that UK leaders accept that world-power status was now behind them, and seek instead to rediscover those things that had made Britain great as a modest-sized nation, not 'Great' as an imperial superpower:

> Thus our generation is like one which comes home again from years of distant wandering. We discover affinities with earlier generations of English, generations before the 'expansion of England', who felt no country but this to be their own.[17]

Powell's dislike of what he saw as the residual big-power fantasies of the United Kingdom's leaders took many forms. Most obviously, he berated the notion of 'Commonwealth citizenship' as a post-imperial folly that allowed hundreds of thousands of non-British people to settle in the United Kingdom under what he saw as a bogus and delusional version of *civis Romanus sum*. He came to distrust both the alliance with the United States and the UK possession of nuclear weapons. He mocked the United Kingdom's pretensions (still with us in a more modified form at the time of writing) to a major role in untangling the problems of Rhodesia (now Zimbabwe) and the Middle East.

And the logic of his position (which was not, to be fair, always especially logical) led him also to deprecate Britain's role in the postwar economic and monetary system, one in which Powell again detected the sickly aroma of a grandstanding and a self-importance that did nothing but harm to the country's real interests and made us a laughing stock internationally.

> Look at that great national totem, the pound sterling. It is a matter of national honour, we declare, to uphold the decree of Providence that the pound was created equal to $2.80, give or take two cents .... But of course, it demands certain difficult exertions to maintain. For if the equation is fixed, and the behaviour of one side of the equation – the economy of the outside world – is not in our control, it follows we must be ready to adjust the other side of the equation – our own economy – to fit. But we are not willing to face this. It would be unpleasant, there would be deflation, there might even be some unemployment. So we go along to other countries and threaten to let the price of the pound sterling behave like any other price unless they will lend us money to replenish our reserves and will back the pound with their credit.[18]

The link between great-power delusion and international economic management was even stronger in relation to the London gold market, then the most important in the world. The postwar Bretton Woods economic system had tied the dollar to gold at a fixed rate of $35 an ounce. By the end of the 1960s, this relationship was coming under intense pressure as increasing numbers of investors decided they preferred gold to the inflating US dollar and switched their holdings accordingly. Powell declared that the whole notion was farcical:

Nobody knows what the supply and demand price for gold is, any more than anybody knows what the supply and demand price for accommodation to let in the United Kingdom is, for most of it has been controlled and subsidised for so long that there is no possibility of discovering what the price would be in a free market.[19]

In April 1968, after a desperate battle, supported by the United Kingdom and other leading members of the Bretton Woods system, to maintain this link, the US government admitted partial defeat, and suspended dollar convertibility into gold for all but national governments, thus partially liberalizing the open-market price. Powell commented thus on the outcome:

You probably know the story of the man who grabbed a rope while falling down a dark shaft and just managed to hang on to the end of it. Hour after hour he swung there, enduring agonies of fear and exhaustion, screaming for help. At last his fingers could maintain their hold no longer and he fell – three inches … this week in London the open-market [gold] price was two or three dollars up – yes sir, just two or three dollars.[20]

As we have seen, there were many abandoned official economic targets during the 40 years from 1945 to 1985. But hardly had one target been abandoned than it was replaced by another, such as the switch from pay and price controls to money supply and public debt targeting after 1979. Powell, by contrast, was suggesting that the targets themselves were the problem, part and parcel of a doomed attempt by the British establishment to reassert a world role that had vanished.

Powell himself cared not a jot about relative economic decline:

We do not stop to investigate whether the [international growth] figures have any useful meaning at all, nor whether, if they have, there is any a priori reason to expect to grow at the same rate as Japan or Western Germany or the Philippines.[21]

Enoch Powell as the intellectual father of Third World Britain? There would certainly be an amusing irony in such a notion. However, it pushes the narrative beyond the evidence. There is no doubt Powell deprecated official attempts to build up the UK economy to its 'rightful' place in the world, or that he believed using the same tools to produce jobs and prosperity at home would prove equally fruitless. But modern-day Britain is far from the modest, virtuous parliamentary state that he evoked, living by the principles of the free market but not being dominated by them. What he would have made of our current garish landscape of bank bailouts, political favoritism, millions parked on welfare while millions more are imported to do the jobs of which they are not thought to be capable, inexplicable and contradictory decisions by those in authority and all the rest is hard to imagine. Add in further bizarre third-world features such as political leaders commenting in all solemnity on the fate of fictional characters in soap operas, or the periodic shows of contrition by MPs and others caught up in 'sleaze' scandals and the assurance that this will never happen again (mid-1990s, late 2000s) and it is hard to imagine his accepting any sort of intellectual paternity.

In some ways Nigel Lawson, the Tory radical against whom we earlier contrasted Powell, may have a better claim. Indeed, his ministerial career oddly mirrored developments in Britain as a whole, with an abrupt change of course in 1985 that amounted, in effect, to letting go and hoping for the best.

Mr Lawson entered the public consciousness as one of the hard men of the new regime. When in opposition in September 1978, he wrote an article for *The Times* advocating a rigorous new framework for economic policy, declaring: 'Rules rule: OK?' By October 1985 he was telling a Mansion House dinner that one of the most central of all the rules no longer ruled, OK or otherwise. Money supply targets, he said, had been downgraded – shelved, in effect – and henceforth the inflation rate would be 'judge and jury' of economic policy. Inadvertently, perhaps, the then chancellor had hit on the notion that was to dominate monetary policy in Britain and elsewhere in the 1990s and the 2000s and remains in force today, albeit in a modified form – inflation targeting.

It turned out that Mr Lawson did not really mean it, at least not in the way we would understand inflation targeting, because the following month, and until his resignation in October 1989, he attempted to persuade the government of which he was a member, and in particular Margaret Thatcher, the prime minister, to adopt a quite different approach, targeting the exchange rate. Indeed, it was his disagreements with Mrs Thatcher on the issue of membership of the European Exchange-Rate Mechanism (ERM) that led to his resignation.

The ERM looks superficially like a European-scale Bretton Woods, but it was in fact very different. It had much more in common with inflation targeting, and with the various self-imposed restraints on borrowing and spending dreamed up by subsequent chancellors, whether Gordon Brown's 'golden rule' or George Osborne's 'fiscal mandate'. All these had two things in common that set them apart from the structure of British economic policy making between 1945 and 1985. First, they were variations on the 'one-club golf' of which former prime minister Edward Heath had accused his Conservative successors with regard to over-reliance on interest rates as an economic regulator. As we saw above, the 1945–85 governments employed a range of different tools, and when one went out of favour (for example a fixed dollar exchange rate) another would usually take its place (such as targets for wage and price increases).

Second, pre-1985 governments had employed these tools in the pursuit of a range of objectives, such as full employment, a healthy current account, manageable price inflation and so on. The new tools were employed to meet no objectives other than the successful employment of the new tools. In other words, inflation targeting 'worked' as long as the inflation rate was on target. ERM membership was 'successful' provide the pound was near its central rate of 2.95 against the German mark. Failure in this latter task in September 1992, chorused the political and media class, 'lost the Conservative Party its reputation for economic competence'. Aside from the existence of this 'reputation' (on which boom-to-bust chancellor was it based? Reginald Maudling, Anthony Barber, Mr Lawson himself perhaps?), this viewpoint failed entirely to ask whether there were any real value in holding the pound at that level.

It was the same story with the fiscal regulations, which proved their worth, apparently, simply by being adhered to. When such adherence proved difficult, as it did for both Gordon Brown and George Osborne, the rules would be redrawn in order to make them achievable. In the case of Mr Brown's rules, they were ditched entirely by his successor as chancellor, Alistair Darling, in the storm that followed the 2007 credit crunch.

What this amounted to was a letting go, a giving up on all attempts to keep the United Kingdom as a functioning front-rank economic power, and the beginning of a new era of enormous economic volatility, lurid contrasts in wealth and poverty, a debased public life and a governing

elite whose members were prone to boast ever more loudly
about their 'core principles' as those principles became
ever harder to identify.

Don't worry, be happy: unemployment, the balance of payments, Big Bang

Of all the objectives to which governments had been
committed from 1945 to the mid-1980s, a high and
sustainable level of employment was perhaps pre-eminent.
Even after the mid-1970s, when its achievement became
far more difficult, the goal remained.

> We give a high priority to working for a return to full
> employment. A good job is a basic human right.
> > Labour Party manifesto, 1979

> [We aim] To restore incentives so that hard work pays,
> success is rewarded and genuine new jobs are created
> in an expanding economy.
> > Conservative Party manifesto, 1979

The means by which this happy state was to be achieved
increasingly diverged as the postwar economic consensus
fell apart in the 1970s. It is not our task here to take sides
in those long-ago controversies. But there is a world
of difference between those disagreements and the
suggestion that employment itself was of no fundamental
importance.

Yet voices were being raised to that effect. Here is
Lord Bruce-Gardyne, a former Conservative MP: 'The
producer lobbies regarded it as axiomatic that the
citizen offered a choice between a job and the ability to
afford an Italian washing-machine would choose a job.

Perhaps the outcome of the 1983 election proved them wrong.'[22]

An intermediate suggestion was that the quality of the jobs on offer mattered little. Here, chancellor Nigel Lawson let the cat out of the bag in September 1984, speaking at a meeting of the International Monetary Fund in Washington, when he warned Britain's workforce that many of the jobs of the future would not be 'high tech', or even low-tech, but 'no tech'. This was a remarkable swing-round in official policy, given that the great alibi for the UK government at a time of more than 3 million people unemployed on the so-called claimant count, the traditional measure of those eligible for benefits related to worklessness, was that new jobs would in due time appear in the 'sunrise industries' of the future.

Just as the dilapidated state of much of what was then British Rail was excused in the 1970s and 1980s on the grounds that the then-revolutionary Advanced Passenger Train would whisk train travel into a sleek new future, so in the early years of Margaret Thatcher's 1979–90 time in office, those concerned about unemployment were told that 'rustbelt' jobs would be replaced by those in Britain's own versions of California's 'Silicon Valley' – in Scotland, East Anglia, the Thames Valley corridor and elsewhere.

Ministers were forever pointing to the existence of modestly sized firms with names such as Com-Vac and Digi-Floppy as 'proof' that a second (or was it third?) industrial revolution was under way. Few extensions to the smallest semiconductor plant on the most remote industrial estate were complete without the presence of a grinning politician to preside over the ceremony while burbling about the wonders of the 'silicon chip', as local councillors and journalists worked their way through red wine and sausage rolls while clutching a plastic folder containing the 'press kit'.

Hot on the heels of the International Year of Disabled Persons in 1981, the government declared 1982 to be the year of 'information technology', then an unusual term for most people. Indeed, 'IT82' was to be supervised by the 'information technology minister', Kenneth Baker, whose more prosaic title at the Department of Trade and Industry was minister of post and telecommunications, successor to the job of postmaster general.

Now even the chancellor (Nigel Lawson, as quoted above in 1984) was suggesting the whole idea of a future of high-tech employment was, in part at least, an illusion.

The importance of the link between work (and/or savings) and income has long been taken as read across the political spectrum, a good conservative principle and a good socialist principle as well. Of equal importance is the fact that this link is a key indicator of a developed economy. Underdeveloped countries may find it easier to pay off uneducated or otherwise unproductive and potentially troublesome social groups rather than train them for work. They may similarly prefer to import skilled and eager migrants from countries with better education systems to perform the work for which 'the natives' are deemed incapable. That the United Kingdom has taken this road in the last quarter-century is another exhibit of evidence of its journey to the third world.

In many cases, the disguised unemployed have been reclassified as too sick to work. Between 1979 and 2011, the number of people deemed too ill or disabled to hold down a job increased nearly fourfold, to about 2.1 million people of working age, while the number of those in employment who are non-UK nationals is now 2.5 million.

Another priority target of postwar economic management, of only slightly less importance than full employment, was the balance of payments. The United

Kingdom's solvency, as it was seen, was not up for discussion. Younger, poorer countries might need to run deficits in order to finance their growth and development. This would be funded by the savings of mature first-world countries – such as the United Kingdom. An overvalued exchange rate from 1945 to 1967 made it much more difficult than it need have been to balance the current account, or better still achieve a surplus. Yet it was in balance or in surplus in 17 of the 25 years from 1947 to 1971. By contrast, it was last in surplus in 1983. Every single year since then has seen a deficit.

Funding this rake's progress has been a constant sale of British industrial and other assets to foreigners. By 2011, Britain's net external asset position – the balance of UK ownership of foreign assets after deducting foreign ownership of British assets – was negative, to the tune of nearly £200 billion. This is not surprising, perhaps, given the roster of great British names that have passed into foreign ownership: Rover and Land Rover, Rolls-Royce cars, Bentley, the Mini, British Rail Engineering, Cadbury and Rowntree, to name but a few.

More striking still was the loss of capacity in one of the core areas, perhaps the core area, of British competence: the City. The 'Big Bang' reforms, mentioned earlier in this chapter, were justified initially on the twin grounds that existing arrangements for the trading of securities infringed UK competition laws and that City firms needed outside capital if they were to compete in an era in which exchange controls – the official limitation of movements of currency across Britain's frontiers – had ended.

This necessitated, so the claim went, two big changes. The first was to end the requirement that stockbrokers (who bought and sold shares on behalf of clients) and stockjobbers (who held shares in their own right and made a market in them) be partnerships. The second was to end the requirement, dating back to 1908, that they be separate, in order to avoid conflicts of interest. This rule was known as 'single capacity'.

One oddity of the rush to merge brokers and jobbers, often bundling in a merchant bank as well, which would then sell themselves to the highest bidder – usually a British or overseas banking giant – was that the Lloyd's of London insurance market was at much the same time moving in the opposite direction, separating insurance brokers (who sought cover on behalf of their clients) from the underwriters (who provided the cover). The potential for conflicts of interest was enormous, and indeed scandal enveloped the City within months of the October 1986 shake-up, when government inspectors arrived at the offices of Guinness, the drinks company, to investigate allegations of fraudulent share dealing. To be fair, any wrongdoing relating to Guinness predated the Big Bang, but there were scandals aplenty to come.

From our perspective, however, the extraordinary legacy of Big Bang was the almost complete disappearance within just a few years of those newly bulked-up national champions in the world of investment banking (the umbrella description of the new City titans). Even the most pessimistic forecaster, fearing the impact of competition by new American, European and Japanese entrants to the City, would have expected a hard core of British 'bulge bracket' institutions to survive and thrive. Bank of England thinking at the time suggested perhaps half a dozen. Yet one by one they fell into foreign ownership or simply left the business, despite investment banking being, we were told, something 'Britain does so well'.

The roll call is as mournful as that of the motor industry: SG Warburg, Smith New Court, Barings, Robert Fleming, Schroder Wagg, Kleinwort Grieveson and the rest. Yet official concern was near to zero. 'Ownership', went the argument, 'doesn't matter'.

All this was in the future, however, as the old City was convulsed by the changes. In an eerie foretaste of the 'toxic derivatives' of the 2007 credit crunch, December 1986 saw the collapse in London of the market for 'perps', perpetual floating-rate notes, a somewhat fantastical type of IOU issued by banks and others and with no maturity date. In theory, they paid interest for ever.

About the same time, a bid was made for the respected Extel publishing and news-wire service by a company, Demerger Corporation, whose 'shares' were nothing more than promissory notes secured on the assets of Extel. The company had no assets, and was merely offering Extel shareholders their own company back, minus a cut for Demerger Corporation. In 1987 Saatchi & Saatchi, an advertising agency, was mooted as a buyer for the Midland, one of the country's largest banks, now known as HSBC.

Enormous media excitement was generated by the upheaval, with loving articles and features about the 'talent' that would be employed by the new organizations. These bright and determined young men and women would put in double-figure hours each day in return for six-figure salaries. At times the adulatory coverage verged on the sort of treatment given by communist regimes to 'shock workers' who had exceeded their 'production norms'. Indeed, these heroes and heroines of capitalist labour were to get their very own model town, the new 'Docklands' centred on Canary Wharf in the east of London. The skyscrapers of this 'water city' would provide the appropriate working environment for these latter-day Alexei and Alexandra Stakhanovs, while trendy riverside flats nearby would provide their homes.

Even once Britain lost most of its top-notch banks, this

was apparently not a problem, because the 'players' – the abovementioned shock workers – were British. Even if they weren't, that simply proved London was a magnet for 'global talent'. In this ever-receding hall of mirrors, everything was, and is, just fine.

In a sense, the 1986–87 fascination with 'yuppies' was just one aspect of an emerging fantasy in which London was rapidly acquiring the dream features of a major global metropolis that are today fundamental to the self-image of its leaders, actual and aspiring, and indeed a key aspect of the self-image of Britain as a whole. London, we were told, was now one of three or four 'world cities'. On closer inspection, however, this exciting new status had been achieved simply by deciding that what were once problems were now advantages. The dirt, noise, the crowds, the over-reliance on financial services, impassable roads and pavements and the ludicrous cost of housing are now evidence of its 'vibrant', 'diverse' 'exuberant', 'exciting', 'truly global' identity.

Nothing better sums up the post-1985 dynamic: negatives are now positives, yesterday's concerns are old hat, free-falling to third world status is actually a glorious ascent.

Go with the flow, indeed.

Chapter 6

Up where we belong: is Britain's economic crisis all in the mind?

The spectre showed a spectre's ordinary caprice; it gave no sign of being.

Emily Brontë, *Wuthering Heights*, 1847

There is no doubt that the entrepreneurial spirit represented in this room can build a bright future for our economy. But that hopeful prospect will be pushed even further into the future if your efforts and the efforts of thousands like you are blown off course by these global headwinds .... That is the challenge we face – restoring confidence, removing uncertainty, and doing what we can to change the default answer from 'wait and see' to 'let's go for it'.

Chancellor George Osborne, speaking at the National Business Awards in London, 24 January 2012

You just come over and take a look at the place. It's not doing all that badly ... we still climb Everest and beat plenty of the world at plenty of sports and win Nobel Prizes.

Ian Fleming, *You Only Live Twice*, 1964

Vince Cable, the UK business secretary, spoke to the Policy Exchange think-tank on 16 October 2011. His message was straightforward. To use a cliché beloved of the politicians of yesteryear, Britain can make it:

Where once we led the way as innovators in textiles, shipbuilding and iron and steel production, we now have companies blazing a trail in frontier technologies such as new materials, robotics, software design and some renewable energies. I have recently visited highly successful manufacturing companies in sectors which we seemed to have written off, like bicycles and motorbikes; casting and forgings; machines tools, steel making and large scale car production (which you will remember was a sad joke a generation ago). So it is important we explode the myth that UK manufacturing is moribund.[1]

True, Dr Cable did draw attention to weak spots and vulnerabilities in Britain's economic landscape. But his message was largely upbeat:

We have outstanding manufacturing companies, both large and small .... There are big new industrial investments taking place, even in these difficult times. Airbus has opened its new £400 million factory in Broughton, North Wales in the past fortnight. Jaguar Land Rover is investing £355 million in a new engine plant in Wolverhampton. BMW is ploughing £500 million into its UK production operation. Nissan has chosen to design, develop and make the next-generation Qashqai here because of its success in Sunderland.

Indeed, Jaguar Land Rover's investment was touted shortly afterwards in an interview on the BBC website with John Cridland, director-general of the Confederation of British Industry, on 18 November 2011. The report begins with the reporter Russell Hotten quoting a comment from Mr Cridland:

'[C]an we just acknowledge, please, that also there is a great deal of good stuff going on?'
He reels off a list of business success stories, but a

particular favourite at the moment is the decision by Jaguar Land Rover, owned by India's Tata, to build an engine factory near Wolverhampton. 'Fabulous news,' he says.[2]

For those accustomed to claims that the British economy in general and manufacturing in particular have problems that are both chronic and acute, such flag-waving can seem a little jarring. Where, they may wonder, is this successful world-class economy, and do we need visas to go there? In truth, there has long been a school of thought that asserts that there are in reality few deep-seated economic problems of any sort, and that Britain has solid, sound economic foundations.

Take manufacturing, for example. It is thriving, according to a viewpoint succinctly expressed by the UK Advanced Engineering website, developed jointly by the Whitehall agency UK Trade and Investment and businesses.

> The UK is the world's sixth-largest manufacturer by output (USA and China are at the top – UN figures) and has many globally operating companies. Firms such as Renishaw, Delcam, Group Rhodes and 600 Group are part of major supply chains, including those for aerospace, automotive, defence, oil and gas and medical devices.[3]

In case the message has failed to get through, the website features a drop-down menu the headings of which read: 'World class in aerospace', 'World class in automotive', and with the same prefix, in engineering, design engineering, advanced materials and advanced manufacturing.

Things are chipper in the service sector, too. To take

one example, these quotes are from the UK Higher Education International Unit, an information and policy coordination service jointly funded by various government bodies and Universities UK, which represents vice-chancellors and principals, along with GuildHE, another representative body:

> The UK sells more brainpower per capita than anywhere else in the world. In 2008, this amounted to £118 billion in knowledge services – worth 6.3 per cent of GDP.[4]

> Higher education institutions are worth £59 billion to the UK economy annually and are a major export earner. Through their international activities they are one of the UK's fastest growing sources of export earnings, and last year bought in £5.3 billion.[5]

Even the oldest 'industry' of all, farming, is efficient and productive. Food self-sufficiency in those foodstuffs that can be produced here has risen from about 50 per cent in the mid-twentieth century to more than 70 per cent now. According to the educational and promotional charity Living Countryside the value of farm exports grew from £8.7 billion in 2000 to £14 billion in 2009.[6]

Finally, of course, there is the financial services industry, apparently bloodied but unbowed by the financial crisis. Its case is put in detail by a body that used to be called British Invisibles, but – perhaps having decided that sounded too much like the name of a 1960s science-fiction television drama – has now settled, with an admirable disregard for the space bar, on TheCityUK. Here is its view on the importance of the industry:

The UK is the world's leading exporter of financial services, earning more than ten times US exports of financial services in 2008. Financial services generated a trade surplus of £36 billion in 2010 ... and contributed £124 billion to the UK economy in 2009, accounting for ten per cent of total economic output.[7]

Beyond these different sectors, all of which, apparently, are doing splendidly, there is no shortage of exhortation for us all to focus on the positives and 'not talk Britain down'. Business organizations, ministers, financial journalists and others routinely urge the rest of us to remember that 'there are some good tales out there', that the United Kingdom remains one of the world's largest economies, that our people are amazingly inventive and that there is much that supposedly more dynamic economies can learn from us.

Could our economy prove, in fact, to be the problem that never was? We are happy to make the best possible case in favour of this proposition. In a sense, the best case makes itself. It requires no detailed examination of the performance of industry sectors or of the balance of payments. It can be summed up in one sentence: Britain is a magnet for people and for capital. Neither workers nor money go to places where nothing is happening, they go instead to buzzing centres of economic activity.

On 25 August 2011, the BBC news website reported:

Net migration rose by 21 per cent last year, with 239,000 more people arriving in the UK than those leaving, the Office for National Statistics has revealed.[8]

Money too has been heading for Britain. In its '2011 European Attractiveness Survey', published in May of that year, Ernst & Young stated, 'The UK remains the most attractive destination in Europe for FDI [foreign direct investment].'[9] On top of this, the United Kingdom simply could not have sustained nearly 30 years' worth of current account deficits had the rest of the world not been prepared to lend the money with which to do so. We will look at that more closely later in this chapter. For now, it is sufficient to say that labour and capital are unlikely to be flooding into South Sudan or the North Pole. They go to places where things are happening economically. Britain is such a place.

On top of the world: Britain's national champions

It is hard today to believe that Rolls-Royce was once not only a nationalized industry but one that had been taken into public ownership as a result of its bankruptcy. Back in February 1971, when one of the most famous names in the world of engineering became insolvent, it was possible to believe that the car manufacturing side of the business would have some sort of future, given its status as a supplier of vehicles to the rich and famous. And indeed it thrives to this day, under the ownership of Germany's BMW motor group.

But the exceptional worldwide success of the Rolls-Royce aero-engine business would have seemed somewhat fanciful. Yet today it is a world leader, employing more than 38,000 people, about 45 per cent of whom are outside the United Kingdom. More than simply a maker of aircraft engines, it is involved in supplying power units of all types to th marine, energy, aerospace and defence industries. According to the company's website, 'A Rolls-Royce powered aircraft takes off or lands every 2.5 seconds.'

It is perhaps equally hard today to reflect that the

UK pharmaceutical industry between the wars was, in large part, a collection of cottage industries vulnerable to foreign competition:

> [F]irms remained small and family-run. Those business leaders who might have effected large-scale mergers had their attention elsewhere .... The great national inter-war combines, such as ICI, Unilever and Associated Electrical Industries, each had workforces well in excess of the total number of those manufacturing drugs and medicines. Of the 200 firms in the latter industry in 1935, only 13 employed more than 500 people. The three leading companies accounted for only 18 per cent of total output.[10]

T. A. B. Corley adds:

> The most impressive pharmaceutical innovations between the wars came from May & Baker, using French know-how from Poulenc. In 1934 Rhone-Poulenc, as it had become, acquired control of May & Baker.[11]

The industry looks very different in the twenty-first century. One would perhaps expect a little drum-banging from its trade body, the Association of the British Pharmaceutical Industry, but the facts as listed on its website speak for themselves:

> Earnings from the exports of medicines exceeded imports by £7 billion in 2009 and the industry has been a net earner for Britain throughout all of the past 30 years.
> The industry invested £4.4 billion in UK research and development in 2009 and employs more than

72,000 people, including 27,000 highly-trained
scientists and doctors. In addition, the industry
generates thousands of jobs in related industries. [12]

And then there is the City. Here, the surprise may seem
more that it would even be included on a list of once-
mediocre business sectors that has now found its feet
rather than that anyone could ever have doubted its
world-class status. Surely financial services have always
constituted one area of British dominance?

Far from it. Well within living memory, in the
mid-1970s, the City was in a dire position. Between
January 1973 and December 1974, the then benchmark
London share index, the Financial Times 30, lost more
than 70 per cent of its value. In the middle of this
period, on 1 March 1974, the Conservative government
lost office and was replaced by a Labour administration
which had stood for office on the most left-wing manifesto
in decades. Sterling, whose strength had long been seen
as a cornerstone of the City's global position, was subject
to recurrent crises. It began the decade at an official rate
against the US dollar of $2.40, and its slump below $2
in 1976 saw the government seeking a loan from the
International Monetary Fund.

Even in the early 1980s, there was little sign of the
City breaking out of its downbeat mood. Memories of
the 'go-go' years of the late 1960s and early 1970s were
fresh, as were those of the crash that followed. The days of
the City's swashbuckling Young Turks were seen as very
much in the past rather than the future. Even electronic
share trading seemed history, after the merchant
banks abandoned their Ariel share-dealing system, set up
in 1973.

But whereas the official date of wholesale deregulation
of the City (the Big Bang) on 27 October 1986 has been

seen as firing the starting gun for the revival of the Square Mile as an economic force, the seeds were sown much earlier with the so-called Eurodollar market. This was a market, created in London, for dollars held outside the United States and whose owners were reluctant to repatriate them, not least because of legal restraints on US interest rates. Packaging exiled dollars into loans for both the overseas subsidiaries of US companies and non-American corporations became big business in the City. At the same time, London was building a large base in foreign exchange trading. As we shall see elsewhere in this book, the idea of the City as a business success story was taking root before the Big Bang. In a way, the deregulated stock market of the mid-1980s was the latecomer to the party.

Later in this chapter we shall take a closer look at the balance of payments. For now, suffice it to say that financial services makes the largest single contribution to our surplus in trade in services – £31.5 billion in 2010 out of a total surplus of £58.8 billion. Insurance, which is counted separately, ran a surplus of £3.7 billion.

Finally in our somewhat selective tour of Britain's national champions we come to a collective group that could be loosely titled 'broadcasting and culture'. It would have surprised few people 50 years ago to learn that the BBC would remain, in the twenty-first century, a respected provider of news, culture and entertainment. More surprising would have been the corporation's current size and global reach. Routinely described as the world's largest broadcaster and the world's most trusted media brand, the BBC has been said to be better known round the world than the country in which it is based.

The BBC's global reputation has produced many a touching testimonial from victims of oppression, as well as anecdotes of senior government officials in foreign parts who refused to believe news of a coup or war until it had been reported by the BBC. In a lighter vein, the Burmese pro-democracy leader Aung San Suu Kyi amused many in Britain when, in an interview in June 2011, she recalled during her time under house arrest listening with pleasure on the World Service to the presenter Dave Lee Travis, whose style had long been thought to be somewhat lightweight.

In culture more broadly, Britain is a world champion. According to the website of Arts Council England:

> The creative industries accounted for £59.9 billion or 6.2 per cent of UK Gross Value Added (GVA) in 2007. They grew by an average of five per cent per annum between 1997 and 2007. This compares to an average of three per cent for the whole of the economy over this period. They account for £16.6 billion in exports and nearly two million jobs.[13]

Updating aspects of the Arts Council England numbers, we see that the United Kingdom ran a surplus on 'personal, cultural and recreational' services of £2.5 billion in 2010. Separate figures for 2009, the latest available at the time of writing, show a £929 million surplus in exports over imports of the film industry and a £145 million surplus of exports over imports of the television industry. The creative economy is here.

In two minds: how sure are we about this?

This, then, is our maximum case for the upbeat – or at the very least sanguine – view of the British economy. It is productive and forward-looking. 'Creativity' is not simply a matter of clapperboard-wielding film types or the art galleries of Bond Street (important though these are). It is a way of thinking, of adding value, of deepening and enriching the product or service on offer. In a world of 'commoditization', this is where the future has to lie for developed economies. Britain is already heading into that future.

There is, of course, a quite different school of thought. But oddly, this more pessimistic viewpoint is often to be found intertwined with the 'maximum case' stated above.

Thus in March 2011, Britain's coalition government published *The Plan for Growth*, a strategy document whose key features included the intention 'to encourage investment and exports as a route to a more balanced economy'. That such a rebalancing was badly needed was, as far the plan's authors were concerned, beyond question. Issued under the signatures of the chancellor, George Osborne, and the business secretary, Vince Cable, the plan noted:

> Economic growth was [before the financial crisis] unbalanced across the UK, concentrated in the South East, with other parts of the country increasingly reliant on jobs funded by public spending. Growth relied on a limited number of sectors. Financial services' share of GDP rose from 6.5 per cent in 1997 to 8.5 per cent in 2007, while manufacturing's share nearly halved over the same period, from over 20 per cent to 12.5 per cent .... In terms of jobs, the position was equally stark, with the numbers employed in manufacturing falling from 4.5 million in 1997 to 3 million in 2007.[14]

A picture, then, of unrelieved gloom? On the contrary:

The UK has intrinsic strengths to build on. For
example ... [it] is an open, trading economy with a
flexible labour market, and an attractive investment
location for global companies. English remains the
predominant language of business throughout the
world and the UK's institutions, such as its legal system,
are respected around the world. Overseas companies
choose to use UK courts to settle commercial disputes,
and the UK is the world's second largest exporter of
services. The UK has a world-class research base, with
more top ranking universities, and more Nobel prize-
winners, than any country except the US.[15]

If the casual reader were baffled by the deeply troubled
yet simultaneously world-class British economy, there
was a second source of confusion embedded in the
document. Here is the plan's rationale:

For sustainable growth to be driven by private sector
investment and enterprise, the Government needs to
act in a way that supports growth rather than hampers
it. The UK needs a Plan for Growth.[16]

That seems fairly straightforward. A little later, however,
and we come across this:

The immediate priority was to restore economic
stability. This is an essential precondition for sustainable
economic growth, because businesses will not invest
unless they have confidence that long-term interest rates
will remain stable, and that finance will be available,
on reasonable terms, when they need it. In the June
Budget 2010, the Government set out a credible plan to
tackle the fiscal deficit and restore debt as a percentage
of GDP to a sustainable downward path.[17]

So is the government-sponsored rebalanced economy leading the way out of the recession, and as a consequence balancing the nation's books? Or is it that the balanced books will set the scene for the export powerhouse that will be the rebalanced economy?

Funnily enough, 80 years before *The Plan for Growth*, an official inquiry chaired by a lawyer, Hugh Pattison Macmillan, produced a report on the proper response to the 1929 stock market crash and subsequent depression. The Committee on Finance and Industry is remembered today for the brilliant advocacy of radical policies by the then maverick economist John Maynard Keynes and the participation of Ernest Bevin, the giant of trade unionism who was later to head the wartime production executive and then to serve as foreign secretary. It is tempting for us today to see the Macmillan report as a sort of pre-echo of the policies of the 1945 Labour government.

And indeed bold new policies were suggested, including management of trade, the establishment of state-owned enterprises and new measures to bring finance to industry. But this was only part of the story. As with *The Plan for Growth*, the Macmillan report appears to alternate between suggesting there is little to worry about and then proposing powerful initiatives to deal with these supposedly insignificant problems. Thus on the committee's central preoccupation, the relationship between finance and industry, we learn that:

> British manufacturers and traders have always been able to find cheap accommodation.[18]

This seems pretty conclusive. However:

> Particularly in the matter of investment have our financial institutions been weak.[19]

And the committee's radicalism had its limits. Here is the report's conclusion on the gold standard:

> The Committee concludes ... that the promise of international co-operation and the dependence of this country on overseas trade and on invisible exports make it desirable that we should maintain the gold standard at the present parity.[20]

In short, some things never change, and official reports and plans regarding the UK economy would seem to make up one of those things. Such documents frequently display two fault lines, or axes of contradiction. One is that British industry has terrible, deep-seated problems that require radical surgery, while at the same time it is a world-leader with the scope to exploit the fantastic opportunities that lie ahead. The second is that orthodox financial arrangements – whether for the provision of capital for industry or in macroeconomic terms with regard to fiscal and monetary policy – constitute a root cause of the economy's woes, while at the same time being perfectly adequate for the needs of business finance, and on the macroeconomic side, a precondition for economic success.

More recently, as noted above and as we shall examine in more detail later, financial institutions themselves have been held to be not an entity distinct from commerce and industry but to make up an 'industry' in their own right, and a very successful one too.

So why the uneasy coexistence of two quite different viewpoints in high places? Why the heavy qualification, at the very least, of the optimistic case by the pessimistic one?

Having made the optimistic case as best we can, we have to say that the pessimistic case seems to us to be the more realistic. The maximum case reminds us of nothing so much as a would-be weightwatcher who informs you that they now eat only lettuce and drink only tap water. The fact that they continue to pile on the pounds suggests to you that somehow they are still managing to tuck into a fair amount of pudding.

The proof of this particular pudding is to be found in *The Pink Book*, the annual compendium of the UK balance of payments position, produced by the government's Office for National Statistics.[21] Its 2011 edition adds up the totality of British exports in 2010, broken down into exports of physical goods, services (including insurance, legal services and the like, and earnings from tourism), investment income (the total amount earned on overseas investments) and 'transfers' (which includes payments from the European Union and other bodies). In total, these credits to the current account came to £615 billion, in round numbers.

It then lists the debits: imports of foreign goods and services (including holidays taken abroad), investment income earned in Britain by foreign investors and payments to bodies such as the European Union. These debits come to £652 billion, in round numbers.

In all, there was a current account deficit of about £37 billion. Nor is this unusual. This was not a freak year. From 1984 onwards, the UK current account has been in the red. Those 'success stories' have been nowhere near as numerous or as successful as was needed. Those 'good tales' were clearly outnumbered by the not-so-good, or even the downright dire.

Someone has been raiding the fridge, haven't they?

As we saw above, it has not been all bad news since the exhausted survivors of the trenches headed home in 1918. British industry has not been an unremitting story of failure. John Cridland and those who share his point of view are well within their rights to insist that good things are happening across the economy, on windblown industrial estates and in short-lease offices off back staircases as much as in gleaming corporate head offices and on glittering science-park campuses. Indeed, it is his job so to do: it would be an odd representative of business who spent his time highlighting the shortcomings of his members.

But the numbers do not lie. We have looked at some of the winners. Later we will look at some of the losers: a more significant category, we believe. Before we do so, it will be useful to look at the more detailed *Pink Book* figures to familiarize ourselves with where we seem likely to have ended up by 2014.

We start with trade in goods, in which the United Kingdom had a total deficit of £98.46 billion in 2010. Within this total, far and away the biggest single deficit is in the category of trade in 'finished manufactured goods', £59.8 billion. This breaks down into a deficit on motor cars of £2.75 billion, on other consumer goods of £23.84 billion, on intermediate goods (items such as components that are then incorporated into other goods) of £11.99 billion, on capital goods (those used to manufacture other goods) of £13.3 billion and on ships and aircraft of £4.91 billion. In other words, in not one of the categories of finished goods does the United Kingdom achieve a surplus.

There is a brighter picture in the category of semi-finished goods, although the rays of light here emanated from one sub-category, chemicals, where the United Kingdom ran a surplus of £6.17 billion. In precious stones and silver, it ran a small deficit of £28 million, one that may well widen once the De Beers group moves its diamond auctions from London to Botswana by the end of 2013. And in the category of 'other', which includes goods made of leather, cork, rubber, paper, textile yarn, fabric, iron and steel, there was a deficit of £14.29 billion.

Overall, there was a deficit on semi-manufactured goods of £8.14 billion.

In the category 'basic materials' – including hide, crude rubber, textile fibre and animal fats and oils – the deficit was £2.9 billion, and on coal, gas and electricity it was £5 billion. Trade in crude oil showed a deficit of £3.38 billion and in oil products of £1.34 billion, while in the rag-bag category of 'commodities and transactions not classified according to kind', which ranges from some types of postal packages to some types of gold, there was a small deficit of £419 million, close to being a rounding error in the vasty deeps of Britain's current account deficit.

Finally, and perhaps most seriously in an increasingly uncertain world, the second-biggest deficit after that on finished manufactured goods related to food, beverages and tobacco – a towering £17.36 billion.

This type of 'visible' trade is, of course, only part of the picture. It is quite possible to run a thriving economy without much by way of trade in physical objects. For years, we have been told that the country's future lies in trade in services, and it is entirely true to state that a pound earned by selling an insurance policy (for example) in a foreign market is worth exactly the same as a pound earned by exporting a television set or bag of coal. So how did we do here?

According to *The Pink Book*, we had a healthy surplus in this area. That is the good news. There is some less good news, but we shall look at that in a moment.

The first category is labelled 'transportation', but we find that word rather too redolent of convicts being shipped to overseas penal colonies, so prefer to call it 'international transport'. This covers passenger and freight transport by road, rail, sea and air. We have an overall surplus of £1.62 billion, behind which lies a larger surplus on sea transport but deficits on road, rail and air transport.

There is less good news in the next category, travel, covering both business travel and tourism. The deficit is £11.39 billion, but the clue to this poor performance lies in the detail. There is a modest deficit on business travel of £251 million and there are surpluses on personal travel for health-related reasons of £70 million and for education-related reasons of £4.89 billion.

Alas, in the 'other' personal travel category – essentially tourism – the UK deficit was £16 billion. This is another way of saying we just don't have the weather, and consequently it is probably the single aspect of the current account deficit about which we ought to worry least. True, during the postwar years of exchange control we did manage to achieve some surpluses, but reverting to capital controls to improve our tourism earnings would be considered somewhat drastic.

The next category, communications services, covers postal, courier and telecommunications services, in which the United Kingdom ran a surplus of £944 million.

Insurance showed a surplus of £3.7 billion, unsurprising perhaps, given that Britain houses both the Lloyd's of London market and a range of expert institutions. But this is dwarfed by the big earner, financial services, where the surplus is £26.64 billion measured without including the element known as 'financial intermediation services indirectly measured' or Fisim. This is the implicit charge when a service is paid for not by fees or commission but by the interest-rate difference between borrowing and lending. Including Fisim, the surplus is, as noted above, £31.5 billion.

On computer and information services, the United Kingdom has a surplus of £4.77 billion, while royalties and licence fees generated a surplus of £3.4 billion.

There is almost a clean sweep in terms of a surplus in every sub-category of 'other business services', with only 'operational leasing services' showing a deficit, of £472 million.

Elsewhere, there are healthy surpluses in legal services (£2.8 billion), accounting (£683 million), business management and management consulting (£3.88 billion) and 'architectural, engineering and other technical services' (£4.58 billion).

In the category of 'personal, cultural and recreational services', which includes film, television and other cultural products, the surplus was, as noted earlier, £2.5 billion, while 'government services' – which measures the balance between diplomatic, military and other spending by the United Kingdom abroad against that by other countries and organizations in the United Kingdom – is one of only three 'services' categories to show a deficit, of £1.94 billion. (Travel is the second of these categories, and the third is construction, which recorded a deficit of £11 million in 2010, but has tended to run relatively modest surpluses).

So the good news is, as we wrote earlier, that we have a surplus on services. The bad news is that this surplus, at £58.77 billion, is nowhere near enough to make up for the £98.46 billion deficit on trade in goods.

All is not lost, however. A third big category in the balance of payments concerns income earned abroad, overwhelmingly from investment but including also salaries paid to British employees abroad. In this latter sub-category, the United Kingdom ran a deficit of £389 million, the amount by which our payments to foreign employees outweighed foreign payments to our employees.

Beyond that relatively unimportant sub-category the picture is somewhat brighter. Earnings on direct

investment – that is to say, investment in factories,
businesses, land and so forth – showed a surplus of
£49.35 billion. Not bad going, given that an entire
generation of British people has grown up under the
impression that direct investment was one of those
things that foreigners did so much better than we did,
hence our need to persuade as many of them as possible
to invest in the United Kingdom, especially in depressed
areas in Wales, the north, Northern Ireland, Scotland
and elsewhere.

By contrast, that same generation will have learned,
the British are remarkably good at so-called portfolio
investment, juggling shares, bonds and other securities
far more skilfully than leaden-footed foreigners. Not
according to *The Pink Book* we aren't. In 2010, Britain
ran a deficit on income on investment in shares of
£6.52 billion and on income from investment in bonds
of £12.55 billion.

So-called 'other investment', which fits into neither the
direct investment nor portfolio investment sub-categories,
recorded a deficit of £14.08 billion.

Once other sub-categories are taken into account, the
surplus on income came to £23.04 billion.

Added to the surplus on trade in services, the total –
£81.81 billion – still falls a long way short of the amount
needed to close the deficit on trade in visible goods. And
we have one more category in the current account still
to examine, that covering transfers. This category takes
in the UK contribution to the European Union budget,
along with money sent home by foreigners working in
Britain, taxes paid by British companies abroad, and
social benefits paid by the United Kingdom to people
living outside the country. Of course it also takes in all
such payments made in the other direction, to the United
Kingdom, and calculates a balance. The deficit here

is £20.08 billion, of which payments to the European Union account for £9.11 billion.

Foraging through the details of the current account as we have just done can be dusty work. Some would go further, and argue this work has little value. A country's external trade and payments position is, they would say, merely one measure of its economic virility, and not a very reliable one at that. The current account, they might say, is merely a by-product of the exchange rate, Should you want to 'balance' the books, you should move the currency's external value down a little (to eliminate a deficit) or up a little (to eliminate a surplus). It is merely a question of accounting.

Some may go further, and claim that even if the surpluses and deficits are 'real', that they have some intrinsic reality, they do not matter, being, in the hackneyed phrase, merely the difference between two very large numbers. Worrying about the current account belongs to the late 1960s and the 1970s, to television news broadcasts in which a container was filmed being winched off a ship on to a dockside to a doomy voice-over declaring that 'Britain was in the red again last month'. The balance of payments, you may hear, is one of yesterday's worries, along with 'latchkey children', sex before marriage and the decline in hat wearing. The 'trade gap' belongs with the generation gap in the lumber-room of recent history.

We could not agree less. The current account is perhaps the most acute index of a nation's economic prowess, measuring as it does the extent to which the country relies, or does not rely, on other people's money to fund its standard of living. To say that an exchange-rate adjustment would wipe out the trade deficit is correct, but only in the sense that a sufficiently devalued currency would force us all to work very much harder to buy the same things from abroad. That is not so much a theory as a truism. It is rather like saying that the cream-cake eater we met earlier in this chapter would cease to be fat were they to eat fewer cream cakes and to do some more exercise. Yes indeed. But this notion that because you could activate a Plan B did you wish to do so, there is no need to activate said plan, makes no sense.

One final 'reason' for the alleged unimportance of the current account verges on the nihilistic. This states that any deficit on the current account does not matter because it is, of necessity, always matched by an equal and opposite inflow of funds from abroad. In other words, overseas savers and businesses are lending us the money with which to fund a lifestyle we are not earning. It would be interesting to try that line of argument with a bank manager: your overdraft does not matter, indeed does not really exist, because a matching amount of money has flowed into your account in the form of other people's savings mediated through the bank.

We need waste little time with this sort of argument. But it would be quite right to point out that all the current account figures which we have been examining suffer from being little more than a snapshot, the state of play in one year only. For that reason, right at the end of this chapter, we shall return to *The Pink Book* in search of recent trends, in order to give a fuller picture.

Before then, however, we need to go very much further back, to look at the underside of the British economy during the last near-century, the industries where our inability to overcome weaknesses was to lead, eventually, to the chronic balance of payments deficit with which we are now lumbered.

This category of losers might in retrospect seem obvious, or even self-selecting. It was not so at the time. For example, the formation through merger in 1931 of Electrical & Musical Industries gave Britain a fully integrated world-leading company in the new audiovisual business, making records, record players, radio and television sets. EMI's HMV brand became famous round the world. Yet today, EMI's record interests are being broken up for sale, its audio equipment arm went long ago, and the now-separate HMV record shops have had a torrid time in the face of declining record sales.

The UK automotive industry too once cut a dash. The Morris company, based at Cowley near Oxford, experienced rapid growth, overtaking Ford to seize more than half of the British market by the mid-1920s. In the atmosphere of bullish self-confidence, the company established its own steel-pressing plant at Cowley in the late 1920s, named, perhaps unimaginatively, the Pressed Steel Company. In time it was to produce also the Prestcold range, leading to one of the earliest privatizations when, at the start of the 1980s, it was decided the state had no real need to own a refrigerator manufacturer, Morris having long since passed into public ownership.

In aircraft manufacture, Britain supported a dense undergrowth of businesses, with at least 15 substantial concerns by the standards of the time. Names that reverberate to this day include Hawker Siddeley, Vickers, De Havilland, Handley Page and Gloster.

As was noted in 1995 in a paper by the Department of the Environment, the First World War gave the industry an enormous boost. The Society for British Aircraft Companies (SBAC) was founded in 1916 with 48 members; by 1918, membership had risen to 80, with production having risen to 10,000 units a year, although the end of the war and the switch to civilian aircraft saw SBAC membership fall back to 18 by the early 1920s.

Between the two world wars, companies tended

to specialise in certain types of military aircraft, for
example Gloster, Hawker and Bristol concentrated on
fighters, while Blackburn, Shorts and Supermarine
manufactured flying boats and Fairey produced
light bombers...In 1935, there were 27 companies
producing both civil and military aircraft and a
number of companies producing aero-engines.[22]

In the postwar economy this diverse corporate ecology
came to be seen as a disadvantage, but not so in the
run-up to the Second World War:

> The wartime production of aircraft was directed by
> the Government but all manufacturing was carried
> out by the private sector.[23]

So a new economy of sorts was taking shape in parallel to
the old. George Orwell wrote of its social consequences:

> The place to look for the germs of the future England
> is in light-industry areas and along the arterial roads.
> In Slough, Dagenham, Barnet, Letchworth, Hayes –
> everywhere, indeed, on the outskirts of great towns
> – the old pattern is gradually changing into something
> new. In these vast new wildernesses of glass and brick
> the sharp distinctions of the of the older kind of town,
> with its slums and mansions, or of the country, with its
> manor-houses and squalid cottages, no longer exist ....
> It is a rather restless, cultureless life, centring round
> tinned food, *Picture Post*, the radio and the internal
> combustion engine .... To that civilisation belong the
> ... technicians and the highly-paid skilled workers,
> the airmen and their mechanics, the radio experts,
> film producers, popular journalists and industrial
> chemists. They are the indeterminate stratum at

which the older class distinctions are beginning to break down.[24]

But the old economy had not gone away:

> The evidence of industrial decay was omnipresent
> .... After a brief post-war recovery, the fundamental
> weakness of Britain's traditional export industries –
> coal, cotton and textiles, shipbuilding, engineering
> – all of which had old equipment, old animosities
> and old work-practices, combining to produce
> low productivity, was reflected in chronically high
> unemployment.[25]

The story of British industry and business after the Second World War falls into two distinct phases. We refer here to the actual behaviour of the economy – the policy ideas and economic strategies are covered in Chapter 4. The first, which is the subject of the remainder of this section, ran from 1945 to the late 1960s. The second is covered later.

This first phase gave concrete expression to the notion that the United Kingdom ought to be a major industrial power, with a presence in all existing major business areas – cars, aircraft manufacture, textiles, engineering, chemicals and so forth – and some new ones too, such as nuclear power. It is not an original comment that greater stress was placed on products that could be sold to the public sector, both home and abroad, than those for private consumers. Japan and West Germany, by contrast, developed a much sharper consumer focus. A parallel strand was that work itself ought to be considerably less of an ordeal for the majority of people than it had often been in the past.

'Work can be made universal, pleasant, secure, by

proper planning of the national resources', declared the influential magazine *Picture Post* in January 1941. The dominance of these two strands of thought was remarkably consistent throughout a quarter-century or more after the war. The wrapping may have changed – 'New Elizabethans' gave way to 'the white heat of the technological revolution' – but the thinking did not. Indeed these strands were interwoven to the extent that the more rapidly Britain moved into the industries of the future, the more rapidly its workforce would swap dirty overalls for white coats or collar and tie. Nowhere was this more vividly illustrated than in an industry dear to the nation's hearts, the railways, where with the complete switch by the mid-1960s from steam to diesel, diesel-electric and electric power replaced the sweat and soot of the steam-era driving cab with a comfortable chair for the driver and a modern control panel.

Pursuing this status of 'scientific' industrial giant was easier said than done. The economic inheritance of 1945 was deeply troubled, and not only because of the war:

> It was a mark of how profoundly 20th Century industrial Britain had remained stuck in an early 19th Century rut that even in 1937 exports of cotton (despite having collapsed by three-quarters since 1913) still remained a third more valuable than exports of machinery and two and a half times more than exports of chemicals.[26]

But in the immediate post-war years, there was better news as well.

> The year 1948 was to set new records for production and for exports .... Not only were older staples

such as the pits of the Rhondda or the shipyards of Birkenhead, Newcastle, Barrow or the Clyde in full operation; but newer industries, cars, chemicals, electronics and rubber, and much else besides, were adding much-needed variety to the industrial base of the old 'depressed' regions.[27]

The newest industry of all, the flagship of Britain's postwar economy and a major factor in its claim to be an advanced industrial power, was nuclear energy. In 1956, the facility at Calder Hall in Cumbria became the first nuclear power station in the world to generate power for a grid system.

> [N]uclear power came to be regarded as a British technical triumph. Some scientists even claimed that Britain was the world leader in nuclear generating technology; but that claim related to high volume of output so far, not to low cost.[28]

Professor Myddelton, the author of this comment, adds that, from the start, nuclear power was seen as a matter of national prestige, quoting Margaret Gowing, author of *Independence and Deterrence: Britain and atomic energy 1945–52*.[29] Nine nuclear power stations were opened in the first phase of the programme, from 1955 to 1965, using the Magnox design, and a second phase was started in 1965, using another British design, a modified version of Magnox called the Advanced Gas-cooled Reactor (AGR). Both Magnox and the AGR, wrote Professor Myddelton, 'suffered from serious cost overruns, construction delays and operating problems'. In retrospect, it might have made more sense to buy American nuclear-power technology.

Professor Myddelton continued:

But there was no agreed method of evaluating reactors and the British appraisal failed to convince others. It later became painfully apparent that the AGR had been far from ready for commercial construction, and no overseas buyer ever placed an order for one. The obvious question was whether it would have paid to import reactors from abroad. At this time [the mid-1960s] the British Government was controversially deciding to scrap the TSR-2 bomber in favour of the American F-111, and it might have been awkward to buy American in nuclear power as well.[30]

Mention of the TSR-2 – a low-level nuclear strike aircraft – brings us rather neatly to another of the 'future industries' of postwar Britain, civil and military aviation, covered in more detail in a later chapter.

Throughout the war enormous resources had been poured into Britain's aircraft industries .... The upshot was that by the end of the war the aircraft industry was Britain's biggest.[31]

It was also remarkably feather-bedded:

During the war the private companies that made up the aero industry had effectively been nationalised ... any competition between them to win the various contracts for new types of aircraft put out to tender by the Ministry [of Aircraft Production] came without the peacetime penalty for failure. No company that was part of Britain's vital defence could be allowed to go under simply because it had produced a dud aircraft.[32]

The government had every incentive post-1945 to

rationalize the industry, and the industry had every reason to resist:

> As their final weapon, most of the companies were household names indelibly associated with the famous aircraft and engines that had helped win victory. No politician was eager to be acclaimed by the newspapers as personally responsible for liquidating any of a dozen hallowed icons.[33]

Perhaps as an alternative to wholesale rationalization of the industry, government policy, beginning during wartime, was to pursue the most ambitious possible future for British aviation:

> It was ... the wartime coalition which had taken the original decision that after the war Britain should not only supply all types of aircraft needed by her armed forces, but also compete with the United States in manufacturing and selling civil air transports. If this were not technological overstretch enough, the coalition Government further decided that British constructors should not limit themselves to small short-haul passenger aircraft, even though this 'niche' market was recognised as offering the better prospects of foreign sales, but should challenge the Americans head-on in the most competitive market of all, that for large long-distance air-transports.[34]

Duplication was the order of the day, as three separate companies built three different versions of Britain's nuclear V-bomber (Avro's Vulcan, Handley Page's Victor and the Vickers Valiant). The TSR-2, for which Vickers was the lead contractor, fell victim to Whitehall infighting (the Royal Navy was against it) and to the

United Kingdom's withdrawal from one of the key areas in which it would have operated, the Far East.

In civil aircraft, the emphasis on speed and comfort produced airliners such as the Vickers VC10, and ultimately Concorde (the former's transAtlantic speed record has only ever been beaten by the latter). The arrival of Boeing's 747 'jumbo' at the end of the 1960s suggested there was another possible future for aviation: slower, more cramped, cheaper and carrying very many more passengers. The Anglo-French Concorde was indeed a technical triumph, as was the Hawker Harrier jump jet, for years the only properly working vertical take-off and landing aeroplane in the world. The difference was to be that the Harrier would win major export orders, while Concorde did not.

Rationalization of the aircraft industry did eventually become official policy after defence secretary Duncan Sandys's white paper of 1957.[35] Hamilton-Paterson noted:

> Amalgamations now became official policy. In 1959 Armstrong Siddeley and Bristol's engine division merged to become Bristol Siddeley – which was itself destined to be swallowed up by Rolls-Royce in 1966 to leave Rolls-Royce as the sole surviving major UK aero-engine manufacturer, which it remains to this day. In 1960, virtually all Britain's venerable aircraft companies were summarily bundled up into either the British Aircraft Corporation or Hawker Siddeley Aviation.[36]

The car industry too was experiencing a wave of mergers, with official encouragement. Satisfying untapped domestic demand for cars had provided a relatively easy living during the postwar years, but beyond niche products such as the Mini, Jaguar and the Land Rover, export success had been harder to come by:

[T]he Austin A90 Atlantic convertible ... [a] monstrosity, a provincial Briton's nightmare vision of American taste ... was intended to be the flagship of Austin's export drive in the United States .... Sadly, however, the American motorist failed to buy the Atlantic despite Austin's certainty that it was the car he ought to want. In mark of defeat, unsold Atlantics were shipped back to Britain and converted to right-hand drive.[37]

By the end of the 1960s, Austin, Morris, Jaguar, Triumph, Rover and others had been merged into the British Leyland Motor Corporation, with more than 40 per cent of the British market.

It was in perhaps the quintessentially futuristic industry – that of computers – that Britain looked set to take a decisive lead.

In the UK, many of the early computer projects benefited from technological developments at the three Second World War R&D centres of excellence, namely: Bletchley Park, the Telecommunications Research Establishment and the Admiralty Signal Establishment. Leading scientists and engineers from these centres formed the nucleus of most UK computer design groups in the late 1940s.[38]

Simon Lavington lists the achievements. The world's first commercially available computer was the Ferranti Mark 1 in 1951, based on a Manchester University prototype, while the first business data processing computer was designed by Lyons, the food manufacturer and tea-shop owner. The 'Lyons Electronic Office' (Leo) dated back to 1951.

The British computer industry was fragmented, however, which may explain why the US International

Business Machines (IBM) had by 1962 captured 18 per cent of the UK market. Under official sponsorship, the main computer interests of British Tabulating Machines Ltd (later part of ICT), Elliott Brothers (London) Ltd, English Electric, Ferranti and Leo had, by 1968, been merged into a single British champion in this field: International Computers Ltd.[39] For the British computer industry, the future looked bright indeed.

De-industrial revolution: the 1970s and after

The collapse into insolvency of Rolls-Royce in February 1971, and its subsequent nationalization by Edward Heath's Conservative government, was a thunderclap that heralded stormy times ahead. If any moment marked the end of the long postwar boom, this was surely it.

That is ironic, given that – as we have seen – Rolls-Royce's aero-engine and allied activities are seen today as a pinnacle of British engineering excellence. The emergency state takeover of Rolls-Royce turned out for the best. We can only hope that the future of the nationalized and part-nationalized banks, rescued after the 2007 credit crunch, proves equally happy and successful.

But such a cheery ending was the exception, not the rule, in the 1970s and after. Another car company was rescued during that troubled decade, British Leyland Motor Corporation, which ran out of money, prompting the government to take a majority shareholding in 1975. Very little remains of British Leyland today. Employment in its volume car business Austin Morris stood at about 150,000 in the mid-1970s. With the exception of the 3500 working on the Mini, it is zero today.

By the end of the 1960s it was becoming clear that

British industry was struggling to hold its own in both the home and export markets, and that the big industrial concerns were increasingly unable to maintain the employment levels to which their personnel had become accustomed.

This was the view of Sidney Weighell, then assistant general secretary of the National Union of Railwaymen and later general secretary:

> In my maiden speech to the [1966 Labour Party] … conference I opposed him [Transport and General Workers Union general secretary Frank Cousins] and his union for their views. I received a rough ride from many of the delegates who did not like what I had to say. There were shouts of 'Scab' as I criticised Cousins for his demand that there should be work-sharing in the car industry to protect jobs. 'He talks about 10,000 people in a shake-out in the car industry,' I argued. 'Well, 150,000 of our workers have been shaken out.'[40]

With unemployment rising during the 1970s to the previously unimaginable level of a million and more, industrial conflict sharpened. Michael (now Sir Michael) Edwardes recalled taking over as executive chairman of British Leyland in November 1977:

> In those days there were disputes in half of our 50 British factories day in and day out, and the list often ran to five sheets. Those pages made unhappy reading …. It was to be three years before the daily dispute sheets swindled to the point where I was able to discontinue them.[41]

Furthermore, the national workforce was increasingly drawn to unproductive, bureaucratic employment.

Rather than being the workshop of the world, Britain
was becoming one of the world's secretarial colleges,
with priority given to non-manual clerical and service
occupation.[42]

The two decades after 1970 were convulsive for
manufacturing industry, and laid to rest many of the
hopes (unrealistic as they may have been) of postwar
policy makers. Despite nationalization in 1977 as British
Aerospace (BAe) (which was later privatized), the British
aircraft industry did not emerge as a major exporter
of civilian airliners, and could hope to take part only
through the Airbus consortium. Even here, BAe's
successor company, BAE Systems, sold its Airbus interests
to the European EADS consortium. Notwithstanding
years of subsidies, British Leyland and its successor
company, Austin Rover, did not manage to build
sizeable export markets for the products of a British-
owned car operation. And despite heavy spending on
projects such as the (later scrapped) Advanced Passenger
Train, British rolling stock manufacture is a shadow
of its former self. In early 2012 Britain's last train
factory, the Bombardier plant in Derby, won a short-
term reprieve from threatened closure, but its future
remained uncertain.

British manufacturing industry has suffered longer
and much worse than most others. Between 1973
and 1980, for example, while world industrial output
rose by 13 per cent, there was a fall of ten per cent in
the UK.[43]

Employment has plunged. In the citadel of the trade
unions' 'triple alliance' of steel, rail and coal, numbers
have fallen since about 1980 from 250,000 to about

22,000 (steel), from about 277,500 to 100,000 (railways) and from about 187,000 to 2700 (coal).

Nor were the industries of the future faring very much better, in general. The nuclear power industry, dogged by cost over-runs and public concern about safety, faced a new menace with the 1989 privatization of the electricity services: accountancy. It turned out that when private shareholders were being asked to put up their own money for nuclear assets, they wanted to know precisely how cheap and safe nuclear power really was.

> As the Government prepared to privatise electricity, capital markets for the first time began to consider the costs and benefits of nuclear investment. Since some of the costs lie many years in the future, nuclear power's true 'costs' are bound to be subject to massive uncertainties. But a market regime provides incentives to understand them rather than just accept the estimates put forward by government technocrats.[44]

As for the major-league British computer industry, it very largely disappeared. ICL was bought by another British company, Standard Telephones and Cables (STC) in 1984, and then sold on to Japan's Fujitsu. In the field of high technology, unalloyed successes, such as Cambridge-based microprocessor designer ARM Holdings, are rare.

The fate of the computer industry is, indeed, a textbook case of Britain's apparent inability to turn brainwaves into big money. Centres of excellence in general are thin on the ground. They include specialist engineering companies, the best of Britain's pharmaceutical businesses, legal and accounting services, and upmarket motor vehicles such as Jaguar cars and Triumph motorcycles. But it is all rather like the economy as it would be were it to be run by people from Imperial College, London, with a little help from the law and the accounting profession.

We have left until last the financial services business. For many years, the City was considered not only apart from British business and industry, but partly responsible for the economy's problems, either because it failed to raise funds for industry or because it promoted a strong pound that throttled exports, or both. But by the end of the 1970s the City was beginning to be seen as an industry itself, one that was doing very well. Here is Sir Ian Gilmour, Conservative MP and future cabinet minister, suggesting the country ought perhaps to thank the City for its performance:

> We need not be effusive about it; people in the City are generally quite well rewarded for their efforts. But we should be quietly grateful. The City of London is one of the parts of our economic system that works undeniably well. It makes an indispensable contribution to the balance of payments; and if the rest of the economy was anywhere near as successful, Britain would not have an economic problem.[45]

As we have seen above, financial services do indeed make a large contribution to the balance of payments, of at least £26.6 million on the most conservative estimate with an additional £3.7 billion from insurance. But two pertinent questions to ask are, first, whether this is likely to continue indefinitely, given both regulation and rivalry from Europe and elsewhere, and second, whether the liability to rescue financial institutions in trouble is a price worth paying. Bank rescues in the wake of the 2007 credit crunch reached a cost equivalent to about 100 per cent of gross domestic product.

What distinguished the winners from the losers? One obvious difference relates to government support, not merely in the sense of grants, subsidies and other aid, but the government as a long-term customer. Take pharmaceuticals:

> The rate of structural change in Britain's pharmaceutical industry accelerated markedly .... A principal cause was the government's strategy for both pricing and drug safety, which astutely used market forces that induced firms to adopt more advanced technology.
>
> As a single (monopsonistic) buyer of prescription drugs for the NHS, the Department of Health aimed to keep the cost to the taxpayer as low as possible, without thereby impeding the flow of new and improved drugs. Under the Voluntary (in 1978 renamed the Pharmaceutical) Price Regulation Scheme from 1957 onwards, it fixed drug prices at levels to allow manufacturers a reasonable return on investment. Its formula encouraged expenditure on innovative R & D that promised to yield good returns, and large exporters received added incentives. It also penalised firms that were merely followers.[46]

Then there is Rolls-Royce, whose 1971 rescue was prompted by the need to fulfil orders placed by UK and allied air forces. Indeed, defence spending has been said to support one in ten British manufacturing jobs, and the principal defence contractor BAE Systems is in the global front rank.

By contrast, Concorde apart, the civil aviation industry was very much left to its own devices after about 1970 in terms of strategic direction, as initial post-war official interest waned and the national flag-carrier British Airways cheerfully bought its airplanes from Boeing.

The City's reliance on public money has been its little secret for decades, from the vast earnings provided by the privatization programme of the 1980s and 1990s to beneficial tax regimes and the bank bailouts, this last being not exactly secret but nevertheless remarked upon rather less than may have been expected.

The BBC, of course, is largely funded by a compulsory licence fee, which brings in more than £3.6 billion a year, while the arts too have long received some state support.

State money, interest and patronage have been no guarantee of success – just look at British Leyland. But they have certainly played a big part.

Which way is up? Trends in the balance of payments

The annual balance of payments figures that we looked at earlier were a snapshot, and now longer-term trends need to be examined.

Regarding manufactured goods, the trend since 2000 has been almost uniformly bad. Back then, the total deficit on goods was £33.03 billion, against £98.46 billion in 2010. One exception is the car industry, where a deficit in 2000 of £4.22 billion had shrunk by 2010 to £2.75 billion. On 28 December 2011 *The Daily Telegraph* reported that:

> British car manufacturing could reach an all-time high in the next decade following £4 billion of investment from manufacturers in 2011, according to new research [by the trade body the Society of Motor Manufacturers and Traders]. The country produced 1.9 million cars in 1972, but could break that annual record following announcements in the past 12 months from car makers such as Toyota, Nissan and BMW to expand in the UK.[47]

By the same token, the surplus on services has risen markedly since 2000, from £15.01 billion to £58.77 billion. A £3.29 billion deficit on transport in 2000 has been turned into a £1.61 billion surplus, and a £13.04 billion surplus on financial services has grown to a surplus of £31.49 billion.

None of these figures is adjusted for inflation, so they should be treated with some caution. Nevertheless, inflation affects the successes and the failures equally, thus the comparisons are valid in terms of looking for patterns across the decade in question.

On income, there has been a steady and very strong improvement in the bottom line during the years 2000–10, from a negligible surplus of £1.96 billion to £23.02 billion. Driving this has been a marked upswing on earnings from direct investment, from £17.6 billion to £49.35 billion. By contrast, the balance on portfolio investment has deteriorated from a surplus of £534 million in 2000 to a deficit of £12.55 billion.

Finally, the 'transfers' section of the current account has shown a significant worsening during the decade, from a deficit of £9.77 billion to one of £20.08 billion. A big factor in this has been a sharp increase in the size of net contributions to EU institutions, from £5.4 billion to £9.11 billion.

The British economy has not experienced a near-century of unmitigated failure since 1914. But the chronic quarter-century-long weakness on the current account is not the result of some terrible mistake, but the culmination of steady decline. In particular, the postwar years can be seen to have been marred by a series of strategic mistakes: the concentration on producing big-ticket items for public-sector purchasers rather than top-quality consumer goods, the failure to rationalize earlier (as seen in the car and aircraft industries), wild swings on the part of ministers and officials between intense involvement and indifference (as seen with regard to the computer industry) and a lazy belief by industry that a big 'home' market, first the Commonwealth and later in Europe, was all that was needed for success.

To focus briefly on one specific industry, it is melancholic for those of us of a certain age to note the decline of the mainstream British audiovisual industry, with the disappearance as independent entities of once-great names such as Pye. True, specialist high-value manufacturers such as Naim manufacture renowned audio equipment for a global market. But there is no 'British Sony'.

Similarly, Morgan is world-famous for its classic British sports car. But it is not sales of Morgan vehicles that have brought about the narrowing of the trade gap in cars that we noted above. Rather it has been the operation inside Britain of foreign-owned car plants whose owners are experienced in making reliable vehicles in very high volumes that will appeal to a mass market.

In Britain, it seems, the natives can be as productive as anyone else, provided they are shown the way by managers and owners from more advanced economies. That is how things work in an underdeveloped country.

Chapter 7

The great reckoning

Home art gone, and ta'en thy wages:
Golden lads and girls all must,
As chimney-sweepers, come to dust.

William Shakespeare, *Fidele*, 1623

Most things may never happen: this one will.

Philip Larkin, *Aubade*, 1977

I opened my hands at the room and its furniture, at the computers,
the drinks trolley, at the chandelier, at New York. 'Who's paying
for all this?'
   'You are.'

Martin Amis, *Money*, 1984

Parker's Piece is where town meets gown in Cambridge.
It is a slab of green open space to the south of the city
centre where, it is said, the rules of Association Football
were first drawn up in the nineteenth century. At the
centre of Parker's Piece there is a lamp-post built by the
Sun Foundry in Glasgow, a company that did not outlast
the reign of Queen Victoria. Since the 1970s its local claim
to fame has been words etched on it by a student at what
was then the Cambridge College for Arts and Technology:
'Reality Checkpoint'. The centre of Parker's Piece was
where the cosseted, privileged world of the university
ended and the real world began.
   Britain has arrived at its own Reality Checkpoint,
although like the blissfully unconcerned under-graduates

from Emmanuel and Downing out for a late evening stroll on Parker's Piece, the message has yet to sink in. For the last 100 years, chancellors of the Exchequer of all political hues, Bank of England governors, Treasury mandarins and distinguished academics have warned of the need for the United Kingdom to face up to the facts of life. The message has been a consistent one: times have changed and the country needs to change too. Fierce competition from rival countries means that this is not the time for the United Kingdom to bask in the glories of yesteryear; rather it is the moment to roll up sleeves and use a bit of elbow grease or face the inevitability of decline. Only rarely, and then only briefly, have the clichés made any difference to UK performance, largely because a way has been found to delay the inevitable and necessary adjustment.

Sometimes the United Kingdom has been helped by a booming global economy, as in the 1950s; sometimes governments have boosted demand by making credit more freely available, as they did with disastrous long-term consequences in the early 1970s, the late 1980s and the mid-2000s. Even now, after a recession that left the United Kingdom with its largest peacetime budget deficit, the consensus is that the future is bright once the country has come to terms with its immediate problems. Dr Pangloss, Voltaire's incurable optimist from *Candide*, could learn a thing or two from the ministers who 'bat for Britain' by talking up the United Kingdom's world-class financial services sector, the strength of its science base and the creativity of its cultural industries. Given a fair wind, the debts will be paid down, the economy will be rebalanced, public services will be improved and living standards will rise year after year. Such talk is both delusional and dangerous, a continuation of the quick-fix approach explained in Chapter 4. The next few years will actually see the United Kingdom forced to confront a Great Reckoning: all the ingredients for a witches' brew have been stirred into the cauldron and are gradually coming to the boil.

The first reckoning: getting poorer

For the past 150 years, people in Britain have expected to get richer each year. Sometimes, during particularly grim periods, those expectations have not been met, but on average the economy has grown by 2–2.5 per cent a year. New techniques and more efficient ways of working have made Britain more productive, and workers have shared the benefits. In the second half of the twentieth century, living standards doubled every 30 years or so, and the luxuries of the 1950s became the consumer staples of the 2000s. Women no longer use a mangle for the washing: even the poorest families today expect to have a television, a telephone and a refrigerator, items that would only have been found in the better-off households six decades ago.

But shortly after the turn of the millennium, this trend faltered. First there was a slowing down in the rate of growth in real incomes, then a stagnation, and finally there was a fall. The weakness of unions meant that employees struggled to receive what Marx called the fruits of their labour, while even those who did chisel pay increases out of their managements found the gains eroded by inflation.

The high water mark for trade union power was the end of the 1970s, when 58 per cent of the national economic cake was accounted for by wages. Since then, labour's share has dwindled to just below 54 per cent; had it remained unchanged British workers would today have been taking home an extra £60 billion a year, £1000 for every man, woman and child in the country [1]

Finally, there was the deep and long recession, during which time many workers accepted pay cuts rather than be laid off. Once adjusted for inflation, real incomes fell by more than 7 per cent between 2009 and 2012, the biggest three-year drop on record. Even in the brief periods when the economy was actually showing some signs of life, living standards were hit by a rising cost of living, and in 2011 household incomes dropped by 3 per cent. Such a fall was on a scale not seen since the slump of the early 1980s, which was followed by a period of strong growth in living standards as inflation dropped to a low of 2.5 per cent by mid-decade, while earnings growth never fell below 7.5 per cent.

For the current crop of workers, the outlook is not nearly so rosy. Wage settlements are expected to remain low as unemployment edges its way back up towards the 3 million mark, and the Institute for Fiscal Studies (IFS) predicted that it would take until 2015–16 for real household median income, the purchasing power of the average family, to return to levels last seen in 2002–03. [2] A period of five years without growth in real incomes is unusual in Britain; a ten-year period had the experts scrabbling around in the history books for comparisons; a 13-year period of stagnant real incomes would be unprecedented in the modern age.

While unprecedented, the IFS's forecast did not seem outlandish. For real incomes to rise, there would have to be growth in the economy sufficiently strong to generate jobs and higher wages. Each year the Treasury has expressed optimism that the economy's rate of growth would soon recover to its pre-recession trend, and each year that recovery has been put back by 12 months.

The Office for Budget Responsibility (OBR) was

created after the 2010 election as an independent body that would take the politics out of official economic forecasting, yet while commendably untainted by political spin, the OBR's forecasts were nonetheless always wrong, and consistently over-estimated the growth rate. At the end of 2011, the OBR expressed confidence that the United Kingdom would return to its old trend growth rate of 2.3 per cent a year, but admitted that it might take until 2014 for it to do so.[3] Some less optimistic observers said the fact that the economy could only grow by 1 per cent in 2011, a year that also saw inflation rise to more than 5 per cent, reflected the inability of Britain to grow at its old rate. As the tentative recovery of 2009–10 faltered and gave way to a double-dip recession in the winter of 2011–12, those fears of an economy trapped in recurrent bouts of mild stagflation were heightened.[4]

The second reckoning: Britain as the New Marshalsea

There are some growth industries in Britain. One is doorstep lending, in which salespeople extend credit to those households unable to borrow from banks. There are at least 500 companies in this field, which market their services on the basis that a small loan will be able to tide the borrower over until payday, or in many cases the payment of welfare benefits. Interest rates on the loans can be exorbitantly high, with annual rates of 1000 per cent common for those borrowers who fail to pay off the debt speedily. Despite the assumption that those taking out payday loans are doing so to pay for holidays or Christmas presents for their children, research for the housing charity Shelter has shown that they are used by at least 1 million borrowers struggling to pay their rent or mortgage. Around 7 million Britons are falling back on some sort of credit to meet their housing costs.[5]

These days there are no official debtors' prisons in the United Kingdom. The Marshalsea, the model for the prison in Charles Dickens's *Little Dorrit*, slammed its gates shut for the last time in 1842, but the perils of debt are still real for millions of families, who in many cases are one pay cheque or less away from penury. The bank First Direct estimated that 6 million households, probably including many of those borrowing to pay their household bills, would be unable to survive financially for more than five days if they stopped being paid. These families have savings of less than £250 at a time when the average outgoings for a household are in excess of £1500 a month.[6]

Despite the repeated claims by Conservative, Labour and Liberal Democrat ministers that they are creating a nation of thrift, a fifth of households have no savings at all. In the 1980s, Margaret Thatcher vowed that she would extend the idea of a 'property-owning democracy' down the income scale, and controversially allowed council tenants the right to buy their homes at discounted prices. In 1988, at the height of the housing boom, 58 per cent of young people under 35 in the middle and low income groups were mortgage payers, 30 per cent were in socially rented housing and 14 per cent were renting from private landlords. In 2008, when the next housing bubble was about to burst, only 29 per cent of young people on low and middle incomes were buying, while 41 per cent were renting privately. Almost a third of those buying their homes needed the 100 per cent mortgages that lenders were, during the boom years, only too willing to provide.[7]

As Guy Standing notes in *The Precariat,* a new class began to develop in the last in the last years of the twentieth century and the first decade of the twenty-first century, which was remote from the high-flyers of the City on the highest salaries, and the cadres of professionals, technocrats and skilled workers ranked beneath them. This group moved from one low-paid, insecure job to another, often with periods of unemployment in-between, and they used debt to make ends meet.[8]

For those in more secure jobs, an uncomfortably large mortgage was the alternative to living at home with mum and dad until early middle age, while for those on higher incomes debt became a lifestyle choice, a way of gambling on an ever-rising property market or choosing not to defer consumer gratification until such time as they had saved for the new car or the holiday abroad. The means used to finance the expansion of higher education – student loans – meant that young people got the debt habit at a young age. When the coalition government raised tuition fees to a maximum of £9000 a year, a graduate on even a relative modest salary would need to find a way of repaying a debt of £40,000 or more even before they could contemplate buying a home.

The received wisdom is that since the crisis of 2008–09 Britain has gradually been kicking the debt habit. There have been reports from the Bank of England showing that instead of borrowing against the rising value of their homes, a process known as equity withdrawal, Britons have been paying off mortgage debt.[9] Unfortunately, this idea of a nation in detox, willingly putting itself through a process of cold turkey, does not square with the facts. Bank of England research found that 'the fall in housing equity withdrawal since the financial crisis was likely to reflect a fall in the number of housing transactions, with little sign that households in aggregate are making an active effort to pay down debt more quickly than in the past.'[10]

The stock of UK household debt – which only makes up around 20 per cent of the country's total debt – has been rising, not falling. Unlike in the United States, where widespread use of home loan defaults and foreclosures has brought personal debt levels down, lenders in Britain have preferred to pursue a policy of 'extend and pretend': extend the term of the underperforming loan and pretend that the borrower has the ability to pay off the debt on the original, more onerous terms. Lenders have not been showing forbearance from a sense of charity; rather they have been concerned that home repossessions on the sort of scale seen in the early 1990s would lead to a steep drop in property prices, which would have a knock-on effect on the value of the assets held by banks and building societies.

This tendency to brush the problem under the carpet means that Britain has disguised the true state of its mortgage debt problem. The Bank of England estimates that even after a prolonged period of ultra-low interest rates, one in eight mortgages are subject to the forbearance of lenders, while another 2 per cent are formally in arrears. Two-thirds of UK mortgages have floating interest rates, which would leave millions of borrowers in difficulties in the event that the Bank's Monetary Policy Committee decided to push up the cost of borrowing. Research by the consultancy firm McKinsey found that at its current glacial pace, it would take until 2020 for the ratio of household debt to disposable income to return to its long-term trend. 'Overall, the UK needs to steer a difficult course: reduce government deficits and encourage debt reduction – without limiting GDP growth', the study noted.[11] We would put it somewhat stronger than that. Unless the United Kingdom can discover a new growth model, it will prove nigh-on impossible for the economy to grow at the old rate of 2–2.5 per cent a year in the cold-turkey years ahead.

The third reckoning: Britain isn't working

They were young, they were jobless and they were angry. As the Arab Spring unfolded during 2011, these were the words intoned by the reporters doing pieces to camera in Algeria, Egypt and Syria. They could, however, have been applied to many countries in the developed west: to Italy, where the youth unemployment rate is above 30 per cent; to Spain, where one in two young workers cannot find jobs; and to the United Kingdom, where the unemployment total edged above 1 million in late 2011 and was heading for 25 per cent of the under-25 age group by early 2012. One key indicator of a developing nation is its inability to find work for its young people, and by this yardstick the United Kingdom was heading rapidly in the wrong direction.

In part, the problem is about demand for labour. Unemployment came down when the economy was on the up in late 2009 and early 2010, but the jobless total started to rise again as the pace of activity slowed again during 2011. The reforms forced through by the Conservative governments in the 1980s left the United Kingdom with what is known as a flexible labour market: for which read insecure, badly paid and cowed. Even so, there was a limit to the ability of workers to price themselves back into work, and this limit was reached when the economy slowed in the second half of 2011. On arrival in office, George Osborne said that the UK private sector was dynamic enough to create career opportunities for the public sector workers laid off in the government's austerity drive, but as in the song by The

Clash, these were the career opportunities that never knocked.

Instead, for the third time since the late 1970s a Conservative prime minister was contemplating the prospect of explaining away a lengthening of the dole queues to 3 million. In the first two years of David Cameron's premiership, full-time employment was down but part-time unemployment rose. The number of self-employed workers rose, not because Britain was suddenly suffused with a spirit of go-getting entrepreneurship, but because sacked full-time employees were trying to scratch a living from their trades. As one expert on the labour market put it:

> With total unemployment and youth unemployment still on the up, with growth in average earnings very subdued, and with a region like the north-east now registering a 12 per cent unemployment rate, it's clear that the UK jobs market is in a very sorry state.[12]

The regional dimension to unemployment was striking. A list compiled by the Institute for Public Policy Research showing the areas with the greatest mismatch between unemployment claimants and vacancies read like a gazetteer of Britain's old industrial heartlands: West Dumbartonshire, Clackmannanshire, Hartlepool, Blaenau Gwent. In these areas, there were at least 15 people on job seeker's allowance chasing every job, and the scars of mass unemployment were deep and permanent. These were the forgotten parts of Britain, where large numbers of men were parked on long-term sickness benefits in the 1980s, women became the main breadwinners in the newly created jobs in the call centres that replaced the mines and the mills, and joblessness was passed down from generation to generation. In the double-dip recession of 2011–12 the women started to lose their jobs, and female unemployment rose to its highest level since the late 1980s.

This, though, was not just a question of a lack of jobs in the depressed regions. Graduates could no longer expect a degree to be the passport to a job for life: those that could not afford to spend time as an unpaid intern might find themselves working in a job paying little more than the minimum wage which, in a previous era, would have been taken by a school leaver. The jobs that school leavers would once have snapped up – serving behind the counter in sandwich bars, driving the home delivery vans for supermarkets – were now increasingly the preserve of workers from overseas.

The employment minister Chris Grayling said it was 'unacceptable' that the food chain Pret a Manger employed no UK-born workers in many of its London stores.[13] Pret said it welcomed applicants who could demonstrate a passion for food and enjoyed engaging with customers, clearly suggesting that this was true of people from inner-city Warsaw, Bratislava and Riga, but not those from Hackney, Islington and Tower Hamlets. Employers said they hired workers from Eastern Europe because they turned up for work on time, were better educated than their British counterparts and had no attitude problems. They complained that the education system was 'not fit for purpose', and that with a large pool of unemployed workers to choose from, employers were hiring older people with more experience.

David Blanchflower, a labour market expert and once a member of the Bank of England's monetary policy committee said another manifestation of this trend was the increase in the over-60s in the workforce. The typical response of an employer when faced with a young

British-born job applicant was 'We don't want you, we want your grandmother.'[14]

Britain is now on the cusp of its third wave of high unemployment in 30 years. In the election campaign of 1979, the Saatchi & Saatchi advertising company was employed by Margaret Thatcher to come up with some striking images to highlight the failings of the incumbent Labour government. The Saatchi brothers came up with some posters that showed a long line of unemployed workers snaking its way from a job centre, under the strapline 'Labour isn't working'. As even those on the left now concede, it was a brilliant campaign, a telling image of how in the half-decade since the first oil shock the jobless total had risen above 1 million, a level then seen as politically untenable. Looking back, however, the 1970s were the golden years. After the 1979 election unemployment continued to rise, hitting 2 million in 1980 and 3 million in 1982. It returned to that level in the early 1990s and is heading that way again.

The fourth reckoning: the pensions timebomb

Life has been sweet for Royal Dutch Shell for the past decade. Long gone are the days in the 1990s when the price of crude was below $10 a barrel: ever since the drumbeats of war began in Washington in preparation for the toppling of Saddam Hussein, prices have been high and the big oil giants have been coining it in. So when Shell became the last company quoted in London's FTSE 100 to close its final-salary scheme to new entrants, it was time to read the last rites for an era of guaranteed retirement income. If Shell could not afford to maintain its old pension arrangements at a time when the cost of crude oil was well over $100 a barrel, there was not much chance of the rest of British industry – battered by recession and facing strong global competition – doing anything different.

Britain's greying population is gradually waking up to the profound changes that have been wrought to pensions over the past decades: changes that have shifted risk from companies to their workers and made pensions poorer. Workers in Britain are currently just as likely to strike over pensions as over pay, and with good reason. The silent dismantling of final salary pension schemes has a much bigger long-term impact on the living standards of employees than any single pay round.

The anger is understandable. While there have been some highly public examples of pension fraud, starting with Robert Maxwell's looting of the Mirror Group, all workers have to an extent been gulled. They were sold a false prospectus in which the smart people in the City and on Wall Street would look after their money, seeking out opportunities for growth and thereby providing hitherto unknown riches for workers. What actually happened was that the closure of final salary schemes boosted profits and allowed those running companies to pay themselves higher salaries and stuff their own pension pots full of cash, while the returns on the managed funds fell well short of the levels promised. In part this was because the bull market of the 1980s and 1990s came to an end, but it was also the result of management charges that skimmed the gains off the top of pension funds.

The outlook for the coming years is made much bleaker by the ageing of the baby boomer generation, a trend that will see the number of people aged over 65 double to 24 per cent by 2032. This increasingly large cohort of the population will live a lot longer than those who retired in 1980, when a man aged 65 could expect to live for a further 13 years, and a woman of the same age could expect to live until she was 82.

Improvements in medicine, better diets and a fall in the number of people smoking mean that in 2020 a man reaching 65 is likely to survive until he is 86, while his wife will outlive him by a year. In one sense that is good news, but the next generation of pensioners is going to need a steady, reasonable income to enjoy two decades or more of retirement. They will struggle to secure it, even if they work longer before taking their pension.

A report for the think tank Civitas outlined the extent of the problem. In the past 25 years, private sector employers have reduced their contributions to their employees' pensions by two-thirds. Millions of people save less than half as much as they used to for their retirement; and the value of their diminished pool of savings is further eroded by the overcharging by the pensions industry. 'Millions end up with retirement incomes that are as much as 20 per cent lower than they would have had and for some, incomes are 75 per cent lower.'[15]

When they retire, pensioners use their accumulated savings to buy an annuity, based on the size of their pot and their life expectancy. In 1980 a £100,000 pension pot bought an annuity of £17,000 a year; by 2011 that had dropped to £6000 as a result of lower interest rates and increased longevity. Today's workers are going to require extremely large pension pots if they are to enjoy the retirement income of their parents and their grandparents, many of whom enjoyed final salary schemes where they were guaranteed an income in retirement that would be in direct proportion to the time spent working for a company. Forty years of service would normally result in a pension worth two-thirds of final salary. Public sector workers still enjoy final salary pension schemes, even though they now have to pay more for the privilege, but the vast majority of workers do not.

Private pensions are important in Britain because the state pension is far from generous. It would be wrong to say that the UK government is the Scrooge of the 34 nations that belong to the group of rich countries, the Organisation for Economic Co-operation and Development, because there is one country, Mexico, which is meaner (for female workers). But for private pensions to deliver, the economy has to grow strongly, that growth has to be reflected in rising financial markets, and the gains from rising asset prices have to be passed on to those saving in contributory pension schemes. None of those preconditions is now being met: indeed, it is the contention of this book that growth will remain weak, the financial markets will not boom, and even if they do, customers will struggle to see the benefits.

As Peter Morris and Alasdair Palmer note:

> The policies on pensions adopted by governments over the last 25 years have had effects opposite to the ones intended: instead of increasing saving, they have diminished it; instead of increasing people's understanding of what they need to do to achieve an adequate pension, they have sown scepticism, bewilderment and confusion; they have loaded pensions with additional, often unnecessary costs; and they have led to a very serious fall in the level of retirement income that people can expect.[16]

The next generation of pensioners is at the mercy of the financial markets – and the fund managers looking after their savings. That is an uncomfortable place to be, and a recipe for both financial distress and anger when retirees discover that they are old, healthy and broke.

The fifth reckoning: waiting for the lights to go out

Arthur Scargill made many misjudgements when he called a national strike in Britain's coalfields in March 1984. He thought the dispute would be solid without a national ballot, and it wasn't. He chose the spring to call out his members, just as demand for energy was poised for a seasonal decline and stocks at power stations were high. He assumed that the government would buckle as it had a decade earlier, and it didn't. Most importantly, he calculated that the economy would quickly grind to a halt without coal, but chose the moment when production from Britain's North Sea oil fields was about to peak to call a strike that would drag on for a year before miners went back to work. When the National Union of Mineworkers helped bring down Edward Heath's administration in February 1974, it would still be more than a year before the first crude was pumped ashore from the North Sea, but in January 1985 monthly oil production was at a high.

Even so, in one way Mr Scargill has had the last laugh, because his warnings about how the government's energy strategy would lead to the demise of the coal industry and an increasing reliance on imported energy have proved to be correct. The luxury of North Sea oil and gas has meant that nobody aged under 40 can remember the days when electricity showroom windows carried lists of which streets could expect to have their power cut off during the disputes of the 1970s, but Britain already has a serious energy security problem, and it is about to get worse. The ability to keep the lights on has always been one easy way of distinguishing between a developed and developing country: the United Kingdom is perhaps within five years of failing the test.

Coal is already a legacy industry, with more heritage

theme parks then there are working pits. Production has tumbled from more than 200 million tonnes a year at the time of the 1984–85 strike to 17 million tonnes, while the number of colliers has dropped from more than 200,000 to 6000. The deep-seam pits have been mothballed, and it would be too expensive at current global prices to bring them back into production. More than two-thirds of the coal used in Britain is now imported, bringing to mind Aneurin Bevan's comment in 1945 that 'This island is made mainly of coal and surrounded by fish. Only an organizing genius could produce a shortage of coal and fish at the same time.'[17] (Most of the fish stocks have also disappeared, incidentally.)

One-sixth of Britain's electricity comes from nuclear power stations, well down on the peak of 26 per cent in 1997 as a result of old plants being decommissioned. This process will speed up over the coming years. Britain has 19 reactors on ten nuclear sites (seven advanced gas-cooled (AGC) reactors, two Magnox and one pressurized water reactor). Of these, the two Magnox plants and two of the AGR plants are due to close by 2016. Shortly after the Fukushima disaster in Japan, when a tidal wave caused by an offshore earthquake led to a radiation leak, the UK government announced the details of eight new nuclear plants to be built at a cost of £100 billion. Significantly, however, even on the timetable drawn up by ministers (which, history suggests, will not be met), the new capacity will only come on stream almost a decade after the old plants are due to be taken out of service.

Oil production has fallen by more than two-thirds since its peak, while gas production has halved. Energy experts differ on whether peak oil – the moment of maximum extraction – has arrived for the global economy as a whole, but for the United Kingdom peak oil was reached some years ago. The latest estimates suggest that there are 750 million cubic tonnes of possible and proven reserves left in the United Kingdom's slice of the continental shelf in the North Sea, while production in 2010 was 63 million tonnes. Even on the assumption that high oil prices leads to exploitation of some new fields and that the rate of production slows down, within 20 years there will be no oil left to extract, and the United Kingdom will be entirely dependent on imported crude, the stocks of which by then will probably be declining globally, leading to higher prices. From a slow start, renewable energy now provides just under 10 per cent of UK energy, but will need to expand rapidly to compensate for the decline in the contribution made by oil, gas and nuclear.

Engineers have warned that the biggest set of investments and social changes to cut back on energy use will be needed over the coming decades to cope with likely demand and to meet the commitment to cut greenhouse gas emissions by 80 per cent by 2050. A report by the Royal Academy of Engineering in 2010 said Britain needed a vast expansion of wind and solar power, coupled with dozens of new nuclear or 'clean coal' plants.[18] This was sage advice, but the necessary revolution requires two things: lots of investment and a large dollop of sustained political will of the sort only normally seen in wartime. And both, preferably, before the lights start to go out.

The sixth reckoning: taxing times

The case of Her Majesty's Revenue and Customs (HMRC) and Goldman Sachs speaks volumes about the way the tax system operates – or to be more accurate, doesn't operate. Details of how Dave Hartnett, the permanent secretary at HMRC, negotiated a sweetheart deal with the US investment bank were made public by a whistle-blower, who felt the public had the right to know that £10 million in interest charges had been waived. Mr Hartnett admitted, under pressure, that the deal had been a mistake, and announced the date when he would retire with his £1.7 million pension pot. HMRC launched a full internal inquiry into the activities of the whistle-blower, with the threat of the sack or criminal proceedings.

For today's companies, and the people who run them, tax is something to be avoided if all possible. And if not legally avoided, then criminally evaded. One estimate of tax evasion puts the global figure at £2 trillion, of which the UK share is £70 billion, almost on a par with the spending cuts under the coalition government's austerity programme.

In the years before the financial crisis of 2007, the government's position looked much healthier. Tax revenues were buoyant and spending on unemployment was falling. The UK national debt was low, leading to savings on interest payments to the country's creditors. The fiscal strength was illusory, however. Despite repeated warnings from the tax experts at the Institute for Fiscal Studies, the Labour government of 1997–2010 assumed that the increase in tax receipts was permanent, instead of a temporary phenomenon caused by bubbles in the City and the housing market. When the economy tipped into recession, the taxes associated with these two sectors – corporation tax and stamp duty – collapsed, contributing to the hole in the government's finances. In the short term the response was to borrow more, since to have attempted to balance the books in the middle of a downturn would have made the recession even worse. But in the longer term, the government had to find a way of reducing the deficit. It could only do so in one of three ways: it could harvest the fruits of stronger growth, as it had in the boom years; it could increase taxes or be assiduous in collecting the taxes it already imposed; or it could reduce spending on the grounds that the United Kingdom's straitened circumstances necessitated a smaller state.

In reality, ministers have opted for all three at once. They have anticipated a return to robust levels of growth; they have raised tax rates and announced plans to close loopholes; and they have cut Whitehall budgets. Under Mr Osborne's plans, both tax and spending will eventually return to their pre-crisis norms of around 40 per cent of gross domestic product (GDP).

This plan rests on some heroic assumptions. The United Kingdom has yet to find new sources of growth to replace the three engines that powered the last boom – housing, financial services and public spending – and that is why, as we have already noted, the recovery from recession has been slow and intermittent. Globalization has meant that it has become increasingly difficult to collect tax, because company executives hold a trump card in their battles with the tax collectors: the threat of moving offshore. This can persuade even a fiscally challenged administration to cut tax rates or call off the revenue inspectors. Dave Hartnett's argument when challenged over Goldman Sachs was that he was at least getting the bank to pay something, which, he insisted, was better than nothing. When the Labour government announced in 2009 that the top rate of income tax was being raised to 50 per cent, few of those due to pay the levy shared the view of Gladstone, who in his 1853 Budget declared income tax to be 'an engine of gigantic power for great national purposes'. Instead, they got their tax accountants on the case, threatened to move to Zug or Monaco, and began a campaign to have the decision reversed.

Having arrived in office with the motto 'We are all in this together', George Osborne found it politically impossible to cut the top rate of income tax immediately, merely promising that the Treasury would investigate whether the bankers and hedge fund dealers were right to say that the 50 per cent tax band would lead to less revenue being collected. He insisted, when speaking at an UK business lunch at the annual meeting of the World Economic Forum (WEF) in Davos, that the 50 per cent tax rate was 'temporary', and urged executives to mount a campaign against the tax if they thought it was bad for investment and jobs.[19] Most did, unsurprisingly. Companies had already received favourable treatment from a chancellor who admitted to being 'unabashedly pro business': not only were they exempted from the public spending cuts and the tax increases affecting the bulk of the public, they were presented with a four-year rolling programme of corporation tax cuts designed to restore Britain's international competitiveness.

One answer to the problem would be for the government to find new sources of tax revenue that are not internationally mobile. In the meantime, however, weaker growth and the difficulty in collecting taxes from the rich and powerful has meant that more of the burden has fallen on those members of the public who cannot afford expensive tax planners to manage their affairs. Mr Osborne raised VAT to 20 per cent in 2011, a move that proved to be spectacularly self-defeating by pushing up the rate of inflation, which in turn reduced the spending power of consumers, leading to weaker growth. The chancellor also announced savings through public sector pay freezes and cuts in welfare benefits, both of which also reduced the level of demand in the economy.

There is no one international model of the ideal state: some countries have high taxes and high spending, while others have low taxes and spending to match. There are no recorded examples of successful governments that have combined high spending and low taxation, as many developing countries – and some in Europe too – have found to their cost. Britain will soon have to decide what sort of state it wants, and just as importantly, how it plans to raise the taxes to pay for it. A moment of truth is rapidly approaching.

The seventh reckoning: the death embrace of the zombie banks

As the financial crisis of 2007 merged into the Great Recession of 2008–09, there was one constant refrain from the world's central bankers and finance ministers: there would be no repeat of the mistakes that led to two decades of economic stagnation and deflation in Japan. Ben Bernanke, before he became chairman of the Federal Reserve, wrote a treatise on the subject and said that, *in extremis*, governments could shower their populations with cash, winning himself the soubriquet 'helicopter Ben' in the process.[20] In one important respect, policy makers have indeed learned lessons from Japan. Policy makers in Tokyo in the early 1990s were slow to respond when the stock market and property bubbles burst, allowing deflation to set in. As soon as it became clear in late 2008 that global demand was collapsing at a pace not seen since the early 1930s, interest rates were cut sharply, banks were recapitalized and the printing presses were cranked up.

This approach brought criticism from both right and left of the political spectrum. The view of conservatives was that the banking crisis would only be ended when financial institutions purged themselves of their dud loans and the weaker among them were allowed to go bust. Providing them with taxpayer guarantees and pumping them full of taxpayers' money might provide some short-term respite but it was essentially a quack doctor's remedy.

The left considered the crisis to be a once-in-a-lifetime opportunity to bring the banks to order. In the winter of 2008–09 the financial sector was on its knees, and without the support offered by governments there would have been a cull of the City and Wall Street, not to mention some of the shakier German, French, Belgian, Spanish, Irish and Italian banks. The financiers who had grown contemptuous of the state in the triumphalist years following the collapse of communism were now forced to come cap in hand to politicians, and the chance was there to split the banks up, to reimpose the curbs placed on them after the Great Depression. The reforms actually proposed were much milder, partly as a result of the lobbying power of finance and partly because the politicians were concerned that restricting the freedom of such an important sector of the economy would lead to even weaker growth. In 1950 financial concerns were responsible for just 4 per cent of total corporate tax revenues: by the height of the pre-crash boom in 2006 that figure had risen to 40 per cent.

Politicians in the United Kingdom, like those in continental Europe and North America, considered the outcome to be an acceptable compromise. Central banks would help banks get back on their feet by providing ample quantities of cheap money, either by allowing them to borrow at ultra-low interest rates for prolonged periods or by exchanging their government bonds for cash in the process known as quantitative easing (QE).

In return, banks would agree to extend credit to small and medium-sized companies (SMEs); speculative bubbles would be made less likely by tougher new rules on capital and leverage that would (eventually and modestly) restrict the propensity of banks to gamble; and in the United Kingdom, there would be firewalls erected between the retail and investment arms of the big international institutions.

Far from being an acceptable compromise, this was actually the worst of all possible worlds: it led to a contained depression that went on and on. What emerged was a zombie banking system still awash with bad loans, unable or unwilling to lend to the private sector, and yet fundamentally unreformed. Codes of conduct on pay and lending to SMEs by the banks are redolent of the 'solemn and binding' pledges made by Britain's trade unions in the 1970s to show pay restraint. Just like Lord Voldemort in the Harry Potter stories, the banks received a near-fatal blow but somehow survived. They are now gradually rebuilding their strength, and when they have done so will carry on in much the same way as before. The crisis that followed the bankruptcy of Lehman Brothers was the first chapter in a much longer tale, and policy makers will come to regret bailing out the banks while asking for little in return.

Worryingly, the preferred method of supporting both the financial sector and the wider economy – QE – has a tendency to boost growth in those sectors where activity is already strong. Banks had more cash on their books, but with interest rates low they looked for investment opportunities where the returns are highest – emerging markets, property and commodities. The first wave of QE was marked by higher inflation, spiralling food prices and cuts in living standards, and resulted in a much smaller pick-up in growth than central banks had hoped for. They responded with further doses of money creation, downplaying the risk that expanding the money supply so aggressively would lead to hyperinflation. They remained confident that growth would recover, cost of living increases will be kept in check, and that QE can be reversed without causing bond prices to collapse.

We are far less sanguine, seeing 2010 and 2011 as what will come to be seen as the years of the Phony Peace. When the next crash comes, the postmortem examination on the UK economy will conclude that the banks were not fit for purpose, failing in their basic task of taking in savings and recycling them as loans for productive investment. The financial system was kept afloat by vast quantities of newly minted money, growth remained feeble and there were sporadic bursts of inflation.

To make matters, policy makers will be left impotent when the second downturn arrives in 2013, having neither the fiscal room to cut taxes or to raise public spending, nor the monetary leeway to cut interest rates aggressively. Instead, they will be forced to use what are known in the central banking trade as 'unconventional measures'.

The eighth reckoning: euro-sclerosis

Looking back, it's hard to recall how much fuss there once was about whether the United Kingdom should join the single currency. In the first six years of Tony Blair's premiership, the euro question was high on the political agenda, and it remained so up until the point in 2003 when Gordon Brown announced that the five tests he had set for UK membership of the currency union had not been met. The decision provoked criticism among the so-called chattering classes, who said it had been a profound error for the country to delay joining the original Common Market, and that once again the European boat was leaving the harbour with Little Englanders waving from the quayside. Supporters of Mr Brown's decision, ourselves included, liked the nautical metaphor, but argued that the ship in question bore more than a passing resemblance to the *Titanic*.

For the first years of its life the euro was indeed like the ill-fated White Star liner as it steamed serenely across the Atlantic from Queenstown in Ireland towards New York. Like the *Titanic*, the designers of the single currency considered it be unsinkable, and few noticed that monetary union had a design flaw every bit as dangerous as that which meant the liner could sink with the loss of 1500 lives within hours of being ripped open by an iceberg.

In *Titanic* the movie, a boy and girl from different backgrounds meet and fall in love on the ship's maiden voyage. The architects of the euro imagined the same sort of social mobility, with the weaker nations eventually joining their superiors for a stroll round the first-class deck. As the financial crisis played out in the years following 2007, it became clear that this was not life as envisaged by Hollywood; instead there was a large and widening gap between the ultra-competitive countries of Northern Europe, for which there were places in the lifeboats, and the underperforming nations of Southern Europe, for which there was not.

As the Greeks rioted in protest at austerity programmes imposed by the European Union and the International Monetary Fund (IMF), those who had advocated British membership had second thoughts. When the unions in Portugal organized general strikes against tax increases and public sector pay cuts, there was a deafening silence from the pro-euro camp. By the time Spain and Italy were sucked into the affair, even the Liberal Democrats, the party that had been most devoted to Brussels and all its works, decided that being left on the dockside had not been such a bad idea after all.

By early 2012, Greece, Portugal and Ireland were all finding out what it was like to be a supplicant sub-Saharan African nation in need of quick cash to avoid going bust. There were fears that Greece would default on its debts, and that this would lead to a catastrophic run on Europe's fragile banks, already being kept afloat by emergency liquidity injections from the European Central Bank. Europe was in recession and the single currency was fighting for its life.

It was, however, not really a moment for triumphalism from those who had predicted just such a scenario a decade earlier, because Europe was a problem for every other country, both developed and developing. Not only is the European Union the world's biggest market, it is involved in half the global economy's $15 trillion a year trade in goods and services. Almost 50 per cent of UK exports are sent to the 17 countries of the eurozone, so the rapid changes in the structure of the global economy from the early 1990s onwards left the United Kingdom heavily exposed when Europe had its existential crisis. In the five years after 2007 the IMF estimated that China will have grown by 60 per cent, and the emerging economics by 35 per cent. British exporters had little presence in these fast-growing markets, and were instead dependent on the developed world, where the IMF predicted no growth at all in the half-decade after 2007. Europe was the worst-performing part of the rich west.

What was happening in this period was a nation-state version of what the economist Joseph Schumpeter called creative destruction. In the corporate world, this tendency was all too evident: companies that called the market wrong – AOL, Nokia, Yahoo – found themselves in rapid decline, while others – Apple and Google, for example – experienced strong growth. The process was slower and less easy to recognize at the sovereign state level, but a shift in the global economy's centre of gravity was there all the same. The United Kingdom had put most of its eggs in one basket: unfortunately it turned out to be the wrong basket.

A second problem was that the interlinked nature of the financial sector meant that British banks were affected by the problems of eurozone banks. When French, German and Italian banks had difficulties raising short-term money from each other, so did UK banks. When eurozone banks started to become more cautious in their lending practices, so did British banks. Fears that the eurozone crisis might deepen meant the interest rates charged by banks rose, making borrowing dearer for their private sector customers. Europe found itself saddled with its second serious credit crunch – a widespread drop in the availability of loans – in five years, and exported it to the rest of the global economy, including the United Kingdom.

For the United Kingdom, the travails of the eurozone could not have come at a worse time, since the coalition government's entire economic strategy relied on a rebalancing of the economy towards exports. But the insistence of the eurozone in tackling a three-dimensional crisis – high unemployment, uneven growth and poor public finances – with the one-dimensional solution of austerity meant this was nigh-on impossible. Shattered consumer confidence, fragile banks and a drying-up of investment pushed the eurozone back into recession in late 2011, and the IMF warned that the expected contraction of 0.5 per cent in 2012 would be significantly more pronounced should a Greek default cause paralysis across the region.

The ninth reckoning: the revenge of Karl Marx?

The near-meltdown of the world's financial system had been a long time in coming. Over the previous 15 years, the crisis had rippled around the fringes of the developed world, affecting Mexico, Thailand, Indonesia, South Korea, Russia, Brazil and Argentina. Occasionally, as with the dot.com boom and bust in the late 1990s and early 2000s, there were warning signs that the heart of the global economy was at risk from contagion, but these were ignored, such was the fanatical belief in the self-righting qualities of markets.

The American economist Robert Brenner was one of the few who correctly foresaw during the mania for internet stocks that debt and speculation were being used to camouflage deep structural problems.[21] Briefly, when the G20 group of developed and developing countries was established in the autumn of 2008, there was a recognition that global problems demanded global solutions, and for a few months the mood was marked by the sort of international cooperation that had not been seen since the Plaza and Louvre currency accords of the mid-1980s. The mood quickly changed, however, as individual countries pursued their own domestic agendas. Prime ministers and presidents continued to make the right sort of noises about the need for togetherness: they insisted that the need to avoid the tit-for-tat protectionism of the 1930s necessitated the completion of the Doha Round of trade talks, which had been underway since 2011. They dutifully sent negotiators to summits on climate change with the mandate to ensure curbs on greenhouse gases. And they nodded sagely when managers at the IMF urged mutually supportive policies to tackle the imbalances between creditor and debtor countries that had been the primary cause of the 2007 crisis.

The trade talks went uncompleted, the climate change negotiators added to the hot air in the atmosphere, and the imbalances were left intact. Europe looked in on itself; the mood in the United States was more isolationist than at any time since the Second World War; developing countries, having been left to fend for themselves when their economies hit the rocks, felt the rich nations of the west should apply the same rules to themselves. Governments in Beijing and New Delhi made it clear at the climate change talks that their priority was to lift people out of poverty, and that it was up to the United States and Europe, with their long history of pollution, to make the sacrifices needed to check carbon dioxide emissions. A new struggle for Africa developed as China sought the natural resources to sustain a growth rate of 9–10 per cent a year. Financial dislocation, climate change and concern that oil production was close to its peak added up to a potentially devastating triple crunch.

As the fifth anniversary of the crash approached, it was only the willingness of central banks to flood financial markets with cheap money that was holding the global economy together. The Federal Reserve Board in Washington announced its intention of keeping interest rates close to zero until 2014; the Bank of England's quantitative easing programme entered a third phase: the European Central Bank provided unlimited amounts of liquidity for up to three years, so concerned was it by evidence that some of the big names of European banking were in trouble. In more normal times, low borrowing costs tend to be associated with economic health, a sign that countries can grow without inflation. In the period after 2007, quite the opposite was true: only when central banks were confident enough to tighten monetary policy would it be possible to say that the crisis was over.

The central banks could not engineer a lasting solution on their own, because that would require governments to come up with a plan for a more balanced global economy. That, in return, meant a recognition that creditor nations would have to expand their domestic economies so that debtor nations could export more. There was, however, no mechanism for achieving this, and under the rules of the international financial system dating back to the Bretton Woods conference in 1944 the burden of adjustment was supposed to fall on nations running balance of payments deficits. They were supposed to deflate their economies, thereby reducing demand for imports, while simultaneously boosting exports by depreciating their currencies.

The problem for the global economy was that none of the big creditor nations wanted to take on the role adopted by the United States in the decades after the Second World War, when it hastened recovery in Europe and Japan by acting as the global consumer of last resort. On the contrary, the biggest creditor nations – China, Germany and Japan – all actively pursued strategies based on export-led growth, in some cases intervening in the foreign exchange markets to hold down the level of their currencies.

Until life is found on Mars or the encounters with beings from other planets depicted in sci-fi movies are found to have some substance, the idea that every country can have export-led growth is a mathematical absurdity. For one group of countries to export its way out of trouble, another group of countries has to be prepared to increase its imports. Otherwise, the result will inevitably be reduced demand, higher unemployment, deflation, and persistent pressure on central banks to prevent a state of permanent depression turning into a full-scale global slump. This was, in fact, an accurate portrayal of the global economy as it existed in 2012, a state of affairs that Karl Marx would have described as the contradictions of capitalism. Indeed, there were some visitors to Highgate cemetery who said the noise they could hear was not the wind whispering through the headstones but a Germanic chuckle from beyond the grave.

System failure

Each January, just before it convenes its gathering of the global economy's movers and shakers in Davos, the WEF publishes a risk assessment, a survey of what academics, business leaders and policy makers think might go wrong in the years to come.[22] In 2012, the study expressed concern at the growing number of young people with little chance of finding a job, the swelling ranks of elderly people dependent on states deeply in debt, and the expanding gap between rich and poor. The seeds of dystopia were being sown, according to Lee Howell, the WEF managing director responsible for the report, who noted that the 'new malaise is particularly acute in the industrialised countries that historically have been a source of great confidence and bold ideas.'[23]

Britain had had a glimpse of its own dystopia the previous August when riots erupted in London, Manchester and Birmingham. Like Scrooge in *A Christmas Carol*, the country was given a vision of what might be to come in a country where financial markets buckled, the economy flatlined, unemployment rose, public services were cut, inequality increased, the basics of life became more expensive, and pensions became meaner.

David Cameron insisted that the burning and looting were, for the most part, the result of pure criminality. 'This is a great country of great people', said the prime minister, adding that the disorder was not caused by race, poverty or the cuts, but by behaviour – 'people showing indifference to right and wrong, people with a twisted moral code, people with a complete absence of self-restraint'.

This was one explanation of the riots certainly, albeit a complacent one. As we have shown in previous chapters, it has been the tendency of the United Kingdom's leaders to delude themselves about the challenges the nation faces. When the WEF report was presented in Davos, the economist Nouriel Roubini sketched out the specific reasons for the bubbling resentment seen around the world: 1 per cent of people owned 40 per cent of the wealth; one in three people worldwide were poor or unemployed; wages as a share of gross domestic product were at an all-time low and profits were at an all-time high: austerity was creating a vicious circle in which budget cuts were making matters worse, not better. All these factors applied to the United Kingdom, and a few more besides.

An alternative way of looking at the riots is that they represent the start of the Great Reckoning in the United Kingdom, not just for the follies of the previous 30 years of financial deregulation but for a century of relative economic decline.

Robin Blackburn summed up the global crisis in *Age Shock* in the following way:

> The huge imbalance racked up during the boom years of the global economy (1992–2007) were the product

of an ever-widening US deficit and the ever-growing Chinese surplus. Chinese workers or farmers were not paid enough to become good customers for overseas products, while in the US the low paid and the poor (subprime) borrowers were taking on debt – especially housing debt – that they soon found impossible to service.

The over-borrowing and asset bubbles that resulted were aggravated by financial deregulations, and by the greed and subterfuge of the banks. The heedless pursuit of short-term profit led to the largest destruction of value in world history. Huge public deficits had to be incurred to prevent collapse. Now those are to be paid for by slashing public spending and shrinking social protection for many decades to come. The welfare state is to be dismantled at a time when higher unemployment and an ageing population make this a certain recipe for destitution and widening misery.[24]

Everything Blackburn said also applied to the United Kingdom, which had all the US vices without its offsetting virtues. The United Kingdom had the poverty, inequality, debt, and poor skills for those in the low-income groups. What it didn't have was the pre-eminence in key sectors of the global economy such as computers, aerospace and entertainment; the entrepreneurial spirit; the ability to reinvent itself.

This, then, is the state of the modern United Kingdom, a country now at a fork in the road. History suggests there is no iron law of progress, and there have been long periods – after the collapse of Rome, for example – when things have got worse, not better. Despite what the prime minister might like to think, the riots were telling us something. Britain is in deep trouble and ready to blow.

Chapter 8

Desperately seeking Sweden, or Freeport Ho! The search for a development model

We have come to a point where we have been able to begin furnishing the great *folkhemmet* [the people's home]. Our task is to make it pleasant, good and warm, bright and cheerful and free.

Per Albin Hansson, chairman, Swedish Social Democratic Party (later prime minister), Christmas 1927

We have had an open policy for 2,000 years. London is the greatest souk in Europe.

Sir Paul Newall, then lord mayor of London, quoted in *The Guardian*, 22 January 1994

What we in the West call the Third World is really the Real World, in which real things happen, in which real wars are fought, in which there is real room for real development and disaster.

Julie Burchill, *Damaged Gods*, 1986

The different economic and social models available across the world tend to attract national or geographical labels: Rhineland (or Rhenish) capitalism, the Scandinavian model, the Washington Consensus and so on.

They attract also caricatures of the most garish and vivid sort. For example, the United States is – supposedly – the land of the entrepreneur, the individual who starts off in their garage or garden shed and – thanks to a business-friendly climate – makes a billion dollars. Or should that be 'makes their first billion dollars'? Because the sky is the limit in this land of opportunity. Success breeds success, and winning streaks become habit forming. True, there may be failures on the way up. But fear not – the United States is not a country that deprecates people who didn't make it first time round. Indeed, bankers and other lenders rather like an entrepreneur with a bit of 'scar tissue'.

On the other hand, it is a land with a minimal welfare state, a very patchy public education system and high levels of incarceration of people from the poorest sections of society, levels which help hold down the official unemployment totals. Good health care, even after President Obama's reforms, remains highly dependent on personal funds. Hospitals swipe your credit card on admission; should you wish the ambulance to turn on its siren it will cost you extra.

A fine collection of clichés, half-truths and grains of truth? Yes, indeed. But not the only such collection.

Scandinavian capitalism? Lavish welfare, egalitarian managers sitting behind IKEA desks when they are not out on the shop floor, consulting earnestly with the workforce (which they do for most of the time), superb productivity, stylish products and the sort of enlightened social policy that allows prisoners' girlfriends to visit at weekends. On the downside, identity cards are compulsory and parents who actually wish to care for their children rather than consign them to state-run battery farms are leaned on by the authorities.

The East Asian model? Some variations here, even for the inveterate caricature-monger, given we are talking about a large range of cultures, from Tokyo to Manila via 'tiger' economies including Hong Kong, Singapore and Malaysia. Yet certain features are routinely touted to 'explain' the relative success of the Asia-Pacific economies in recent decades: strong families, a culture of trust, deep respect for education and self-betterment, and of course, an extraordinary capacity for hard work. But as with the US model, indeed perhaps more so, do not expect too much from the state should you fall on hard times. The most effective welfare system you are likely to encounter is sitting round your dining table – your family. Not that the lack of a welfare state or a compassionate society means the lack of a state or of a society. Far from it. As a rule, the vibrant free markets of the east are encased within either semi-authoritarian state structures or deeply orthodox societies.

France, as we all know, showers money and attention (often to good effect) on an eclectic, not to say eccentric, range of economic sectors: farming, aerospace and defence, car manufacture, high-speed rail and nuclear energy. Germany eschews the often lurid, although also often choreographed, industrial disputes of France, but shares its neighbour's focus on high technology, and excels at advanced manufacturing. While the French state, in theory, is deeply involved in the life of the citizen, its ministrations are frequently rejected (sometimes violently so) and derided. By contrast, Germany's prizing of individual liberty seems often to express itself in a type of regimented bohemianism: in radical politics, in the arts and literature.

This collection of archetypes, stereotypes and occasionally true-to-types is great fun. It is certainly rather less crude and more useful than simply claiming that all Japanese salarymen live in rabbit-hutch flats and that the inhabitants of the European Union's Mediterranean member-states have razor-sharp memories when it comes to their entitlements and chronic amnesia when it comes to paying their taxes.

The notion that the United Kingdom has to choose

from a number of economic and social models on offer
round the world is not new, and neither is the parallel
idea that Britain's leaders have, from time to time,
behaved like dissatisfied motorists and traded in one
model for another.

Thus the post-war 'settlement' of parliamentary
socialism and a planned economy did not, on the face
of it, remain settled for very long. Developments in the
second half of the 1950s – the acceptance of heavy traffic
in town centres, the spread of supermarkets, the arrival
of commercial television – suggested a swing towards the
American market model and away from the paternalism
that infused both European social democracy and centre-
right Christian democracy.

Ten years after that, and the 'scientific', managerialist
economy promoted by both Labour's Harold Wilson and
his Conservative counterpart Edward Heath appeared
to herald another switch, this time away from the
wasteful and meretricious aspects of the 'affluent society'
and towards a proper and fruitful use of the nation's
resources. The model here was something of a hybrid,
mixing French 'indicative planning' with the United
States of the space programme and the state-guided
'miracle economies' of Germany and Italy.

Yet many of these changes were more apparent than
real, and the post-1945 settlement was more enduring
than it might seem. Its bedrock was the full-employment
welfare state. On this foundation, emphases could switch,
but such switches tended to be largely presentational.
Nor did the real level of partisanship come close to
what an outsider might have expected from reading the
newspapers and attending public meetings.

After all, the great expansion of university education
from the early 1960s onwards – a quintessentially
Labour-ish project – was launched by a Conservative

government. The Theft Act 1968, which made life harder for burglars and easier for the police officers trying to arrest and convict them, was a piece of Labour legislation. The Tories did not dismantle the National Health Service; Labour did not dismantle commercial television.

Furthermore, many economic and social projects could have been ascribed to any of the three sub-models listed above. Was the motorway network an expression of socialist planning, of US-style transport priorities or of the 'dynamic' Britain of the 1960s? Suitably modified, the same question could be asked of the nuclear power programme, of comprehensive schools (little different in principle from US high schools), of British participation in the Concorde project, of state-sponsored amalgamations in the car industry, of the aspiration of Newcastle-upon-Tyne's council leader T. Dan Smith (Labour) to turn his city into 'the Brasilia of the north', of official encouragement for greater efficiencies in agriculture, and so on.

By the mid-1970s, when this fundamentally unified albeit hybrid model started to fall apart, the consensus that supported it fractured as well, with inspiration sought farther afield in terms of economic and social models that might be transplantable to a Britain that seemed in terminal decline. It may seem amusing today to recall that the workplace self-management supposedly practised in Tito's Yugoslavia seemed to offer inspiration to some on the left and to people elsewhere at what was a time of bitter industrial strife. Meanwhile, the Conservatives, demoralized by their defeat in the February 1974 'miners' strike' election, were in no position immediately to offer an alternative. Labour's Tony Benn feared the Tories might be planning to use the notion of cooperative self-management for their own ends:

A new school of thought now developing within the Conservative Party and among industrialists looks at co-operatives in a way that creates new dangers for the trade unions. Some Conservatives would like workers to confront directly the disciplines of the market economy through co-operatives. In this way they hope to create a new framework in industry in which capital can withdraw to a banking function, only funding co-operatives that are successful in fighting market forces. This is also what lies behind 'market socialism'. Industrialists who are ready to fund co-operatives see this as a way to withdraw from their role as managers of labour in the front line, letting the workers fight market forces alone.[1]

In the event, the economic and social model that emerged from the ten years of turmoil from 1974 to 1984 had little room for worker-managers, although worker-owners had enjoyed a brief vogue after the 1982 privatization sale to its own employees of the road haulage business renamed National Freight Consortium. Earlier in the book, we describe the economic management from the mid-1980s onwards as the 'no-strategy strategy'. But that does not mean that no distinctive economic model had come into being. On the contrary, the outlines of this model emerged fairly quickly and remained remarkably unchanged until the Great Recession of 2008–09. The chief features were:

- Government withdrawal from almost all aspects of the ownership of businesses and the direction of industry and commerce in general, including indifference to most takeovers by foreign purchasers of British economic assets. Deregulation of services, including law, finance and accountancy. Remaining regulatory matters such as competition policy, monetary policy and infrastructure planning handed over to independent agencies composed of experts, the assumption being that such decisions are essentially technical.

- The privatization not only of state-owned enterprises but also of functions previously thought 'natural' public sector responsibilities, including water supply and sewerage, ownership of some major roads, the cleaning of NHS hospitals, the management of prisons and the transport of prisoners. Widespread attempts in those areas remaining in public hands to introduce simulated market conditions.

- The retention of most welfare entitlements, along with the NHS and the state school system, with the expense of such services defrayed in part by tighter eligibility criteria, the delinking of cash benefit upgrades from the more generous measures of the cost of living, official campaigns against wrongful claiming and the rationing of health and education through hospital waiting lists and a shortage of desirable schools.

- A generally more intrusive attitude by the state and its agencies to the private life of the citizen, with campaigns of a manner that 50 years ago would have been used to instruct children in the dangers of fireworks or the need to observe the kerb drill now aimed at adults, and covering every imaginable subject from drinking and diet to sexual health, safety in the home, hand washing and the correct use of a refrigerator.

Of this hybrid, it would be easy to state that the first two aspects are borrowed from the American economic model and the last two from European social democracy, not least because there is much truth in such an assertion. And the intertwining of a liberalization of money and things with 'deliberalization' of individual lives has been remarked upon before, not least by ourselves. Indeed, there may be many who believe the breaking of the Post Office monopoly on telephone services and the customer's ability to switch from one bewildering electricity supply tariff to another of equal incomprehensibility is a poor exchange for the freedom to smoke in pubs or help out with social activities without needing a criminal records check.

Even here the traffic has not been entirely in one direction. For example, there is much less liberality in some product markets than 50 years ago. Should you doubt this, try selling home-made jam from a market stall, or indeed any other sort of home-made food product. By contrast, some aspects of personal conduct are now less restricted than they were then, one obvious example being the lifting of the ban on gay people serving in the armed forces. It matters little that this liberalization is of benefit to only a small number of people, while the greater general restrictions imposed on personal life affect many more. Perhaps those who wish to purchase home-made jam are also in a minority. It is the principle that is important.

At this point it is tempting to say there are no general economic and social models from which we can seek inspiration for turning Britain from a de-developing to a developing nation. One has only to look at current attempts by the German government, paymaster of the eurozone, to impose its own fiscal, industrial and economic model on the troubled southern members of the single-currency bloc to see a textbook example of the folly of assuming that Country X is successful because its economic model works well, rather than considering the possibility that the economic model works well because it is located in Country X. By the same token, in most cases Person A probably does not have a well-paid and interesting job because they have an agreeable house and enviable living standards; rather, the causality is likely to be the other way round. Finally, when we notice the economic and social differences between even fairly similar countries – the Nordic nations, for example, or the United Kingdom and Ireland – the difficulties of trying to learn from the experiences of others in trying to construct a development model seem overwhelming. Why not let Sweden be Sweden, America be America, and create our own model from the ground up?

A British model is indeed what we need, and it will bear an unmistakably British stamp. But it will not be conjured out of thin air, ignoring principles and practices from elsewhere. It would be more than a little arrogant were we to suggest we have nothing to learn from others. As for the difficulty of transplanting aspects of other economic models to our own country, this can be largely overcome by breaking those models down into self-contained aspects that can be examined objectively, without the distorting effects of cultural and national conditions.

Thus what could be loosely described as the European social democratic model can be said to consist of the following features, all of which are independent of one another and each one of which could, in theory, be implemented without the need for the implementation of any of the others. In no particular order:

- State involvement in the economy, through a number of channels: ownership of individual businesses or even whole industries, 'picking winners' with accompanying subsidies and other assistance, subsidies for land, energy and transport costs, deliberate use of the government's power as a customer to achieve desired outcomes, use of the tax system to try to shape economic activity. Intimate and constant involvement in the promotion and direction of exports as part of a permanent interest in the health of the balance of payments. Possible establishment of a sovereign wealth fund, as has happened in Norway.

- Detailed intervention in the labour market, both through the close regulation of employment terms and conditions and through attempts to manage the supply of and demand for certain types of labour, particularly skilled labour, through labour power planning, including the encouragement of some school and degree courses over others. Employment rights tend to be wide-ranging and to expand over time. Stringent health and safety regulations.

- The provision of universal benefits, payable to all qualifying persons with no means testing or other 'targeting'. Such payments can range from child-support benefits at one end of the human lifespan to funeral grants at the other. From time to time, there are suggestions of going further and paying a 'citizen wage' to all adults, it then being up to the individual to build on this plinth should they wish to enjoy a higher standard of living.

- The provision of 'blue light' welfare services at low or no cost at the point of need: unemployment and sickness-related benefits, healthcare, care for the elderly and very frail, care for those with mental and physical disabilities, care in the home and provision of essential aids for those who need them, such as wheelchairs. Even when such conditions last for years, they are still very much the product of an emergency, in contrast to the state of affairs covered in our next point.

- Redistribution of wealth. If the previous point covered misfortunes of the type that could happen to anyone, whether the loss of a job or a serious illness, wealth redistribution would be likely to be of benefit chiefly to those whose circumstances are blighted in some way from birth. Rather than plunging into a hole and needing to be rescued, these are people already living below economic sea-level. Supporters of redistribution tend to be those who ascribe a large element of chance to human affairs, even in the outcomes of people from remarkably similar backgrounds, let alone those from wildly different circumstances. Critics are more likely to consider individuals responsible for their own success or failure.

• The purchase by the state of goods and services on behalf of some or all citizens that can be and often are purchased by people acting in a private capacity. Housing is the most important of these (housing in the sense of a family home, rather than the emergency accommodation provided for homeless people in most developed countries). Others include payments for bus and railway services, child care, opera and theatre tickets, university courses and home insulation. On the face of it, this category would appear the most vulnerable to challenge, given that it coexists with a private sector in which citizens make their own purchasing decisions and pay for them with their own money. Yet not only do the beneficiaries become strongly attached to these benefits, justifications on grounds of the public good are usually available – the benefit to the environment from train rather than car use, for example.

Nowhere have we mentioned school-age education. There is a good reason for this. The global consensus behind the desirability of schooling that is free or nearly free and attendance at which is mandatory is so strong as to erase school-age education as a defining feature of a social democracy. Here is Alison Wolfe, professor of education at London University and a renowned sceptic about many aspects of the world's obsession with education:

> [I] do not want to deny or belittle in any way the importance of good in-depth, school-based education for all the world's citizens. The basic 'academic' skills with which primary and secondary education are concerned are also the main tools of survival in a developed economy, a precondition for running modern society, and, not least, a gateway to individual opportunity, enlightenment and knowledge which go way beyond the immediate concerns of work and occupation.[2]

These, then, are our six 'variables', our moving parts, in the social-democratic model. We turn now to their free-market equivalents.

- Wide-ranging commercial freedom unhampered by any overarching official economic strategy. The government restricts itself to the enforcement of property rights, including through the registration of patents, and the arbitration through the civil courts of financial and contractual disputes, although even here the state may encourage parties in such cases to seek independent arbitration rather than burden the public courts. Official activism, where it exists at all, takes the form of aggressive use of taxes, tariffs and 'regulatory breaks' to grab business from other jurisdictions. The authorities may also make available public land for development at knock-down prices, but otherwise play little direct role in the economy. The priority is to keep markets open and functioning.

- A hands-off approach to employment matters, to the extent that even talk in official circles about 'flexible labour markets' sounds too interventionist. Employment contracts, as with all contracts, are believed to be essentially private and ought to be safe from official interference. Workplace rights are one such interference with contracts, thus are kept to a minimum. Health and safety regulations are rigorously tested for cost-effectiveness. There are no 'labour market policies', and there is official indifference to the sort of work people choose to do, and even, provided they can support themselves, to whether they work at all.

- The ease of establishing a business and the minimum of regulation once it is established. A free-market jurisdiction may well regulate a company with regard to its line of work, for example enforcing hygiene laws against a drug or food manufacturer or safety regulations in relation to a transport concern. But it will barely regulate companies as companies, beyond some minimum requirements for filing accounts. High levels of privacy for business owners and their clients will be assured. For those wishing to conceal their involvement or exposure, anonymous bearer shares and bearer bonds will be available. There will be minimal money-laundering regulations

- The streamlining of welfare into a basic insurance system for 'blue light' events only, including unemployment. There will be no element of wealth redistribution, merely a rudimentary service covering the sudden dire need for food, shelter, unemployment relief and medical attention. All services are aimed at coping with such crises, with no wider purpose. There is no purchase of non-urgent goods such as rail transport or social housing, and there are no subsidies for the arts or for university education. Translation services are available only to those charged with criminal offences or in need of accessing an emergency service.

- Tax rates are very low, raising sufficient revenue only to meet a strictly limited public sector remit in terms of services, with possibly a 'flat' system for income tax. There are no incentives anywhere in the tax system, which is fiscally neutral – that is, it is designed in order that nobody ever makes a decision simply on grounds of tax or subsidy. Reliefs and loopholes are also abolished. Corporate tax rates are set at very low levels or even abolished, on the ground that companies have no independent existence and the tax they pay is an extra levy on shareholders. There is no a priori assumption that the tax authorities have any right to an overview of the taxpayer's affairs.

- Priority is given to re-establishing the genuine freedom of commercial entities to choose with whom they do business and on what terms. Anti-discrimination legislation is cut back sharply, in order that business is put on the same legal footing as its customers in terms of entering or declining a commercial relationship without needing to justify such a decision. If a customer can quite legally refuse to use a pub because the landlord is from Trinidad or because the barmaid lives with a woman, why is the reverse not true? Prejudices, corporate and personal, are treated merely as preferences. They may carry a price tag in terms of lost opportunities, but that is none of the state's business.

It may seem that the first set of variables, those attaching to a social-democratic market economy, are more familiar to British eyes than the second, those attaching to our imagined free-market economy. But that is because even free-market aspects of the British system as it stands tend to be couched in vaguely social-democratic language, with much stress on 'opportunity', 'openness', 'diversity' and so on. Our free-market shopping list may sound harsh, but that is because the underlying ideas are rarely spelled out quite so bluntly.

Just before we go any further …

… who says we need a 'development model' at all?

The United Kingdom has slid down the league table of economic performance since 1914 – gradually at first, then more rapidly following the Second World War. This process is going to continue; by 2040 and perhaps sooner than that, the United Kingdom will have dropped out of the list of the ten biggest economies in the world.

Does this matter? In one sense, no. Provided the United Kingdom gets richer decade by decade, it does not matter that other countries will be getting richer more quickly. Given that countries like India, Brazil, Indonesia and Turkey lag behind in terms of incomes and technological know-how, a period of catching up is both inevitable and desirable. Furthermore, it would not matter even were these emerging giants to become richer than us in absolute terms. Were the average Turk or Brazilian to be wealthier than the average Londoner, Ulsterman or Yorkshirewoman, that would be unimportant provided British living standards continued to rise and the economy continued to generate the surplus wealth needed for both commercial investment and the purchase of social goods such as medical treatments and other types of welfare.

But this is a big proviso. As we hope this book has made clear, the United Kingdom is currently a de-developing nation, a submerging market. The danger is not that we will lose our place in some global club or other. Such an outcome may dent the pride of our leaders as they are denied a place in a prestigious venue, but would be of little concern to ordinary people. The genuine worry is that we will endure falling real living standards – actually get worse off.

It has happened before, but only for short bursts. That said, a list of the late twentieth-century years in which real incomes fell reads like a list of all those years beloved of twenty-first-century crime writers seeking gritty and downbeat scenarios for their murder thrillers: 1974, 1976, 1977 and 1981. It happened again in 2010 and 2011, which suggests it is becoming something of a modern-day habit.

To arrest and reverse our current 'submerging' status, we need a development model. More than one is on offer. But one has to be chosen. For simplicity's sake, we have boiled them down to the two abovementioned alternatives, the social-democratic model and the full-blooded free-market model. Justified protests would suggest that this is not so much simple as simplistic. Apart from the different varieties of social market democracy on offer, not to mention the variations of more or less free markets, there are even some hybrids.

Singapore, for example, thrives on hard work, competition, free trade and an unsentimental labour market. It ought to be a set-piece example of a 'freeport'. Indeed it actually is a port, one of the largest in the world. But it is also a highly paternalistic society whose rulers (we use the plural, assuming there has ever really been more than one, the country's first prime minister Lee Kuan Yew) have, since independence in 1965, left little to chance in guiding the country's economy and society. There is even an official campaign to promote marriage, and Singapore's economic future is developing under close government guidance. As the *World Factbook* of the US Central Intelligence Agency put it: 'Singapore has attracted major investments in pharmaceuticals and medical technology production and will continue efforts to establish Singapore as south-east Asia's financial and high-tech hub.'[3]

Germany, on the other hand, is in many ways the quintessential social market economy. The phrase might have originated there. But is has no national minimum wage, its commitment to 'hard money' low-inflation policies is renowned (or perhaps notorious), and the government's official fact book declares, 'Germany is a social market economy, in other words the state guarantees the free play of entrepreneurial forces, while at the same time endeavouring to maintain the social balance.' The ordering of that sentence may be significant, as may the contrast between the 'guarantee' and the 'endeavour', particularly in light of the observable fact that the country's awesome export machine has, in recent years, been able to navigate trouble in world markets through agreements with the trade unions to hold down wages.

Instinctively, however, we seem able to tell the difference between the social-democratic and the free-market models of capitalism, and also between the successful and less successful versions of each variant. Here is Dambisa Moyo, in her highly praised 2011 book *How the West was Lost*:

> While it is true that socialist-leaning states are clearly relatively well developed and engineered in Germany and across Scandinavia, well developed but perhaps badly designed in Greece and Italy, the trouble is that the US is on a path to creating the worst and most venal form of welfare state (poorly developed and designed).[4]

We quote this passage not to express either agreement or disagreement but merely to give one example of what seems an ease of identification. So if we accept – with lots of caveats and grey areas – that our possible development model can be drawn from one of two very broad economic models, the next question is inevitably which one, in general, to choose. This need not be entirely an either/ or choice. From the 12 points listed above, expressing six key features of each respective model, it is clear that a modest amount of mixing and matching is possible. For example, a permissive approach to the founding and regulation of companies as entities – point three on the free-market list – could happily coexist with most of the points on the social-market list. Similarly, the provision of first-class 'blue light' emergency health and welfare services free at the point of use, the fourth point on the social-market list, could be slotted into our free-market economy without too much trouble, other than on the fiscal side – either tax rates would have to be lifted off rock bottom or expenditure elsewhere would need to be cut.

But there are limits to such accommodation, unsurprising given the very different philosophies that give rise to the respective models. That said, are there any solid materialistic reasons for preferring one to the other? In short, which is more likely to deliver the goods?

Let us consult the CIA *World Factbook* and start with the country whose name heads this chapter, Sweden.

Its gross domestic product per head was $40,600 in 2011, its unemployment rate was 7.6 per cent and figures for the percentage of its population living below the poverty line were unavailable. Its 'Gini index', measuring inequality in the distribution of family income, stood at 23, the index being constructed so that a perfectly equal distribution would give a reading of zero and a perfectly unequal distribution would give a reading of 100.

Swinging to what many see as the opposite pole, the United States had GDP per head of $48,100, an unemployment rate of 9.1 per cent and 15.1 per cent of the population is thought to be living below the poverty line. The US Gini index reading is 45.

What about France, so proud of its social model and republican values? GDP per head was $35,000, there was an unemployment rate of 9.1 per cent and 6.2 per cent of the population was below the poverty line. France's Gini index reading was 32.7.

Finally, Hong Kong, the Far Eastern exemplar of capitalism red in tooth and claw. Its GDP per capita was $49,300, it had 3.3 per cent unemployment and figures for the percentage of the population living below the poverty line are not available. Its Gini index reading is 53.3.

Where to start with all this? To a very large extent, it is a matter of personal preference whether one chooses to be taken aback by Sweden's low Gini index reading or Hong Kong's high one, by France's high unemployment rate or its low Gini index reading, by the high US GDP per head or by its high percentage of people living below the poverty line.

True, looked at one way the Swedish model would seem the overall winner. Sweden's unemployment rate is lower than that of France or the United States, and its GDP per head easily outstrips that of France, while its Gini index reading is among the lowest in the world. But it is also the fifteenth most highly taxed country on earth. Among developed nations only Finland (13th), Denmark (12th) and Norway (ninth) pay a higher share of GDP in tax. It is significant that all are exemplars of the Scandinavian social model, although the top 15 does contain two oddities: the European mini-state of San Marino (tenth) and Britain's Falkland Islands territory (eighth).

Does the sense of social well-being generated by a low Gini index reading compensate for such high rates of tax? Ultimately that has to be a personal judgement, one that is translated many millions of times through the democratic process until a national view is arrived at. *De gustibus non est disputandum*: there is no arguing about taste, personally or at a social level. In this spirit, we will look briefly at how both models could be adapted to British needs.

Magnetic north: time for a high-fibre economic diet?

One model, beloved of the British left over many years and more recently finding favour among David Cameron's Conservatives, is that of Scandinavian welfare capitalism and its variants in the European social-democratic model, as practised in France, Germany, Italy and elsewhere. The 'Swedish model' has been enormously influential over the decades, even – or perhaps especially – among those unaware of the origin of their ideas. Between the wars, this was a sort of 'fourth way', different not only from communism and fascism but also from what seemed to be hidebound and helpless parliamentary states, apparently incapable of coping with the horrors of the depression. Extensive welfare provision, first-class transport, education and healthcare and an active partnership between the state and the private sector seemed to point the way ahead for a shattered postwar Europe. Unlike Roosevelt's New Deal, these were no emergency measures but a (presumed) new, permanent social settlement. With the end of hostilities, the Swedish model rapidly became the Scandinavian model, and its DNA could be found throughout postwar democratic western Europe, to the extent that it seems fitting that West German chancellor Willy Brandt was himself part-Norwegian.

For a twenty-first-century United Kingdom looking to settle upon a model for economic development, the attractions of going to the source of modern European social democracy and 'turning Scandinavian' are obvious. The Nordic countries are small and extremely prosperous nations, in part because they have not been obsessed with their place in league tables or 'punching above their weight'. They appear to have pulled off the three-card trick: very high living standards, generous social welfare and a healthy trade balance with the rest of the world. Norway even has a sizeable sovereign wealth fund, in contrast to the United Kingdom's empty public coffers. Periodically the model is declared to be dead – only to return to life.

One immediate objection is that the United Kingdom lacks the social coherence needed to make a Nordic-type social market system function properly. On this reading, social democracy is not a piece of machinery that can be lugged round from one setting to another, but a natural outgrowth of local cultural conditions, a delicate plant, cuttings from which are difficult to transplant. Perhaps so, but that does not mean British soil is entirely unsuited for this purpose. In January 2012 the Trades Union Congress published a research paper, 'German lessons: developing industrial policy in the UK', which, in calling for a new approach based on 'equality, fairness and mutuality', stated, in a telling line: '[T]he German social market economy is culturally cherished in Germany, in much the same way that the National Health Service is cherished in the UK.'[5]

Quite so. Social democracy in postwar Britain developed rather differently from that elsewhere in Europe, more ambitious to begin with, but later less resilient in the face of a disillusion with collective solutions to national problems that swept the western world after the oil crises of the 1970s. But it left its mark all the same, of which the NHS is the most enduring. There is a mood to be nurtured, should we wish to do so.

But the difficulties are daunting. To describe the social-democratic model in terms of its functioning is wholly inadequate. To say that the Nordic countries dispense superb social benefits while selling lots of good-quality products on world markets is rather like describing police work entirely in terms of wrestling suspects to the ground and applying handcuffs. Behind the mechanics of a Norway, a Sweden or a Germany lie a bundle of attitudes, a set of social norms. Before we get to the welfare state we need to think about a state of mind.

The plain fact is that to be a Sweden or a Denmark, Britain would require a cultural revolution, ending the search for another quick fix and instead buckling down to many years of hard work. If we wish to join the Nordic club we have very long way to go. GDP per head in Finland is 6.2 per cent higher than in Britain, in Denmark 10.6 per cent higher, in Norway 32.6 per cent higher and in Sweden 11.5 per cent higher.

The social-democratic route to growth is easily described but very hard to follow. Britain would need across the board cooperation between government, the trade unions and big business to build exports, to invest for the long term and to buckle down to the unglamorous business of improving supply chains, giving smaller businesses a fair shake in order both to create the dense undergrowth of specialist firms that the economy will need and to provide the breeding ground for the corporate giants of tomorrow. Cooperation on pay and prices would be essential, but how likely is it?

The not entirely happy British history of this sort of corporatism is not encouraging. Labour's five-year National Plan, launched in 1965, was a dead letter before the party's June 1970 election defeat, its ambitious growth targets unmet. Pay and price controls in the grim climate of the 1970s held for a while, then collapsed in winters of industrial strife (1973–74, 1978–79). Export drives with official backing have had limited success, to put it mildly. Above all, an individualistic streak on both sides of industry has weakened all such collective efforts, whether it came from skilled craftspeople determined to preserve their wage differentials in relation to less skilled workers or the Ford motor group, which broke from the government pay norm and helped trigger the winter of discontent.

In short, are the British prepared to be conformist enough for long enough to see the policy through? Because taking this route would require nothing less than a series of revolutions: in education, facing up to the fact that many schools are failing their pupils; in industrial policy, so that the government provides support rather than sticking to an albeit inconsistent laissez-faire approach; in financial services, to break the power of the City over the economy, smashing up the big banks; and in the property market, to ensure through a saner tax system that the economy no longer endures the endless cycles of boom–bust that have pockmarked the past 40 years. And it will require lots of sacrifice and a series of self-denying ordnances right across the economic scene: on pay, prices, planning, monopolistic behaviour and political opportunism.

Above all, it will need energetic and intelligent

government allied to a serious and deeply engaged public, able to stick to a steady line of policy over very many years. That's a tall order.

Nor is it quite the end of the story, because the social-democratic model rests on a very much more equal society, equal not merely in terms of 'respect' and 'diversity' and other relatively cost-free concessions to various social groups, but also in distribution of wealth. Britain's Gini index reading is 21 per cent higher than Finland's, 14.7 per cent higher than Denmark's, 26.4 per cent higher than Norway's and 32.3 per cent higher than Sweden's.

Here is a bracingly realistic appraisal of Britain's attitude to inequality, from Evan Davies – then the economics correspondent for BBC television's *Newsnight* programme and now a presenter of *Today* on BBC Radio Four:

> Personally, I suspect that most of us would not be willing to pay a very high price for universal equal access to non-urgent health services. The prevalent feeling would surely be that for health – and education, housing and food – everybody should have access to a reasonable level. One might deduce these values from the fact that the public tolerate inequalities in housing and food and make not even a token effort to eradicate them.[6]

More recently Tamzen Isacsson of Nobel Media, writing in *The Daily Telegraph,* shared her experience of Sweden's lavish child support system with British readers under the headline 'We're just not ready to be Swedes, Dave', a reference to the prime minister's apparent enthusiasm for aspects of the Nordic model. A supporter herself of the Swedish way of doing things, she made it clear Sweden's welfare state does not come cheap:

In the end, we all pay for it through higher taxes and the higher cost of living in Sweden.

Food, taxis and household services are expensive, petrol is dear and the state extracts a phenomenal amount of tax from alcohol. It is hard to imagine Cameron getting similar levies through Parliament. But these are the spending priorities that the Swedish people have chosen.[7]

Could we ever choose similar priorities? Possibly. What are thought of as immutable national and social characteristics change over time. For much of the nineteenth century Germans were seen by many as somewhat unworldly characters: romantics, intellectuals and poets. Until well into living memory, the abiding western image of Singapore was of a sleazy, rather lazy glamour, befitting the Old East of the Raffles Hotel and Somerset Maugham.

Entrepot a go-go: into the enterprise zone?

Diametrically opposed to the Scandinavian model is what may be termed 'Freeport Britain'. This model, equally valid, would turn the country into a vast enterprise zone. Tariffs would be slashed to zero, planning controls swept away, almost all official form-filling requirements on business abolished, taxes cut to the lowest possible level, immigration regarded as benign, higher education completely privatized, financial regulation reduced to the minimum on the basis of *caveat emptor*, the abolition of the Department for Business, the downsizing of the Treasury into a small Ministry of Finance with no wider responsibilities, the reduction of local government to a single-tier system with strictly limited funds and functions, the ending of transfer payments to the Welsh and Scottish governments, the replacement of the NHS and welfare system with a simple, basic insurance-funded service, and the use of wholesale market solutions in education and other public services.

Phew! Is this bumper shopping list for real?

Not perhaps all of it, all at once. Indeed, some items could be dropped permanently. It is possible to conceive of a Freeport Britain that featured strict planning controls, strict immigration controls or both, the point being that the gales of free-market competition could continue to blow despite these constraints. But the overall structure of such an economic model would be of a commercial and industrial free-fire area in which the winners get to keep most of their winnings and the losers, should they wish to cease striving and rely on public assistance, enjoy only a very basic standard of living.

Government would focus on the 'sovereign' functions of the state: defence, law and order and other forms of public protection, such as against natural disasters and epidemics. In sharp contrast to the social-market model, ministers would have no official views on a swathe of subjects, from 'healthy eating' to the desirability of having more women on company boards.

Freeport Britain would be very different from the supposed market economy from 1985 to 2008. There would be no corporate welfare, as seen from the 1987 rescue of the imperilled British Petroleum share offer to the 2008 rescue of Royal Bank of Scotland. There would be no 'enterprise grants', or other handouts. No preferential treatment for British firms in, for example, the allocation of airport slots. No trade missions abroad. No legal aid for companies. No political patronage. No bailouts. It would not be a quick fix, but an indefinite determination to live by the ebb and flow of the global market.

Ministers would take no interest in bankers' bonuses, but nor would they ride to the rescue of failing banks. Large swathes of the official statistics sector would be closed down, as ministers would similarly take no interest in phenomena such as the balance of payments. Nigel Lawson, chancellor from 1983 to 1989, once dismissed a large trade deficit as 'noise in the system'. Ministers in Freeport Britain would go further and unplug the loudspeakers.

In contrast to the Thatcher–Blair system, Freeport Britain would be intellectually consistent. There would be huge inequalities of wealth, but total equality of treatment by the state – ministers would be equally indifferent to the individual and the corporation. Nobody would be 'too big to fail' because corporate failure would be a fact of life, as would the collateral damage to people and businesses in the supply chain of insolvent large companies. Due diligence would be the responsibility of each and every counterparty in a transaction with a business of any size, the plumber and contract cleaner as much as the investment bank. In place of implicit and explicit taxpayer guarantees would emerge a genuinely self-regulating marketplace. Just as motorists would drive rather more carefully were they to be deprived of seat-belts, air-bags and 'crumple zones', so all concerned would learn to take great care when choosing with whom to do business were they to be aware that losses are potentially unlimited and that government-underwritten compensation arrangements are few and far between.

Oddly, however, although Freeport Britain would undoubtedly be an 'enterprise economy', there would be little by way of enterprise propaganda from ministers and officials. There would, indeed, be little propaganda of any sort, it not being considered the job of the state to 'change attitudes' among the population other than in specific, limited and uncontroversial areas, such as campaigning against drink driving or advising children not to accept sweets from strangers. The 'enterprise economy' would not be an aspiration, to be pursued by government and encouraged by official exhortations to the public. Rather it would simply be the environment in which people lived. The authorities in Freeport Britain would no more urge people to be entrepreneurial than the authorities in Guernsey would urge that small island's inhabitants to live near the sea.

One point of similarity with a social-market Britain would be a distrust of international posturing and overseas entanglements such as Afghanistan. Freeport Britain would show little interest in 'punching above our weight' in world affairs. Foreign involvements of any sort – military or diplomatic – would be subject to a rigorous cost–benefit analysis. This would not rule out enduring and close relationships, such as those with the remaining UK overseas territories, or armed interventions of a sort that could protect British trading interests, such as action against piracy in the Indian Ocean. But 'vanity' foreign policy would be a thing of the past.

Indeed, even those international commitments that might seem to be amenable to Freeport Britain, such as membership of the World Trade Organization and International Monetary Fund, would be treated with considerable suspicion. Just as those quintessential freeports, Macao and Tangier, stayed out of the postwar Bretton Woods system, so Freeport Britain would prefer the reality of free trade, day in, day out, to the theory of it as espoused in conference rooms and at major diplomatic gatherings. All these bodies are more about rule making than they are about trading, and should anyone need a warning about the likely development of a treaty organization supposedly set up to facilitate cross-border commerce, they need only look at the European Union and its vast schedule of 'competences'. Freeport Britain agrees with the late Enoch Powell:

> One of the beauties of free trade is that it is a-political: you do not have to browbeat or overrule anybody else in order to enjoy its blessings for yourself. It is a game at which, like Patience, one can play; and like common sense it can be practiced with impunity and advantage in the midst of a crazy world.[8]

There are many enterprise zones and freeports round the world, from Shannon in Ireland to Jebel Ali in the Persian Gulf, and each has a border with the parent nation. Freeport Britain would have no such border. There would be no 'other side'. The enterprise zone would be all there was.

This may sound rather bleak, just as social-market Britain may sound rather bossy. But the founding philosophy of Freeport Britain, while open to challenge, would rest on something deeper and more profound than an aversion to paying taxes or a fondness for small government. It would be deeper even than a love of free trade and is rooted in the notion of the sovereign rights of the individual As Deepak Lal put it:

> These are [John Stuart] Mill's principles of liberty: a person can undertake any feasible action which does not harm others or break an obligation. The burden of proof lies on someone who wants to prohibit an individual's actions. This process is equivalent to the presumed innocence of the accused unless found guilty by due process.[9]

There would be no room, in other words, for official action against institutions, whether lap-dancing clubs or private schools, on grounds that they 'send the wrong message' or 'exacerbate social divisions'. Nor against individuals on the ground that their words or actions may 'cause offence'.

But as with social-market Britain, the question has to be whether Freeport Britain would prove acceptable to the public as an economic model. The bracing winds of competition and the chilling absence of much by way of subsidy or welfare payments might simply prove too arctic by far for a population used to living in an economic temperate zone. The experience of the Thatcher years is not especially encouraging: public enthusiasm for cut-price privatization shares and council houses dwarfed any real sign of an upsurge in entrepreneurship. Indeed, as noted in the Bank of England's quarterly *Inflation Report* for February 2012, rates of self-employment, despite the increase mentioned earlier in the 1980s, have tended since to rise and fall in an inverse relationship to the labour market, with those displaced from salaried jobs going it alone until the chance comes to re-enter the world of employment. The old joke about 'consultant' being the title given to a jobless person in Surrey would seem to have some validity.

Finally, even in its incipient third world condition, Britain continues to have an influential intelligentsia to whom public support for the theatre, the BBC, libraries, universities, museums, art galleries and musical performances is not merely a luxury that may be axed in hard times, but the essence of a civilized society. They feel the same way about the NHS and the welfare state. As far as they are concerned, Freeport Britain would scarcely be worth living in.

In plain sight: the long road ahead

It is easy to romanticize both of our economic models, for protagonists of one or the other to peer into the future wearing the rosiest of tinted spectacles. Seen through the prism of this sort of wishful thinking, social-market Britain is a crime-free, litter-free, classless society in which thoughtful citizens work hard, engage in wholesome leisure pursuits and participate fully in community life. Public services are first class. Everything works properly.

Similarly, Freeport Britain is vibrant, if a little chaotic, exciting and prosperous. Images of Cape Town, Cairo and Istanbul blur into one. Great ships sway at anchor, sailors hit the town with bulging pay packets as the jukebox in the waterfront café plays Jacques Brel's greatest hits.

This sort of 'thinking' should be resisted. Whichever model is chosen, the road ahead is going to be very tough indeed. That is the lot of developing countries – they have to develop, and that means no more quick fixes and a great deal of hard work. Even getting to developing status is going to involve serious negotiation, given that implementing either of our development models will require at the very least a reconfigured relationship between the United Kingdom and the institutions of the European Union.

It is true that, to an extent, our two models are caricatures. It can be argued also that any 'British model' ought to mix and match far more than we have suggested is likely, that the choice is less black and white. That may be so, although the level of debate and eventual consensus will probably need to be higher in adopting a hybrid model than for a more straightforward scheme of development.

Imagine a house in London whose inhabitants,

whether related to each other or not, know the bailiff will be arriving in the morning. Some suggest they should point their mini-van west in search of a new life, towards Wales and the West Country. Others insist the north of England and Scotland offer better prospects. Getting agreement will be difficult. It would be many times more so were anyone to suggest that the best course of action was a complex arrangement in which their time would be split between the Black Mountains and the Scottish lowlands.

It can be argued also that many of the most important aspects of national life are not covered in our sketches of the two economic models. What about crime and penal policy? Will there be a permissive or a restrictive approach to personal insolvency or divorce? How will inheritance law work?

It is true that these are among the most intimate aspects of any human society, and the answers to these questions tells us pretty much the essence of that society. But ironically, these issues can be addressed and readdressed as the years goes by. Yes, they are of critical importance, but they always will be, regardless of the economic state of the country concerned. By contrast, there is very little time in which we can choose an economic development plan and take the equally important decision to see it through. It is later than we think.

Chapter 9

Hanging on in there:
investment during the crisis

The market adage is, 'buy low, sell high' – which always gets a laugh when I tell novice traders that this is the secret to achieving staggering wealth. It is.

David James Norman, writing in *City AM* newspaper,
31 May 2011

'Money by right means if you can, if not, by any means, money.

Horace (65 BC–8 BC), *Epistles*

'And there are ways to profit from general misfortune. In case you're interested, Margot, you'll find descriptions in my latest book, *Depressions and Disasters: How to Make Money from Them*. Incidentally, it's selling very well.'

'If you don't mind,' Margot said, 'I'll pass. It seems a bit like cornering vaccine in an outbreak of bubonic plague.'

Arthur Hailey, *The Moneychangers*, 1975

This is not a book of share tips. Nor is it a compendium of investment principles, or a guide to the proper analysing of company shares or government bonds. You will not find much by way of price/earnings ratios, dividend yields or interest cover. The share-price 'charts' beloved of so-called technical analysts will be absent. Such topics are covered admirably, some would say over-extensively, in the business section of any good bookshop.

Nor is this chapter concerned with investment during a downturn. This is a proper subject, and one covered in other works. The precise definition of business cycles is elusive, but most accept the so-called Kitchin cycle of three to five years – the standard business cycle – and many accept also the longer Juglar cycle of nine to eleven years (essentially encompassing two Kitchin cycles). The 'long wave', the so-called Kondratiev cycle, is much more controversial. Gaining an understanding of successful investment strategy during the prolonged downswing of either of the longer cycles is a valuable exercise. It is, alas, one that will have to be carried out beyond the pages of this book.

Then there are the guides to surviving and thriving during a depression, or indeed a period of roaring inflation. Oddly, they tend to make the same sorts of suggestions, involving the paying down of excessive debt and the acquisition of 'solid' assets – property, land, blue-chip shares and so on. This is not one of those.

Finally, we do not intend to trespass on the territory of what may be called the survivalist school of investment. This chapter is not going to tell you how to hang on to your assets as society breaks down and armed gangs roam the countryside. There is an excellent reason for this: as we do not believe society is going to break down in this manner, we see little point in advising you as to the best way to cope with such a contingency. The transition to a third world economy will not, we believe, be the story of a catastrophic collapse of law and order and social organization. A third world economy is simply a different sort of economy with different rules for investment and different risks.

If this chapter has an overriding purpose it is to help to guard against readers trying to play the new game by the old rules. We are put in mind of an hilarious moment in the 2011 *Dr Who* Christmas special in which a group of heavily armed futuristic troopers are arresting a time-travelling 1940s housewife. After burbling about their personal 'issues', the troopers lay down their weapons out of 'respect' for their captive. At which point she reaches into her ration-coupon overcoat, produces an old service revolver and takes them prisoner.

There is no sure-fire way to avoid being a hostage to changing times. But this chapter, we hope, will lay down habits of thought that may serve you well in the future.

Conventional investment is rather like archery or golf, in that it is easy to describe but hard to do well. An 'active' investment portfolio – one that is managed in order to acquire and dispose of assets at the most propitious time – is shaken up in line with developments in the wider economy, or rather in line with expected developments. Not all portfolios are actively managed in this way. Some merely track an index of major shares; others feature carefully selected investments, shares and other assets, that are then held over a long period. But the active portfolio will be managed in such a way as to maximize returns by anticipating and profiting from developments in the economy.

Put very simply, when the economy is in an 'up' phase – or a boom, if you prefer – certain types of investments make good sense, and during the 'down' phase, or bust, a different set of investments is profitable. In the former period, these include investments in house building and related activities, luxury goods, big-ticket consumer items, cars, travel and tourism, entertainment, specialist retailing, bars and restaurants and untested technologies.

In the latter period, so-called defensive investments come to the fore. These are, in essence, investments in things that people will still consume (because they have to) during a recession: food and beverages, gas, fuel, electrical power, basic clothing and footwear, and medicines.

Listing these investment areas is the easy part. But timing is an obvious essential in switching in and out of them. When driving round a sharp bend, braking and steering need to be in hand well before the car reaches the corner in question. Similarly, there is little profit to be had from piling into property investment, for example, in the last stages of a boom, the point by which the wise investor will long since have cashed in.

In parallel with this economic investment cycle is an inflation investment cycle. Or perhaps 'spectrum' would be a better word. When inflation starts to pick up and interest rates are still low, investment moves from low-yielding cash to first, near-cash instruments such as government bonds and other fixed-interest products, thence to shares – blue chip at first, then more risky equities – and thence to direct property development and the bankrolling of business start-ups, films and theatrical productions. At each stage, the investor is seeking higher returns as inflation gathers strength. By the final phase of the inflationary blow-out, investors will be piling into unproductive assets whose value is inflating more quickly than the general price level: fine wines, gold coins, vintage cars, paintings and silverware.

At this point, interest rates ought to have risen to a level that makes cash an attractive investment once more. In a din of collapsing asset prices, investors return to cash and the cycle is complete.

As with the economic investment cycle, the wise investor tries to stay ahead of the game. Nobody wishes to be left holding a batch of overpriced wine or real estate just as the market starts to fall apart. In the case of both cycles, the smart operator will be out of each asset phase before the peak is reached. If there is another 10 or even 20 per cent rise in the price still to go, so be it. Let someone else have the rise – and the risk. The key point is to ensure there will be someone willing to take the asset off your hands at the same or a higher price than you paid for it – 'liquidity', in the jargon, or 'the greater fool theory' to use the more cynical expression.

This is, of course, very much easier said than done. Hardened professionals struggle to work out where we are in the investment cycle at any given time. One illustrious stockbroking firm called the top of the London stock market at the end of 1985, sparing its clients the share-price plunge of October 1987 but also denying them the great gains of 1986 and most of 1987. It was not merely over-enthusiastic young people and unsavoury spivs who failed to spot the obscenely bloated state of house prices in 1988–89 and again in the mid-2000s: economists and bankers were equally impervious to the evidence. The roaraway dollar of the early 1980s was a one-way bet – until it turned tail. Few noticed in 1981 that the long bear market in UK government bonds was over.

Furthermore, some will hotly dispute our outline of conventional investment thinking. They may insist that momentum and 'weight of money' are what drive asset prices. Or they may claim that careful research of a handful of underpriced assets, usually but not always the shares of neglected companies, is the key to investment success (the approach favoured by Lord Keynes in the later part of his asset-management career). Some may demand what they see as due respect for the abovementioned charts of share, currency and other prices, on the ground that the charts show what investors have actually done with their money rather than what analysts believe they ought to have done with it.

Regardless of which model is preferred, we argue that conventional investment is ceasing to be conventional in any meaningful sense, and that the United Kingdom's decline to developing country status places the whole nature of savings and investment in a completely different context.

World turned upside down: political risk in the third world marketplace

From the above, it is clear that making good investment decisions is extraordinarily difficult even in the calm and orderly world of, let us say, the oak-panelled office of a private bank in Geneva or Zurich. Spotting in advance the turns in the economy and the market requires good judgement, a lack of wishful thinking and a forensic intelligence. Assessing the counters on the board is hard enough even when there are no distractions. But Britain's de-developing economy magnifies these difficulties many times over. In part, this is because a malfunctioning economy is, by definition, less likely to provide a satisfactory home for savings and investments than one that works properly. We shall look at that in more detail later. But for now, we turn to a central problem facing investors in underdeveloped countries: political risk. Ordinary risk is when the counters do not move round the board in the way you had hoped. Political risk is when someone comes and knocks the board over, accidentally or otherwise.

In the United Kingdom of 2014 and beyond, political risk will take many forms. But perhaps the most fundamental will be the risk of a constitutional crisis. As noted elsewhere, there are a number of potential flashpoints in this regard: Westminster versus Edinburgh, Britain versus Brussels, ministers versus the Supreme Court and the European Court of Human Rights in Strasbourg, and the House of Commons versus the proposed elected House of Lords or 'senate'. Any one of these crises could have severe implications for investment, most obviously in the field of government securities and similar.

The long boom in gilt-edged stock is almost certainly over, given one last lease of life by the Bank of England's quantitative easing scheme, under which the Bank prints new money and uses it to buy securities (mainly gilts) from the private sector. That the scheme, in effect, lets the government print the money that it then lends to itself is disguised by the stipulation that the gilts in question must first be in private hands before being bought by the Bank. This is reminiscent of the tactics used by some publicly quoted firms to get round the rules on so-called related-party transactions, in which arm's-length decision making is required when any deal involves potential conflict of interest, such as the purchase by the public company of a private company owned by one of the directors. Two 'independent' directors are wheeled in to execute the final handshake, thus preserving the appearance of an arm's-length deal.

Gilts, along with sterling, are likely to prove the first casualty of any clash that calls into question the fundamental authority of the state. In the case of proposals for Scottish independence, the very physical frontiers of the state could be thrown into doubt. In the final analysis, sterling and gilts are simply two types of paper issued by the same government. In their different ways, both are IOUs. Their fortunes are intimately linked. A student may have two different bank accounts, but only one set of resources. Regardless of the proliferation of chequebooks and debit cards, an impoverished undergraduate remains just that.

Muddying the waters further in terms of the gilt

market and political stability is the proposal to allow
the Scottish government to issue its own bonds. At the
time of writing, their status in terms of whether they
would form part of the United Kingdom's national debt
is unclear. The linked question of whether there would
be any limits on the amount that could be raised in this
way has also yet to be addressed. The hazards here are
obvious: without such limits, the Treasury in London
could find itself standing behind substantial borrowings
of which it disapproves and over the servicing of which it
has no control. But any restrictions imposed by London
could cause an enormous furore north of the border.
International investors would almost certainly lump
Scotland's debts in with those of the United Kingdom. All
this is without raising the question of whether 'Scottish
gilts' would qualify as part of the capital base for Scottish
(or indeed English) banks, another neuralgic issue with
enormous implications for investors.

Perhaps the most sensitive issue of all relates to
Scotland's likely credit rating, and whether the country
poses a serious default risk. Then there is the prospect
of a Scottish government (or one of the other devolved
administrations) switching back and forth on levels of
taxation and other levies, creating constant uncertainty,
although the Westminster authorities are quite capable
of behaving in the same manner, as we shall see shortly.

One final impact of constitutional devolution upon the
economic scene, and hence the outlook for investment, is
the increasing likelihood of clashing legal systems across
the internal borders of the United Kingdom, notably in
relation to Scotland but increasingly elsewhere. It is true
that Scotland has kept its own legal system for hundreds
of years and it has rubbed along well enough with the
English system during that time. It is true also that from
1921 to 1972 the Northern Ireland government was able

to act on and to introduce legislation about all but a few key matters, such as defence, foreign affairs and some taxes (although this may not be the happiest example to cite). But Scotland now has a Parliament that can, if it wishes, make laws without reference to any other part of the country on a wide range of matters. Wales is in the process of following suit. Corporate or other assets that lay across 'internal' borders could thus be subject to different legal regimes. That could be difficult enough, but what would happen were one jurisdiction to claim oversight of all of a company or other asset on the ground that its head office or its most important aspect was based within its borders?

Different tax regimes within the United Kingdom – Scotland has already some tax-varying power – would ratchet up the potential for such turf wars, as different fiscal jurisdictions staked their claims to the take from companies and wealthy individuals.

All this could be managed were there to be a robust umpire at the heart of the UK system, adjudicating on such matters, the decisions of which would be final. Such a body would need the consent of all sides to the constitutional settlement. It would also, preferably, need to be very old and long-established.

In the event, the actual body charged with this umpiring role enjoys neither of these benefits. The Supreme Court of the United Kingdom is not old (it started work only in October 2009) and its role in nationalist-ruled Scotland is already controversial, given it is charged both with hearing appeals in criminal cases with a human-rights dimension and with judging, if asked by either Scotland's law officers or by the UK government, whether the subject matter of a particular bill passed by the Scottish Parliament is within its powers to legislate.

If devolution is one potential minefield for the

investor in terms of political risk, it is far from alone. For example, a serious challenge to the creditworthiness of the state arises south of the border, in the new elected upper house. Since 1911, the House of Lords has been excluded from so-called money bills, in essence the Budget and related legislation. Peers have no powers over these types of bills because control of taxation and spending is rightly seen as at the core of the functions of a democratic legislature. And for as long as the House of Lords remained unelected, this position held good, although from the 1990s onwards the Lords – now largely appointed, with only 94 hereditary peers remaining – increasingly inched into purely economic affairs as well as industry and overseas trade, its more traditional areas of economic interest.

But an elected upper house will surely prove impossible to exclude from financial legislation? Nick Clegg, the deputy prime minister and Cabinet member with special responsibility for constitutional reform, has suggested that such a body could be kept out of budgetary matters by the simple expedient of writing into law that this is so. Over time, however, we believe that trying to restrain elected senators with legal niceties will prove as futile as trying to restrain the Edinburgh government.

Another fiscal flashpoint is in the relationship between the Supreme Court and elected representatives in relation to taxing and spending. Already the chancellor has to vouch for the fact that various measures are compliant with the Human Rights Act and assorted 'equalities' criteria. The likelihood has to be that, sooner or later, the highest judges in the land will overturn a key fiscal measure, essentially overriding the will of the electorate on matters of taxing and spending, which, along with fighting wars and signing peace treaties, is at the core of what makes a country a sovereign state. It can be claimed, although many disagree and the recent travails of the eurozone would seem to argue against it, that a country can share its currency and monetary policy with another country and still be a sovereign state. Similarly, a country or group of countries can choose to outsource its monetary policy to experts within its own frontiers and still remain democratically governed. The United Kingdom, the eurozone and the United States fall into this category.

But there is no precedent for a democratic country outsourcing fiscal decisions to a supposedly dispassionate unelected group. When that group is made up of judges, and far from having been given the job of ruling on fiscal decisions they have simply grabbed it for themselves, then the stage is set for a major confrontation. It is no exaggeration to say that this is the stuff of which civil wars are made.

A second and equally hazardous type of political risk is that arising from arbitrary confiscation of income or assets. A first world economy may include a severely circumscribed private sector, steeply progressive taxes, a large public sector and a wealth tax. Many do, or have done so. Others may do so in future. But what in this context distinguishes a developed from an undeveloped economy is the security of property and contract where applicable. In other words, changes to taxation, regulation and property law likely to have a serious impact on a group of people's lawful enjoyment of their possessions are flagged up well in advance, discussed at great length and implemented, if at all, only after the fullest consideration. This allows those affected to plan ahead, and in the case of tradable assets such as shares, it gives time for the value of those assets to adjust to the new reality.

Britain's great wave of nationalization after the war

was accompanied by proper arrangements for paying fair compensation to the private shareholders whose assets were being taken into public ownership. It was the same story with the more low-key nationalizations of the 1970s. The special tribunal set up to hear appeals relating to the taking into public ownership of aerospace and shipbuilding in the mid-1970s was scheduled for winding up only in 2012, many years after the industries concerned had been returned to private hands.

By contrast, third world economies are much more likely to be disfigured by arbitrary and random confiscation of property, either by physical force, in the worst cases; or as seems to be the pattern in Britain, through unannounced sudden changes to the regimes of taxes and subsidies; or in the case of the individual, through the pillorying of the individual concerned in the 'court of public opinion'.

To take this last category first, it is quite proper for ministers to have a view on the salaries of those employed at all levels of the public sector. Indeed, they – or a suitably independent body – ought to set those salaries. Stretching a point, it could be argued that the remuneration of all directors of limited-liability entities is a legitimate area for ministerial intervention, given that limited liability is, in effect, a gift from the public to the private sector. Furthermore, at a time of great economic difficulty it is arguable that ministers are entitled to impose limits on pay for all groups of employees, as happened in the United Kingdom from 1972 to 1974, and again from 1975 to 1978.

Finally, should it be thought a senior external appointment to a public sector position has somehow obtained unfair contract terms, it is right that this should be investigated and possible avenues for redress on behalf of the taxpayer be looked at.

The case of Stephen Hester, chief executive of the state-owned Royal Bank of Scotland, in January 2012 fitted none of these categories. A former investment banker, he had been hired by the previous Labour administration to bring the bank back to profitability and lower the level of risk involved in the 82 per cent public stake. Early in 2012, it emerged that the board had approved a bonus for Mr Hester of £963,000, payable in shares. At that point the 'court of public opinion' decided he ought to get nothing, and after days of intense pressure he waived his bonus on 30 January.

Chancellor George Osborne said it was a 'sensible and welcome' decision that now let Mr Hester focus on getting back billions of pounds for the taxpayer. In any other context, it would have been extraordinary had someone's employer (Mr Osborne's relationship, in effect, with Mr Hester) congratulated the employee on not taking money or other earnings to which they were entitled, and gone on to suggest that the absence of this troublesome entitlement would now allow the employee concerned to do his job more effectively.

Funnily enough, strife-torn Syria was in the news on the day Mr Hester waived his bonus. There was no obvious connection, other than that the treatment the previous year of Syria's ambassador to London ought to have given fair warning of the instincts of the political and administrative class in twenty-first-century Britain.

Dr Sami Khiyami had been invited to the wedding of Prince William and Kate Middleton, which took place on 29 April 2011. But his likely presence as a guest was becoming increasingly controversial as the event grew near, as Syria reacted in an ever more heavy-handed way to domestic protest. Little however, could be done – as Nick Clegg pointed out, 'who attended the Royal wedding was a matter for the Royal Family, not the Government'.[1]

Shortly afterwards the Foreign Office announced on 28 April that it would after all take a hand in this 'family wedding', and had withdrawn the invitation: '[T]he Foreign Secretary [William Hague] has decided that the presence of the Syrian ambassador at the Royal Wedding would be unacceptable and that he should not attend.'

Time was when the United Kingdom prided itself on doing the right thing even though the heavens were likely to fall – the 1973 arrival in the teeth of much public hostility of 30,000 Asians expelled from Uganda is one example. Of course, the public dignity of the Syrian ambassador scarcely compares with the forced expulsion of families from their homeland on Africa's east coast only to end up homeless at *inter alia* a former army base at Maresfield in Sussex. If anything he more closely resembled a foreign apologist for the Asians' persecutor, the late Ugandan tyrant Idi Amin, than any of Amin's victims.

But that is the whole point. There would have been little courage required to stand by an invitation to the representative of a universally admired public figure such as Nelson Mandela. Doing the right thing is only courageous when it is unpopular, sometimes deeply so.

True, this self-image of stiff-necked rectitude in all such matters was not always supported by the United Kingdom's actual behaviour. But now 'getting it right', doing things properly, scarcely seems to be a priority of any sort. It is one thing to temper justice with mercy. It is another to abandon probity for the sake of good publicity.

What goes for individuals' pay packets goes also for company profits. In the Budget of 23 March 2011, the Treasury sprang a £2 billion a year tax raid on North Sea oil companies. They were unpopular, so why not? The idea of a so-called 'mansion tax' on the most expensive residential properties is forever doing the rounds in government circles. New taxes are proposed, and sometimes levied, on a range of sporadically unpopular phenomena: alcohol, bankers' bonuses, car-parking spaces, patio heaters and many others. What is lawful or even praiseworthy one moment can quickly become a pariah activity, singled out for punitive treatment.

Beyond the strictly fiscal field, various regulatory regimes can have much the same effect in terms of depriving people and businesses of their assets. Obvious areas include regulation of financial products, foodstuffs, over-the-counter medicines, licensed premises and public entertainment. It is not the fact that the authorities seek to impose regulations in these and other areas that is odd or surprising. It would be strange were they not to do so. What is bizarre is the apparently random and often contradictory nature of the regulatory approach, often swinging wildly between deregulation and reregulation, as seen in casino gambling and pub opening hours.

Selecting investments in such a climate is fraught with obvious hazards. A regulatory change can wipe out a business every bit as easily as can an abrupt change in taxation.

A third and deeply frightening form of political risk arises from civil disorder and the widespread destruction of property. The rioting that swept through British cities between 4 and 10 August 2011 caused hundreds of millions of pounds' worth of damage, and subjected business premises to looting and outright destruction. The performance of the police, lamentable in the early days of the disorder, drew widespread criticism. For many, the rioting marked a qualitative change in the social climate.

Usually peaceful suburbs were under siege; meanwhile, there was increasing violence in other towns. The Government belatedly appeared to regain control in London but the electorate's trust that the cavalry would show up if they call 999 has been shattered. It no longer feels as if we live in a civilised country.[2]

In Southall, Sikhs, some armed with ceremonial swords and hockey sticks, took to the streets to defend homes, businesses and places of worship. But for those lacking such a community response capability, the riots will have given pause for extensive thought about the location and security of physical business investments. Of course, such investments can always be insured against wanton violence, but the certainty that the insurer will pay up is itself a feature of a first world economy. Interference with the terms and conditions of insurance contracts has become commonplace, as judges, ministers and officials seek to use the insurance industry to pursue non-commercial goals, as with the prohibition of taking into account actuarial differences between men and women. The near-certainty that disorder on a similar scale will be repeated, and the doubt whether the police response will be any more effectual next time, would seem to weigh heavily against any investments that involve an extensive physical presence in urban areas: bars, restaurants, residential letting, warehouses, transport depots, and of course the rioters' first target: retailing.

Even outside the traditional inner-city areas, wise investors will want to keep the identifiable physical presence of their investments to a minimum.

Some will say we have missed areas of political risk that ought to have been given prominence, not least the prospect of one unstable coalition government after another, reflecting deep divisions within the electorate. There may be those who believe a key cause of political instability is the mixture of increasing levels of tax-dodging combined with a ravenous appetite for public goods, the very combination that helped give us the economic goriness that is Greece. Terrorism, the taking up of arms against the state by its own subjects – whether affiliates of Al-Qaeda or variations on the Continuity IRA – is given too little prominence, others may claim. What of inflation, fuelled by hundreds of billions of pounds of Bank of England funny money, the so-called quantitative easing scheme? What of the 'lost generation' of the young unemployed, combustible material, surely, for political extremists?

We take on board these criticisms and believe the threats listed are real and present dangers. That we gave prominence to other political risks reflected our personal judgement.

But we have less respect for those who insist the concept of political risk has no place in a mature democracy, that it belongs in Nigeria or Peru but not here. That political risk is something found only in third world countries.

Quite so.

Everything you know is wrong: structuring business and investment in a third world economy

The structure of your investment vehicle or vehicles is as important as the choice of the investments themselves. Conventional wisdom has it that the public limited company – a limited liability entity that is entitled to offer its shares to the public – is, all things being equal, the premier choice for the investor, as the manager of investments (such as a pension fund or other asset-management company), as the direct repository of investors' funds in terms of the purchase of their shares, and for the more successful professional investor, as the vehicle through which investments are managed. These are the big beasts of the financial scene. Use their asset-management services, buy their shares, set up a PLC of your own, should you be rich enough, and then you can issue your own shares, allowing other investors to buy a piece of your investment success.

This is the conventional wisdom. And it is wrong.

In a third world economy, the PLC is a sitting target. PLCs may be big beasts. So were the dinosaurs. Since the days of President Theodore Roosevelt, incorporated businesses have been expected to submit to surveillance and regulation in return for the privilege of limited liability. But in a developing country, this routine and entirely proper expectation is overlaid with bizarre and random demands from the state: switches in taxation, 'crackdowns' on high executive pay, and submission to 'codes of conduct' on a huge range of subjects from the availability of work experience to displays of sweets in places where children might see them.

Just one government body, the Financial Reporting Council, produces reams of regulations and recom-mendations on auditing standards, boardroom structures, accounting standards, actuarial practice and the standards of 'stewardship' expected from institutional shareholders. And this is just one body with a piece of the action in terms of 'corporate governance', a vague notion that, in true third world style, has swung round 180 degrees in its brief history. In the mid-1980s, it was thought hard-pressed managers needed protecting from greedy shareholders who would cash in the moment a bidder came along, while more recently the emphasis has been on keeping potentially maverick managers (and the huge bonuses they are thought to covet) under control.

Of course the routine, admonitory regulation of business activity is a given of a civilized society. But what we are discussing here is its opposite: random, sporadic official interference with business for a wide range of often-contradictory reasons and with little regard for the consequences. As British business has slipped down the international league table for competitiveness, so corporate governance bureaucracy has blossomed, in much the same way as Britain's dwindling sporting prowess has been matched by a flowering in the budgets and status of assorted sport 'governing bodies', busily conducting drug tests, banning and suspending sportspeople, investigating 'inappropriate betting activity' by players, and so forth.

No business activity, however small-scale or innocuous, can ever hope to be completely exempt from official notice. In government publicity for the Disability Discrimination Act 2005, for example, self-employed tradespeople were warned that if they had a website, they would need to ensure it was accessible to people with disabilities.

A correctly structured investment vehicle can provide a much smaller target for the authorities, giving greater freedom of manoeuvre to participants. And the design of this structure is dictated in large part by the fact that official interference 'bites' most severely at the junction between different types of economic actors: employer–employee, customer–supplier, fund manager–investor, shareholder–manager. By constructing a partnership or syndicate within which as many of these relationships as possible can be relabelled as those of a business partner, a structure can be created that is far less prone to interference and the abrupt swiping of resources by the third-world state than is the conventional PLC or even private limited company.

As an individual investor, you can join such a grouping as a partner. As a businessperson you might well choose to structure your business activity in this way, as far as is possible. The key objective is to create a truly private community of economic interests that contain as few as possible of the 'moving parts' at which official interference is directed.

Some types of businesses are easier to structure in this way than others. A transport company, for example, is unlikely to bring all its customers within the fold, unless it enjoys very long-term contracts with a small number of important clients. Much the same is probably true of a restaurant business. But such a structure would seem tailor-made for an investment company. Relabelling the participants as business partners means that huge amounts of regulation and interference directed at relationships between people of different status are eliminated.

We are coming close here to what Professor Ian Angell of the London School of Economics has called the difference between 'communities of law' and 'communities of trust'. The conventional PLC is an example of the former, with both its own operations and its relationships with customers and employees closely regulated. The community of law, when functioning properly, is the jewel in the crown of the first-world economy. It allows people to do business with people they have never met and are never going to meet, over immense distances and in very large quantities. It makes possible rapid economic growth because it allows for specialization and economies of scale. But for it to work, the legal framework must be predictable and impartial.

Once the legal and regulatory framework becomes prone to interference and manipulation for goals that have nothing to do with its original purpose – and when those goals themselves keep changing, from 'more enterprise' one week to 'greater social mobility' the next – the community of law becomes a much less attractive model and the community of trust much more so.

A community of trust, as the name implies, is a much more personal and legally informal structure. Participants are much more likely to know each other, and admission to such a community will rely on personal recommendation. To join a community of law, such as British Gas or Tesco, it is necessary only to buy some shares in a deep and liquid market. No such option is likely to be available when joining a community of trust.

Furthermore, paperwork and formal contracts play a less prevalent role in communities of trust than in communities of law. Apart from anything else, written records can create openings for regulation and interference, if only to the extent that they may be justiciable in the civil courts.

Official suspicion of communities of trust has traditionally been fuelled by the belief that they are vehicles for tax evasion. There is no a priori reason why this should be so. It is obviously the case that an absence of some aspects of formal book-keeping may be conducive to tax dodging, but there has never been much evidence that involvement in the affairs of a limited-liability company or similar enterprise is proof against such behaviour.

A more telling criticism is that economies dominated by communities of trust grow more slowly. Notwithstanding the hongs of Canton and Hong Kong and similar trading houses elsewhere in the Far East, this is likely to be proved overall to be correct. Growth is likely to be more patchy, both in general terms and geographically, in an economy where communities of trust play a significant role. This is inevitable when the important factor of personal relationships is inserted into the processes of trade and investment. But for the purposes of this chapter, that is not our concern.

One final and very critical aspect of such a business and investment structure is its total disconnection from any type of benefit, in cash or kind, distributed by the state. The list includes limited liability status (including limited liability partnership status), government grants, charitable status, offers of funding from state-backed venture capital funds, participation in government schemes to guarantee business loans or debts, and state funding for trainees or apprentices. He who pays the piper will, one way or another, end up calling the tune. In a well-regulated social democracy with extensive public-sector participation in the economy and many business assistance schemes, it may well make sense for business or investors to take advantage of them. Or they may prefer to emulate the frontier spirit of the most rugged brand of American-style free enterprise. Either way, there is a proper choice to be made. But no business person or investor ought to get entangled with the dysfunctional third world UK state. No good will come of it. *And what about preventive tax treatment*

The magnificent seven: some fruitful lines of enquiry

As we said at the start of this chapter, we do not have a list of share tips or other specific investment advice that will see our readers through what is bound to be a painful and volatile time, even were work to begin right now on 'redeveloping' the British economy. But we do have some suggestions, some general notions ('principles' sounds a little hifalutin') that we believe should inform asset allocation in submerging market Britain.

First and foremost, disabuse yourself of the idea that the United Kingdom's is simply an (albeit-troubled) ordinary Group of Seven economy. The surest way to lose money is to fail to recognize that submerging market Britain's investment landscape is prone to volatility and political interference.

These leads to our second axiom: keep your exits clear. The March 2011 surprise tax raid on North Sea oil and gas companies to fund a populist subsidy of fuel prices will not prove a one-off.

A third point to bear in mind is that, as we discussed at some length above, the best investments and investment vehicles are those that have the lowest profiles on the official radar. You could call them 'stealth investments'.

That said, and in a suitably diffident spirit, we offer some possible areas for fruitful enquiry.

First, companies and organizations offering genuinely private personal services: health, education, personal security, valuable work-related training. By 'genuinely', we mean that the provider is taking neither cash subsidies from the taxpayer nor subsidies in kind, such as charitable status, given that those who do so leave themselves open to interference. As state-provided or at least funded services in these areas become ever more burdened with bizarre requirements, often contradictory, from the official class, the demand for those that are completely independent will grow. We have no wish to second-guess the likely outcome of reforms currently in hand in all of these areas. We would ask you simply to look at the record of all such reforms over the last 25 years and take a clear-eyed view of whether you think independent provision in these areas is likely to become more or less popular.

A word of caution: your due diligence ought to include the most detailed scrutiny of just how independent these providers really are. At the first sign of involvement in government schemes, or the acceptance of public money, you ought to consider pulling out. The same goes for taking benefits in kind, in particular charitable status. There really is no such thing as a free lunch when it comes to taking handouts of any sort from a submerging market state.

A second area of fruitful investigation ought to include the providers of stand-alone domestic equipment: generators, air-conditioners, water-filtration systems, self-contained gas supplies, emergency computer back-up devices and similar. We do not backtrack for a moment from our earlier contention that a total breakdown of organized society, along the lines of the 1970s television dramas *Survivors* (1975) and *Quatermass* (1979), is not on the cards. But neither do we believe that the (reasonably) smoothly running public services and utilities of recent decades will continue as they are. We foresee brownouts and blackouts with regard to the electricity supply, water shortages, interruptions to gas supplies and breaks in the coverage of fixed-line and mobile telephone services.

Anybody able to supply equipment that will allow people to bypass the worst effects of such disruptions ought to be in a position to command high prices, so this presents a potentially lucrative home for investment. It ought not to be underestimated just how physically and emotionally dependent the public has become on all these utilities, electric power in particular, even compared with the 1970s, the last period of widespread interruption to the current. Gone are the days, for example, when a gas boiler could be lit with a match. Today they are sealed units operated by electricity. As for the dependence on computer systems – themselves highly vulnerable to problems in the electricity supply and telephone services – this provides huge opportunities for businesses able to offer comprehensive back-up that enables users to both keep connections open and perhaps equally important, save their data.

Third, on perhaps a happier note, there should be growth opportunities in the value of companies able to supply equipment allowing people to insulate themselves from the vagaries of smoking bans, drink-driving crackdowns and proposed calorie-counted restaurant menus by becoming, at home, their own bartender, restaurateur, cinema owner and so forth. The recent trend for 'pop-up restaurants' in people's own homes is, we believe, an early example of this. Suppliers of home brew and home-fermentation kits will flourish as drink taxes are inevitably ramped up. Such kits, too often a joke in the past, are likely to become more sophisticated, as will their products. Brewers and vineyards will complain vociferously about 'unfair competition' but there will be little that can be done about it. There ought also to be opportunities to invest in private, informal dining and drinking clubs, based in homes and other private premises, but care will need to be taken to ensure such investment does not amount to an admission that the establishment concerned is in effect a business that is flouting licensing and other laws. There ought to be ways round this, not least by employing the partnership/ syndicate principles outlined above.

Indeed, what is true for 'informal' bars and eateries ought also to hold good for theatrical and cinema clubs and private venues for live performance of all types, not to mention private museums and art galleries. As mainstream venues stagger under the weight of burdensome health, safety, 'accessibility' and 'diversity' regulations, smaller, more exclusive establishments ought to have a bright future. But again, great care must be taken to ensure that investment in such an establishment is not taken by the authorities as proof of the existence of something that ought to come within their purview. The club or syndicate principle ought to provide substantial protection in this area, but it is unlikely to be total protection, especially given the penchant for judges in a submerging market economy to make up bits of law as they go along to suit their own prejudices, rather than sticking to statute and precedent.

Fourth, food production and manufacture. Behind the smoke and fury of volatile commodity prices, there is a clear trend emerging – Britain is paying more for food and is going to have to pay still more. Not for decades has a stake in a farm seemed so attractive, especially an arable farm, given its insulation from rises in feed prices. The brave talk at the turn of the century about eliminating farm subsidies and allowing British farmers either to pay their way in the world or pack in agriculture and turn their farms into golf courses sounds like the chatter of a bygone age – which, in a sense, it is.

There will be big panics over food shortages. Anybody living in outer suburbs or market towns during the heavy winters of 2009–10 and 2010–11 will remember the reaction once it dawned on the local population that, if they were unable to use the main roads, then neither could the delivery fleets of Tesco, Sainsbury's, Asda and Morrisons. Supermarket shelves were stripped bare in a matter of hours. Yet that will be nothing compared with the frenzied stockpiling likely to accompany what will probably be repeated panics in the future. Ministers will make ineffectual noises about 'tackling hoarding'. Chickens and even pigs will be kept in back gardens. Thefts of crops and livestock from farms will become as common as metal thefts are now. Rural police forces will complain they can do little to stop the rustlers, because of lack of resources –

another opportunity for the private security businesses mentioned above.

Fifth, other basic commodities. What is true for goods is true also for metal, minerals, oil and gas. The late 1990s, when oil tankers roamed the oceans unable to find anywhere to dock as nobody wanted their cargo, are long gone. Oil is more than ten times the price of that time. Base metals have done well, as has bullion. It is a truism that none of these investments is for the faint-hearted. But should you judge that their price, expressed the only way it can be, in inflating paper currencies, will continue to rise, then the strategy of buy and hold suggests itself.

Sixth, we turn to land and property. On the face of it, this is a perverse area to which to drawn attention. Is not real estate likely to be a prime target for taxation and even confiscation? Indeed is it not, because of its fixed nature, likely to bear an ever-heavier burden of taxation in years ahead, as more fleet-footed targets either depart our shores or engage in ever more intricate tax planning? Not for nothing is property known in romance languages as 'immobile goods'. It cannot go anywhere. Truly, this is a sitting duck.

All true. Yet we believe there are opportunities with regard to the most carefully chosen sorts of properties, either in remote yet desirable locations or in the roundly despised but inevitably sought-after gated communities. The trick is to spot properties whose desirability on the one hand and whose taxation profile on the other have, for whatever reason, diverged and are likely to remain divergent. The most obvious example of this is a residential property whose book value remains below the threshold for the proposed (and quite likely to be implemented) 'mansion tax' but on which the profit on the original purchase price remains substantial.

Seventh, businesses involved in the provision of reliable

and resilient private channels for cash transmission, medicine distribution, the movement of valuables and the transport, both physical and electronic, of important documents are likely to find their services much in demand. Publicly owned or regulated channels are likely to continue to disappoint; in third world style, their many failures will be shrugged off by super-abundant managers, none of whom will accept irresponsibility. Discreet, reliable, entirely private services will, we believe, step into the gap.

Another type of what may be called point-to-point communication may well also. flourish as various drawbacks to online communication make themselves ever more evident, not least that 'online is forever', in that somewhere a copy of everything you ever sent anybody is likely to be lurking. That covers love letters, detailed proposals for dubious business dealings, and everything in between. Online is also open and universally accessible, or if you prefer hopelessly insecure, regardless of how many services are available supposedly to encrypt information. Hence the huge number of US State Department cables that a leaker was able to download on to a small personal computer drive and supply to the WikiLeaks site. Apparently the Post-It note has made a big comeback in US government circles. Understandably so – it cannot be hacked into. Finally, a rather more ominous aspect of the WikiLeaks affair of 2010–11 arose from the announcement that a number of payments services would not process contributions to WikiLeaks. This was an aspect of the online cashless society that had not exactly been broadcast. What would be banned next? Communist Party membership fees perhaps, or blue-movie subscriptions. Suddenly, good, old-fashioned cash was looking a whole lot more attractive.

In short, point-to-point services will not be confined to movements of physical objects, important though these will be, but will also deal with communication. We anticipate a noticeable comeback for those services that have no server, no memory, no hard drive and no other users of that particular channel: telephone calls, letters, telexes and the traditional point-to-point fax machine.

These areas are, of course, fairly defensive in nature. But there is scope for the daring investor to 'game' third world Britain, riding upwards the share prices of those who pocket large government contracts – IT consultants, defence companies, suppliers of dubious 'training and evaluation' services to central and local government – and with luck, bailing out before the inevitable project cancellation. But beware. There will be those better informed than you are who are likely to have cashed out before you have the chance. Furthermore, there is always the danger that you will fall for the sales patter from these businesses as they play the patriotism card, insisting that 'Britain can make it' and that the service they have been contracted to provide to the public sector will be 'world class'. Should you swallow this sort of thing it is likely you will lose a substantial amount of your investment.

It is far better, if less admirable perhaps, to think like an expatriate. See both your investments and the British economy as a whole through a foreigners' eyes, even if – or perhaps especially if – you personally are as British as roast beef and light ale. Expats are far more fully insulated against sentiment and wishful thinking. They keep their escape routes clear, as we recommend above. They keep a second passport handy, when possible. They do not leave their assets in vulnerable locations where they can be subjected without warning to special levies and taxes. Such imposts may be justified on grounds of fairness and social justice. Expats may well be wholeheartedly in favour of both, but they doubt that the dysfunctional state machine is likely to use their resources properly to these ends, and prefer to make their own disbursements. Expats are unimpressed by politicians' claims that 'we are all in this together', a sort-of latter-day reprise of the Dunkirk spirit. They see clearly the fractious convoy of powerful interest groups – finance, the public sector, defence contractors and so forth – that make up the British establishment.

It would be easy to dismiss our expats as unattractive figures. Perhaps they are. Yet how many of the battered commuters that stream every day into our big cities, London in particular, already display some of these characteristics? To them, the city is no more attractive than an oil-rig, a place to earn good money before heading home in evenings, weekends and holidays to begin 'real' life with family and loved ones, far from the dirt, the crowds, the traffic jams, endless police sirens, disrupted public transport and general aggravation.

Furthermore, their lack of wishful thinking make these characters uniquely well placed to judge the question we raised at the start of this chapter, the extent to which a malfunctioning economy is, by definition, less likely to provide a satisfactory home for savings and investments than one that works properly.

There will be those who claim that the very turbulence and insecurity inherent in a submerging market economy will make it easier rather than harder to make money from clever investment decisions. The steady-state of a first world economy offers fewer opportunities for a real killing, they will say. After all, there are rather more billionaires to be found per head of population in Russia and China than there are in Austria or Switzerland. For the strong-hearted, the third world is the place to be.

That is one view. Another would take as its starting

point the truly grim outlook for British society painted by author Graeme Maxton in *The End of Progress: How modern economics has failed us*.[3] Maxton's starting point is that not only is the United Kingdom heading into the relegation zone to developing status, pretty much the whole developed world is doing so. Water, food and energy are about to become scarce. So is money. The flabby, over-indebted west is in no position to compete in the sharp-elbowed climate of tomorrow. The United Kingdom, perhaps, is one of the least well-equipped in this department.

Furthermore, Maxton warns, post-industrial Britain will not be some downshifter's paradise, in which the rat race becomes a thing of the past, along with dreary suburban conformity, pointless materialistic aspirations and terrified acquiescence in the workplace instructions of The Man. This is not television's *The Good Life* (1975). Indeed, Maxton seems to think it rather more likely to prove The Bad Life. It will become more urban (as petrol cost rises make transport more expensive), diets will worsen (as people eat more cheap, filling, stodgy food) and so will health (as the price of medicines rises).

The trouble with making profitable investments against such a background is twofold. One, the majority of the population will be buying standardized, low-value commodity products, for the simple reason that few people will be able to afford anything else. That is not a promising environment for the investor. And two, the political temptation to interfere in the distribution of consumer goods in order to try to underwrite some of the staples of life will be hard to resist. Maxton foresees rationing of some goods.

All that said, even the downbeat consumer landscape that he foresees is not likely to prove an investment-free zone. And persuasive though his book is, we have made it clear that we do not foresee long periods of a quasi-Soviet Britain in which a downtrodden citizenry shuffles from one queue to another. Indeed, the third world future that we forecast would in many ways be rather garish and over-lit.

In this new climate, one piece of sound advice for the investor is never to buy anything for nostalgic or sentimental reasons. We greatly admire the spirit of the grand Hungarian lady in this scene set just after the First World War, but cannot recommend her investment strategy:

> 'Where have you been for the past few months? Don't you know what has happened? We have a socialist government! At any moment we – you, I, people like us – will be removed from our property, our land will be taken away. And you – you choose this time to go and buy back your house!'
>
> 'And my land.'
>
> Alfred blew his cheeks out and let the air escape in a hiss of irritation. 'What on earth are you doing, Luiza Kaldy, buying something you may only have for a day!'[4]

More bracingly realistic is the advice in what is if not the best certainly the funniest and most stylishly-written investment guide of the last 30 years, *The Zurich Axioms* by Max Gunther:

> Do not get rooted in long-range plans or long-term investments. Instead react to events as they unfold in the present. Put your money into ventures as they present themselves and withdraw it from hazards as they loom up. Value the freedom of movement that will allow you to do this. Don't ever sign that freedom away.[5]

All this may sound, as with the accusation made in the Arthur Hailey quotation at the head of this chapter, like trying to corner the market in a vaccine while a plague rages. We do not agree, and believe we are merely offering what we hope are realistic lines of enquiry for people seeking to protect their assets during the nadir of Britain's submerging market status.

Climbing out that nadir will require some equally realistic thinking, to which we now turn.

Chapter 10

After the illusions

The world in the next century is going to look more like Africa than like Europe.

Iris Murdoch, *The Book and the Brotherhood*, 1987

'Where does this all leave us, sir?'
'Things are moving fast.'
'We're getting near the end, you mean?'
'We were always near the end.'

Colin Dexter, *The Remorseful Day*, 1999

I see you stand like greyhounds in the slips,
Straining upon the start. The game's afoot:
Follow your spirit.

William Shakespeare, *Henry V*, c. 1599

It was getting on for 5.30 in the afternoon when Geoff Hurst lashed in a shot from the edge of the penalty area at Wembley Stadium to seal England's 4–2 victory over West Germany in the World Cup final. Never again has English football scaled the heights that it did on Saturday 30 July 1966 in North London; the story ever since has been one of supreme underachievement as other nations have exposed the limitations of the country that invented the 'beautiful game'.

At first, it was only traditional rivals that put England in the shade: the Germans, the Italians, the Brazilians, the Argentinians. More recently, however, the national team has struggled to cope with the challenge from the game's lesser lights, drawing with Algeria and the United States in the group stages of the 2010 World Cup in South Africa before being thrashed 4–1 by the Germans in the first knockout round.

There was plenty of soul-searching when the lavishly paid England 'stars' flew home in humiliation. In the past, excuses for World Cup failure have been that the hot weather sapped the players' strength; that they were not used to games at high altitude; that they had been missing key players; that British coaches were light years behind their continental counterparts. In 2006 the story was that they had been distracted by the presence in the German spa town of Baden Baden of their shopaholic wives and girlfriends; four years later in South Africa it was that they were pining for the so-called WAGs in their monastic footballing retreat, their lovelorn state rendering each player incapable of passing the ball to one of their team mates. Other familiar get-outs were that England had been robbed by dodgy referees, by foreign players with a strong thespian bent or by just plain bad luck, but none of these really applied to a tournament played in South Africa in winter when a full-strength England was – despite, it has to be admitted, one blatant refereeing blunder – beaten by a demonstrably superior German team. The English team was even managed by an Italian, the Football Association having apparently come to the conclusion that if Japanese management could breathe new life into what had appeared to be a doomed car industry, Fabio Capello, with an illustrious curriculum vitae that included spells at AC Milan and Real Madrid, could do the same for 11 men kicking a ball around on a large lawn. He couldn't, it transpired.

After due deliberation, the pundits (of whom there were many) concluded that it was not really Capello's fault and that the English game had been going south for decades, with the one-off triumph in 1966 masking the scale of the relative decline. This was a reasonable assessment. The teams from other countries were more skilful, had been better coached from an early age, and played an altogether more dynamic version of the game than the one-dimensional plodding fare served up by England at Wembley, which in keeping with the spirit of Concorde had been rebuilt since the glory days of 1966 at many times the original budget. True, the English premiership was considered to be the most exciting in the world, but most of the star players were mercenaries from overseas, attracted by salaries of £100,000-plus a week made possible by selling the television rights to Rupert Murdoch's BSkyB.

The mood of national sporting introspection did not, however, last long, and when England qualified with relative ease (under Capello) for the next international competition, the 2012 European championships hosted jointly by Poland and the Ukraine, there was once again talk about the merits of the English game – the physical strength, the never-say-die spirit – and how there really was not all that much to choose between the boys with the three lions on the shirt and the Dutch, the Italians and the Spanish.

Football is not, of course, the only sport exported from these islands in the nineteenth century in which the 'old country' now finds itself routinely upstaged by foreign rivals: cricket, rugby and tennis are three others. Even so, the parallels between the national game and the national economy are particularly stark: the complacency, the failure to adapt, the many false dawns, the way imported talent has shown up the deficiencies of the domestic workforces, and the belief that with one or two tweaks all will be well again. The tendency of football clubs to live well beyond their means, paying wages they cannot remotely afford, is in keeping with the British way of doing things.

There are periods of gloomy introspection in which a determination to remedy deep-seated ills is professed, accompanied typically by the appointment of a new manager with go-ahead ideas, and followed by a couple of encouraging results. This gives rise to talk of a new dawn for English football; a new dawn which, alas, always proves to be false. The boom–bust cycle applies to football just as much as it does to the economy, only with fewer highs and rather more lows. For many clubs, the most important man at the ground is no longer the chairman, the manager or the star striker, but the administrator appointed by the creditors to get a grip on the insolvent club's affairs. Since 1992, half the members of the Football League have been in administration. More recently, Portsmouth became the first of the elite Premier League to go the same way.

As with the economy, there have been plenty of warning signs of impending or actual decline: the 1–0 defeat by the United States in 1950; the 6–3 hammering by Hungary in 1953 in what was the first defeat for England at Wembley by a team from outside the British Isles; the failure to qualify for successive world cups in the 1970s. All were ignored or quickly forgotten. Despite not having won anything for 46 years, there remains to this day a belief that England is the slumbering giant of world football.

Ominously, if anything the Walter Mitty tendency is even more apparent in those charged with running the national economy.

Downward bound: life in the relegation zone

It is perhaps worth, at this point, recapping the main themes of this book. Britain has been in relative decline for more than a century, and none of the many remedies that have been tried has worked. The past decade has highlighted the country's structural weaknesses: its narrow industrial focus; its dysfunctional financial sector that serves itself but not the wider business community; the heavy dependency on debt, both public and private; the chronic balance of payments problem; the greater vulnerability to inflation than other nations; the lack of work for graduates; the inadequacy of an education system that has left more than a million people aged under 25 without work while jobs are taken by better-qualified migrant workers; the severing of the country both by geography and income; the growing insecurity of energy supplies. In 2009 and 2010, the government borrowed £1 for every £10 produced by the economy, the sort of fiscal profligacy that Britain had only previously resorted to when engaged in a life or death struggle with Napoleon, Kaiser Wilhelm II and Hitler. This time, the borrowing was to shore up Britain's banks. As one observer put it:

> Except perhaps in America and Ireland, no democratic country has ever imposed so great a burden on its ordinary citizens for the benefit and protection of that country's wealthiest elite. The worst kleptocrats of Africa and Asia must be watching in astonishment. They never knew it could be this easy.[1]

To be sure, there will be those who will say that the United Kingdom also has some innate strengths, and we would agree with them. It is, for now, a stable democracy, where it is relatively easy to set up a business and where foreign investors do not for the moment fear that their assets will be appropriated by an unfriendly government, although growing problems in this area are identified in Chapter 9. Central London's property market, kept buoyant by demand from Russian oligarchs, Indian magnates and Chinese billionaires while prices elsewhere in the country have sagged, is evidence that the world's super-rich currently feel comfortable in Belgravia and Mayfair.

Over the past decade, it has been fortunate that the United Kingdom has had its own currency and has been able to run an independent monetary policy. Without that flexibility, the recession would have been even deeper and longer, the austerity even more painful. There are sectors of the global economy, pharmaceuticals and aerospace in particular, where Britain more than holds its own. The army, the BBC and the leading UK universities are all not-for-profit organizations that remain world-class in their different ways, although all three are threatened by the country's descent into submerging market status. There are actors, architects, film directors, lawyers and designers who are ranked among the best. London, warts and all, is one of the world's great cities, although that greatness is likely to shrink as the warts grow.

Our point is that the strengths are outweighed by the weaknesses, and will soon be overwhelmed by them. To us, the lost decade of growth, the falling real incomes, the gap between rich and poor, the cuts in public spending, the drying up of North Sea oil, the hollowing out of manufacturing and the overweening power of the financial sector are all indicative of an economy going south. The pretence of being a military power was exposed during the air strikes against Libya, when the Royal Air Force had to be lent missiles by the Pentagon because it did not have enough of its own. The United Kingdom has a malfunctioning economy, vast liabilities and is close to going broke. The official view of the United Kingdom a decade hence is of a country in harmony, with balanced public finances, an appropriate mixture of private-sector entrepreneurship in health and education; the right mixture of finance and manufacturing; a gleaming new infrastructure and new sources of sustainable energy. The alternative vision is of a country where the state is shrinking not through choice but through penury, the search is still on for new sources of growth, the infrastructure projects are mothballed for lack of money, and the plans to harness the wind, the tides and the sun are still on the drawing board. History suggests the latter is the more likely direction of travel, and if Britain is to avoid becoming shabbier, meaner and poorer, weaknesses need to be addressed before it is too late.

To continue with our sporting theme, there is no reason why countries – any more than football teams – should retain their place in the league table. Take this list: Accrington Stanley, Aston Villa, Blackburn Rovers, Bolton Wanderers, Burnley, Derby County, Everton, Notts County, Preston North End, Stoke, West Bromwich Albion and Wolverhampton Wanderers. These clubs, all from the Midlands and the north of England, were the 12 founder members of the Football League in 1888, when Britain's economic centre of gravity was in its industrial heartlands and the challenge from Germany and the United States was just starting to become apparent. In the 2011–12 season, seven of this illustrious dozen were still in the elite group of clubs in the English premiership, although four of them were battling against relegation, and none of the other three – Aston Villa, Everton and Stoke – were challenging for the title. As the gap between them and the top clubs widened, fans of Villa and Everton had to comfort themselves with the knowledge that there had once been a time when they were winning trophies and were considered the best in the land.

In the context of this book, the United States and Germany are Manchester United and Arsenal: teams that have been through the occasional bad period, often lasting for some years, in which they have struggled but have always found a way of reinvigorating themselves, and as a result, have performed consistently well for the past 100 years. Britain is not yet an Accrington Stanley or a Notts County, both playing in a lower division and with little hope of regaining their place among the elite. That fate may well be in store unless the rot is stopped, and there are plenty of big clubs that have slipped rapidly down through the divisions. It would be tempting to categorize the United Kingdom as an Everton or an Aston Villa, a club not just with a great tradition, but with the potential to compete once again for the game's big prizes. That, though, is the sort of fantasy beloved of football fans, who live on past glory and hope, despite all the recent evidence to the contrary, that the glory days will one day come back. In reality, the events of the past five years have exposed the United Kingdom for what it really is: a Bolton Wanderers or a Wolverhampton Wanderers, a club close to the bottom of the premier league of nations, short of cash, heading in the wrong direction and facing a long, hard battle to avoid relegation. There is a footballing cliché that the table does not lie, but that cliché could apply with equal force to the performance of the British economy – slow-growing, unproductive, unequal, unbalanced and living beyond its means.

Be that as it may, the fantasy lives on that the United Kingdom is just a couple of policy reforms and a slice of luck away from a seat back at the top table. As we finished writing this book, the government was extolling the virtues of apprenticeships as one of the cures for youth unemployment, then rising steadily towards 25 per cent of all those under 25. While these conjured up images of a mediaeval stone mason teaching his indentured employee how to adorn gothic cathedrals with gargoyles, the reality was that many were simply 12-week training courses provided by private-sector firms with no guaranteed jobs at the end. Historically apprenticeships had always been a form of cheap labour, but for the young worker there had been the promise of a 'trade' at the end of it. Learning how to stack a shelf at Tesco or how to collect the shopping trolleys from the far-flung corners of the car park at Asda does not really live up to the sepia-tinted image.

Meanwhile, the Labour opposition was looking (once again) with envious eyes at the German model, seen as the essence of a modern, prosperous, sustainable social-democratic state. Under Tony Blair and Gordon Brown, Labour had flirted with Rhenish capitalism, but soon abandoned ideas such as workers' participation on boards and the need to forge long-term relationships between companies and their bankers in favour of what was seen as the more 'dynamic' American model. Only when the aforementioned 'dynamism' resulted in the most serious financial and economic crisis in eight decades did Labour decide that there might be something in the German way of doing things after all. As has been proved on many occasions and in many different countries, admiring the Germans is one thing; importing the model lock, stock and barrel is another. The chances of the United Kingdom becoming the next Germany are currently on a par with England winning the next World Cup in Brazil.

As we have tried to show in this book, the problems go deeper than that. We don't profess to have a miracle cure, and are suspicious of those who say that one exists, because the evidence of the past 100 years is that all the supposed instant remedies have proved to be the potions of quack doctors. But there are lessons to be learned, not just from the postwar history of the developed world, but also from the emerging market economies that are rapidly approaching in Britain's rear-view mirror. These lessons have to be fully assimilated and acted upon, because the time for illusion is over. It is not just a question of adopting a different system of taxation or limiting the ability of the commercial banks to create credit – however commendable those individual ideas may be in themselves.

One hundred years of pretending to be a 'big beast' have to end, and end now. There has to be an acceptance, like that in Germany, France and Japan in 1945, that the country has hit rock bottom and needs to change. In football, this happens all the time; a new manager goes to a struggling club and proceeds to clear out the dead wood. This has never happened to the United Kingdom, and even now the country does not seem ready for the sort of cathartic moment that the defeated Axis powers had at the end of the Second World War. Our fear is that even now there is a belief that all will be well, that something will turn up, that Britain will muddle through. The temptation, as ever, will be to look at the events of the past decade as another occasion where disaster was averted by a whisker. The reality is, however, that this is not an economic Dunkirk, a miraculous escape from disaster; it is an economic Suez, the moment when the United Kingdom has to face the truth about its diminished status in the world.

Let's take our sporting analogy one stage further. Imagine that the United Kingdom is a struggling Premier League football team and that a new manager has just been appointed to avoid the drop. What would he say? In our view, his rebuilding programme would have four distinct themes: an honest appraisal of the club's predicament; better coaching; the need for a strong central spine to the team; and the recognition that the decline will continue unless the players themselves want to change. The successful developing countries in Asia have broadly followed this approach: they have owned up, they have brained up, they have built up and they have worked their way up. Here in Britain, we may think that there is nothing to be learned from South Korea, Taiwan or the People's Republic of China, but that would be a mistake.

Champions League? You're having a laugh

The United Kingdom's was not the only economy to suffer during the Great Recession of 2008–09. Other countries – notably the manufacturing powerhouses of Germany and Japan – suffered bigger falls in output, as a slump in confidence and a lack of finance led to a contraction in production and trade. The 7 per cent drop in the UK gross domestic product was certainly large, but what really set the United Kingdom apart from France, Germany or the United States among the developed countries, and China, India and Brazil among the leading emerging nations, was the sluggishness of the recovery. The reason was simple: the United Kingdom was like a team far too dependent on two or three star players – financial services, the housing market and public spending – all of which had seen better days. Bank of England research (2012), for example, showed that the collapse of the housing bubble was responsible for a quarter of the drop in UK output during the recession of 2008–09.

Money had been sprayed around during the half-decade from 2007 to 2012, with the Treasury borrowing £500 billion to fund public spending and the Bank of

England creating a further £325 billion of electronic money through the gilt-buying programme known as quantitative easing. But the return on that investment had been poor: the economy grew by less than 1 per cent in 2011 and was expected to expand even more feebly in 2012. This, in short, was a country not nearly as strong as it thought it was. When the Institute for Fiscal Studies (IFS), the independent think-tank, published its assessment of the state of the nation ahead of the 2012 Budget, it concluded: 'The UK likely re-entered recession at the end of 2011. Near term prospects are bleak with a number of headwinds hampering the economy'.[2] In the longer term, it was assumed by the Bank of England, the Treasury and the IFS that the economy would be rebalanced and that growth would pick up to its old pre-crisis rate.

One of the 'headwinds' identified by the IFS was the severe budgetary pain planned by the government. The think-tank noted that despite having been in power for almost two years, the Conservative-Liberal Democrat coalition had barely begun to deliver on its promised austerity, with 94 per cent of the cuts in current spending by Whitehall departments and local government still to come. 'The impact of the remaining cuts to the services provided is difficult to predict; they are of a scale that has not been delivered in the UK since at least the Second World War.'[3] Famine was to follow feast, since the belt-tightening followed the largest sustained increase in public spending since 1945.

Yet for all its tough talk, the coalition government formed after the 2010 general election was pursuing the continuation of the politics of the past 100 years: faux modernization to disguise decline. The mantra for the coalition was that under the previous Labour government, Tony Blair and Gordon Brown had acted like a couple of spendthrift Premier League managers, wasting money on a stadium they could not afford and paying inflated salaries for players of little talent. Productivity figures for the public sector showed that there was more than a little truth in this accusation.

For David Cameron, the solution was a return to good husbandry. The United Kingdom would once again live within its means. Takings at the turnstiles plus the money from the club's sponsors would equal the players' wage bill and the cost of looking after the stadium. To be sure, the United Kingdom was a country that wanted to rise up the international league table and welcome the best foreign talent, but it would do so only once it had put its financial house in order. The government set great store by the judgment of the credit-rating agencies, notwithstanding the abject failure of Standard & Poor's, Moody's and Fitch to provide any warning about the sub-prime mortgage crisis that provided the trigger for the Great Crash of 2007. It came as something of a blow to the chancellor, George Osborne, to find in February 2012 that one of the rating agencies, Moody's, was threatening to strip the United Kingdom of its prized triple-A rating on the grounds that an economy hindered by austerity might grow too slowly to get to grips with its debts. In March 2012, Fitch revised its outlook on the United Kingdom to 'negative'.

Like all chancellors before him, Mr Osborne insisted that he had a strategy for growth, a strategy that with its mélange of red-tape cutting, tax incentives for business and nice fat contracts for infrastructure companies sounded remarkably similar to all the other (failed) growth strategies of the recent past. The government's boast was that the United Kingdom had the full confidence of the financial markets, which is why it was not in the same boat as the benighted eurozone countries that were having regular visits from International Monetary Fund (IMF) and European Union officials demanding structural adjustment to their economies in return for financial assistance.

As usual, there was a certain amount of self-delusion involved in this analysis. There was to be fair some reward for the government's willingness to tackle the budget deficit, but the real reason the United Kingdom was treated differently from Greece, Ireland, Portugal, Spain and Italy was that it had not joined the European monetary union. Those countries with deep-seated economic problems inside the single currency felt the pressure from the financial markets through the interest rate payable on their debt; those outside – like the United Kingdom – saw their currencies take the strain first. The pound was 25 per cent lower in 2012 than it had been five years earlier. Even then the depreciation, unlike those in the 1980s and 1990s, was insufficient to clear the UK current account deficit: the size of the productive base was no longer big enough.

In an attempt to mitigate the impact of the squeeze on 'front-line services' (a favourite phrase of politicians), the coalition decided to ransack various welfare payments – in particular, housing benefit and child benefit – and to scale back on public sector pensions. Some may see this move as a sign that David Cameron and Nick Clegg had chosen a full-blooded free-market model for the United Kingdom after weighing up the other options. The reality was much more banal and in keeping with the theme of this book: the raid on welfare was a classic manoeuvre of third world leaders to help themselves to the resources of a group or groups of people thought to be unpopular, whether the police, public sector officialdom or the very poor. Boris Johnson, the mayor of London, let the cat out of the bag when he attacked the plans to cap housing benefit at £400 a week on the grounds that it would lead to 'Kosovo-style cleansing' in the capital. Another unnamed Conservative MP told Benedict Brogan of *The Daily Telegraph* that the changes would be akin to the Highland clearances, the forced displacement of Scottish communities in the eighteenth and nineteenth centuries. In Westminster, a borough in which there were virtually no privately rented properties for less than £400 a week, some schools said almost half their pupils were affected, with families moved into bed and breakfast accommodation or homeless hostels.[4]

At the other end of the income scale, the government stripped the former chief executive of the Royal Bank of Scotland, Sir Fred Goodwin, of the knighthood awarded to him for 'services to banking' by the former Labour administration. He had been personally responsible for the ruinous decision to buy the Dutch bank ABN Amro, and came to be seen as the unacceptable face of the City. His reward for the biggest corporate loss in British financial history (£24.1 billion) was a pension of £350,000 a year. Sir Fred was by all accounts an abrasive character, and judging by his record, spectacularly incompetent. Yet, without getting embroiled in an argument about whether the United Kingdom should have an honours system at all, there was something unsettling about the government decision, taken at a time when public hostility towards bankers, inflamed by falling real incomes for the bulk of the population, was running high. For the most part, only someone who has committed a serious criminal offence can expect to be deprived of an honour in the United Kingdom, and it was hard to take issue with those who said he proved to be a convenient scapegoat. One Conservative MP told Sky News that it was the sort of action that might be expected of Russia's prime minister, Vladimir Putin.

Shooting practice

Britain may still be a member of the G7 group of major industrialized countries, but when it comes to education it has already been relegated. Every two years, the Organisation for Economic Co-operation and Development (OECD) conducts an international study to measure how well 15-year-old children are doing at school. The latest results of the Programme for International Student Assessment (PISA) showed that out of 65 countries, Britain was ranked 25th for reading, 28th for maths and 16th for science.[5] Four years earlier, when 57 countries were involved in the study, the rankings had been 17th, 24th and 14th respectively.

The OECD findings are interesting in two respects. First, they suggest that there is something in the claim that the reason pupils in Britain are attaining higher grades in exam results is that the tests are getting easier. Even if there is no 'grade inflation' going on and British children are actually more intelligent than those of previous generations, the slide down the PISA rankings show that other countries are making even more rapid advances. This is not for the want of extra resources, for in the decade that he was prime minister Tony Blair made good on his pledge to make 'education, education, education' the central theme of his government. The number of teachers and teaching assistants increased, pay rose in real terms and there was an eightfold increase in investment in new schools. Spending on education rose to the international average. Even so, Labour's 13 years in power ended with concerns about the decline in the number of pupils studying foreign languages, the quality of science teaching, the need for some universities to give new maths undergraduates crash programmes to bring them up to the necessary level to start their courses, and the lack of numeracy and literacy skills among those entering the labour market. A Confederation of British Industry survey in 2011 of more than 500 employers found that 42 per cent were unhappy about the levels of literacy among school and college leavers, while 35 per cent grumbled about numeracy standards.[6] Chiming with the PISA study, employers found that job candidates who had been educated overseas tended to be better prepared for work.

Developing countries seeking promotion to the Premier League understand the importance of education. In Mao's China, the Communist Party made a priority of the four 'modernizations': agriculture, industry, defence, and science and technology. When he came to power in 1978, Deng Xiaopeng insisted that science and technology was the key to growth and the eradication of poverty. The need to upgrade China's technical and scientific skills was acknowledged, and best practice imported from other countries. China is now both the fastest-growing economy in the world and the country that scores highest in the OECD's PISA rankings. Illiteracy among the young and middle-aged has fallen from 80 per cent in 1950 to less than 5 per cent today; in a country of 1.4 billion people, there is now almost universal primary school education; there has been a rapid increase in the number of universities, which turn out almost 20 million undergraduates a year; a further 700,000 Chinese students are educated overseas. The proportion of the national budget devoted to education has increased by one percentage point in every year since 1998. Parents have to supplement public spending with tuition fees, but most pay up in the belief that education is the key to a better life. In China, 'education, education, education' is not an aspiration, it is a fact.

China is not the only developing country to have

made the link between education and economic success. In 1960, per capita incomes in South Korea were on a par with those in Afghanistan and Nigeria: four decades of investment in schools, vocational education and universities meant that by the start of the new millennium South Korea was no longer considered a developing country.

Finland (third), Singapore (fifth) and Japan (eighth) made sure that their investment in education was best utilized. All three countries ensured that the brightest and the best graduates went into teaching rather than, as has been the case in the United Kingdom and the United States (17th), into finance or law.

Sporadic attempts have been made by governments of both left and right to woo graduates with first-class degrees away from their computer screens in the City of London and into the classroom. Most have resisted the temptation to swap a salary of £100,000 a year at an investment bank for a third as much at the chalkface. Far from following the example set by China, South Korea or Singapore, there have been signs that the United Kingdom has started to ape the less successful developing economies. Barking Borough Council in East London said a shortage of primary school places meant it was drawing up plans to convert an empty Woolworths store into a classroom and teach children in two shifts. The idea was that one group of pupils would be taught between 8 am and 2 pm, with another group of five to 11-year-olds clocking on for their time at the chalkface from 2 pm to 7 pm. With the government admitting that it would need an extra 450,000 places in school by 2015, it was clear the United Kingdom was suffering, on a smaller scale, from the same sort of problems faced by the financially embarrassed nations of sub-Saharan Africa, where a lack of capacity often means class sizes of 100 and more, and pupils sitting in makeshift classrooms.[7]

A team game

Over the decades, there has been a clear pattern to the behaviour of the British economy. In times of strong growth, household spending has been the main factor behind rising output. Consumption has exceeded production, and as a result, imports have exceeded exports. The balance of payments has deteriorated and inflation has tended to pick up, until such point as the Treasury or the Bank of England has raised interest rates and pushed the economy into recession. During the downswing consumer spending has dropped back, but the productive capacity of the economy has tended to suffer even more. The fall in the value of the pound during the recession has made British exports more competitive, but the hollowing out of industrial capacity has made it harder and harder to exploit fully the benefits of a cheaper currency. So, whereas the devaluation of the late 1960s resulted in a healthy trade surplus, the depreciation during the financial crisis of 2007–08 led simply to a smaller trade deficit. The process has been rather like a dentist asked repeatedly to repair the same tooth: each time it needs to be filled a bit more has to be drilled out, eventually leaving only a fragile shell behind.

The outlook is made worse by three other developments: much tougher competition from overseas; much lower levels of activity in the financial sector, which has in the past been the mainstay of earnings from so-called 'invisible' trade; and the increasingly large deficit in oil and gas, made worse by rising global energy prices. The

UK response to these developments has been to bang the drum for free trade, to reject the idea of a major activist industrial strategy – although a minor-key version has been published by the Department for Business – and to assume that a lower exchange rate and some severe belt-tightening by the state will lead to a rebalancing of the economy. It is not an approach that has been followed by the most successful developing economies, including – it has to be said – the United Kingdom in the days when it was struggling for global dominance.

There are two ways a developing economy can rebalance. One is if the policies are imposed from outside, usually through one of the IMF's 'structural adjustment' programmes. These involve a squeeze on the domestic economy designed to push resources towards the productive side of the economy, coupled with a currency devaluation that allows the goods coming out of factories to compete more successfully in world markets. Alternatively, and usually more fruitfully, countries devise their own strategies for industrial expansion and export-led growth. This normally involves some form of national development plan, in which policy makers analyse the problem, decide on their priorities and seek to remove any obstacles in the way of achieving success.

It should be stressed that such a plan can as easily opt for the 'Freeport' model as the more structured types of economic strategy that the word 'plan' may imply. A plan with a small 'p' need not lead to Planning with a large one. The Hong Kong economy, for example, did not happen by accident, but was carefully nurtured by British officials and may well be sustained by their Chinese counterparts. What is absolutely essential is that the plan addresses real, rather than illusory, problems.

In the UK context, the central problem is relatively simple: with each economic cycle it has become more difficult for the country to pay its way in the world. There will be a short-term improvement while the squeeze is in force, but as soon as there is any let-up in austerity, the nation will revert to type. Consumers will start to spend freely on their credit cards and borrow against the rising value of their homes; the pound will strengthen on the foreign exchanges, making imports less expensive and exports dearer; the balance of payments will dive deeper into the red; manufacturing will account for a smaller share of national output when the economy is expanding and will contract during the subsequent recession.

So what does a developing country do in these circumstances? Again, it is quite straightforward. It decides where the opportunities for growth are, chooses quite deliberately the sectors it wishes to nurture, and goes about building them up. This can be a detailed, hands-on process with close official involvement, or it can be a looser arrangement. But even a more arm's-length approach is still an approach. Favourable tax, regulatory and planning policies do not happen by themselves. Public land does not make itself available for factory units, warehousing, retail and the rest. Politicians and officials have to make it so.

Indeed, as we showed in a previous chapter, Margaret Thatcher's supposedly non-interventionist Conservative government in the 1980s picked upon finance as the sector in which the United Kingdom had a global comparative advantage, a not unreasonable judgement given London's pivotal role as a commercial and banking hub dating back centuries. It goes without saying that finance will continue to be important for the health of the UK economy. What matters is whether the City can be regulated in such a way that its activities do not result in orgiastic speculation, and that finance is part of a team effort, in which other sectors have the chance to prosper.

The City of London was cosseted in a fashion no different from the way in which Japan nurtured Panasonic and Toyota: both Conservative and Labour governments would go in to bat for Britain's financial services sector much more vigorously than they would ever defend the interests of manufacturing firms facing the full blast of low-cost competition from East Asia. The protection offered to the City is a cause for optimism for advocates both of more economic planning and of a more laissez-faire approach. For those seeking industrial planning and targeted development as the way out of our woes, Westminster's careful tending of the financial sector shows that an active industrial strategy can work. It shows that there is nothing, in theory, to stop governments from deciding – as the Germans have done, for example – to make a priority out of building up environmental industries, both because Britain will soon be in desperate need of alternative sources of energy, and because the efforts to tackle climate change will ensure high profits for companies that pioneer anti-pollution technologies. Money for the investment could have been provided by channelling part of the Bank of England's quantitative easing programme into the development of low-carbon energy, and into refurbishing Britain's housing stock to make it more fuel-efficient.

For those who put more faith in market forces, government promotion of the City can be seen as a rather different sort of success story, one that began with ministerial action to clear away the closed shops that had dominated the Square Mile (the Stock Exchange's tight circles of brokers and jobbers, the Accepting Houses Committee for merchant banks and so forth) and open up the City to all the talents.

On a more discouraging note, to both schools of thought in terms of development models, the choice of the City as a national champion more than a quarter of a century ago has tended to crowd out other sectors of the economy, particularly in the apportionment of graduate talent.

For those preferring a planned economic strategy, the dominance of the City poses deep questions. The diversion of top talent means other countries have been quicker than has the United Kingdom to spot the opportunities provided not just by the environmental sector but by the other sunrise industries of the twenty-first century: digital, robotics, genetics, biotechnology. Already, the United Kingdom is playing catch-up.

Both schools of thought wish to rebuild the productive capacity of the economy, but for each the answers are not as obvious as they may at first appear.

Free-market supporters may see the whole thing in a less complex way: if the City is overly dominant, then cut back any overt or covert state support and give other sectors of the economy some room to breathe.

Those seeking a full-blooded planned strategy may be tempted to say that the answer would be a good old-fashioned dose of protectionism (something Britain was not averse to in the seventeenth and eighteenth centuries), but this is putting the cart before the horse. There is not much point in throwing up tariff barriers and leaving the World Trade Organization (WTO) (which is what full-throated protectionism would necessitate) unless there is something to protect. At present there is not, and the priority therefore is to decide which industries the United Kingdom can hope to excel at, and then use the full range of instruments at the government's disposal – grants, procurement, regulation, tax breaks, subsidies – to ensure that they are strong enough to cope with global competition. For advocates of strategic planning, the latest in a century-long saga of missed opportunities was the failure to turn either Northern Rock (100 per cent nationalized) or the Royal Bank of Scotland (80 per cent nationalized) into a state investment bank with the remit of providing a long-term source of cheap funding to manufacturing.

There may, of course, be a time when such a blueprint for national renewal comes into conflict with EU or WTO rules. At that point, policy makers will have to decide whether the best interests of the nation are served by the sort of infant industry protection that has served the leading developing nations so well, or by an adherence to free trade. As the Cambridge economist Ha-Joon Chang has noted, there is no recorded example of a country successfully making the leap from developing to developed status without the use of protectionism.[8] That includes the United States, Germany, Japan, China, Taiwan, South Korea, and of course the United Kingdom.

But if detailed strategic planning could bring Britain into conflict with its international obligations as they are currently configured, and could therefore lead to a renegotiation or rupture with the organizations concerned, much the same is true of a more free-market model. On the face of it this may seem odd. Is free trade not the orthodoxy in Europe, America and many other places besides? Indeed, in one form or another, has it not been so since 1945? The European Union is a free-trading single market. Why would anyone object to an United Kingdom that practised what the free-traders preach? It would be rather as if the supposedly peace-loving United Nations were to criticize Switzerland for being too peaceful.

However, the global model known loosely as free

trade is in fact managed trade, governed by hugely complex agreements that have sought over the years to accommodate the concerns and interests of all participants, large and small. And the European Union's single market is not a free-fire trade zone but a club with very detailed rules.

As with the strategic planning model, policy makers will need to think hard where they believe the country's best long-term interests lie.

A winning mentality

Flicking through Britain's television channels is a curiously revealing experience. There are the costume dramas such as *Downton Abbey* and *Upstairs Downstairs*, designed to conjure up a feeling of warm nostalgia for the days when Britain was great, society was ordered and everybody knew their place. There are the medical soaps, which either – as in the case of *Call the Midwife* – hark back to the idealism that marked the early days of the National Health Service or else, with *Casualty* and *Holby City*, intersperse the case histories with political messages about hospital reorganizations, the tension between medical staff and bureaucrats and the ever-present threat of cuts. Sport still fills up large chunks of airtime, as do game shows and cooking classes fronted by celebrity chefs. One unexpected bonus of the recession has been the reduction in so-called 'property porn', programmes designed for those lusting after a bigger or a more expensive home.

Strangest of all, perhaps, has been the rise and rise of the talent show, a genre that in the 1970s amounted to little more than the low-key *Opportunity Knocks*, but which by the second decade of the twenty-first century had become an industry all of its own, with the tabloids full of stories not just about the contestants vying for fame and fortune but about the judges deciding their fate. The shows come in all shapes and sizes. There have been contests for girls who want to play the role of Maria in *The Sound of Music* and contests for those who want to be the next Gordon Ramsay or Jamie Oliver. *Big Brother* was a programme that appeared to have been loosely based on Jean-Paul Sartre's maxim that 'hell is other people', since it involved locking a group of individuals of incompatible personality types into a house, keeping them under 24-hour CCTV surveillance and inviting the public to eject them one by one. *The Apprentice* brought a similar format to the world of business: the idea here was to select 16 young entrepreneurs, for the most part long on ego and short on talent, and watch them being torn to pieces by Lord Alan Sugar, a British businessman of some renown. It proved a strangely compulsive format.

The biggest shows of all, however, are *The X Factor* and *Britain's Got Talent*, programmes in which thousands of hopefuls are gradually whittled down to one winning group or solo artist. For the winners, and sometimes the runners-up, the television exposure is the equivalent of The Beatles winning their first record contract with Parlophone in 1962, a meal ticket for life. Inevitably, though, the vast majority do not see their dreams fulfilled and, often tearfully, have to reconcile themselves to a less glamorous future behind the supermarket check-out or on the construction site.

It is commonplace to state that *The X Factor* and *Britain's Got Talent* are emblematic of the current state of the country, but we would disagree with that judgement. That is not because we think Britain lacks talent: that is certainly not the case now, and never has been. There is, though, a sharp contrast between the ferocious ambition that radiates out of the talent show contestants unhappy with their lot in life, and the complacency of the national mood. What do the talent show wannabees tell us? That modern Britain is failing large numbers of people desperate to better themselves and gain respect. That the world does not owe us a living just because we were the first to industrialize and were once, not that long ago, the most powerful nation in the world. That hard work is the secret of success. That there is a hunger for change and that it is possible to make it, if we decide that we have had enough of trying to muddle through in the customary British way. Let's be clear, though: muddling through represents a choice in itself, and will almost certainly lead to a more rapid descent into developing country status.

For almost a century, the United Kingdom has deluded herself, first into believing that the days of global dominance will return, then into thinking that the symptoms of decline can be relatively easily tackled. More latterly, the conviction has been that the United Kingdom is on its way back from the trough reached in the third quarter of the twentieth century. These were all illusions, and by 2014 they will be all used up.

We have not chosen that date merely to bookend Britain's 100 years of decline, convenient though the anniversary is. Respected commentators including the investment bank Lazard have identified a huge wall of banking and commercial debt due for refinancing at about that time. There are serious doubts whether it will be possible. Taken together with squeezed supplies of energy, metals and food, this is going to confront the west with an existential crisis, a great reckoning that will affect all developed countries. But the United Kingdom will be hit harder than most. It has been on a quarter-century rake's progress that has seen it sell its economic assets into foreign hands to finance a standard of living it has not been earning. This has left it with a hopelessly unbalanced, unhealthy economic structure, an economy that does not work, and as a candidate for third world membership.

When the last illusions are stripped away, we will need to choose a development model and stick to it. But there are two caveats. First, we do not have all the time in the world to decide what sort of economy we want to have. Second, when we do decide – whatever we decide – will matter, in large part, only to ourselves. One hundred years after the guns of August, the rest of the caravan has well and truly moved on.

Notes

Introduction: One hundred all out

1. Available at: www.guardian.co.uk/uk/2012/mar/21/budget-speech-2012-full-text (accessed 20 April 2012).
2. Office for National Statistics, available at http://www.statistics.gov.uk/hub/index.html (accessed December 2011).
3. New Economics Foundation (NEF) 2004, *Chasing Progress*, available at: http://neweconomics.org/publications/chasing-progress (accessed 16 April 2012).
4. *Economist*, 'Lost economic time: the Proust index', 25 February 2012, available at: www.economist.com/node/21548255 (accessed 16 April 2012).
5. Mike Brewer, James Browne and Robert Joyce, 'Universal Credit not enough to prevent a decade of rising poverty', press release, Institute for Fiscal Studies, October 2011, available at: www.ifs.org.uk/publications/57109 (accessed 16 April 2012).
6. House of Commons Committee for Culture, Media and Sport (2003) 'A London Olympic Bid for 2012', HC 268, 21 January.
7. *The Daily Mail*, 'Olympic sell-out! 91% of souvenirs made abroad', 4 February 2012.

1 June 1914: A snapshot as the storm breaks

1. Quoted in Roy Hattersley, *David Lloyd George: The great outsider*, Little, Brown, 2010.
2. Quoted in Robert Skidelsky, *John Maynard Keynes: Hopes betrayed 1883–1920*, Macmillan, 1983.
3. Ibid.
4. David Lloyd George, *War Memoirs*, vol. 1, Ivor Nicholson & Watson, 1933.
5. Douglas Jay, *Sterling: A plea for moderation*, Sidgwick & Jackson, 1985.
6. A. J. P. Taylor, *English History 1914–1945*, Clarendon Press, 1965.
7. Benjamin Seebohm Rowntree, *Poverty: A study of town life*, Macmillan, 1901.
8. Ken Follett, *Fall of Giants*, Pan Macmillan, 2010.
9. Neil Monnery, *Safe as Houses*, Publishing Partnership, 2011.
10. Christopher Andrew, *The Defence of the Realm*, Allen Lane, 2009.
11. See e.g. Roderick Floud, *The Economic History of Britain since 1700*, Cambridge University Press, 1994.
12. Ibid.
13. Andrew Tylecoat, *The Long Wave in the World Economy: The current crisis in historical perspective*, Routledge, 1991.
14. Lyon Playfair, Letters to the Schools Inquiry Commission. In *Memoirs and*

Correspondence of Lyon Playfair: First Lord Playfair of St. Andrews (1899), ed. T. W. Reid, Harpers, 1867.

15. Ibid.
16. HM Government, *Report of the Royal Commission on Technical Instruction*, HMSO, 1884.
17. Correlli Barnett, *The Audit of War*, Macmillan, 1986.
18. Ibid.
19. Sidney Pollard, *The Economic History of Britain since 1700*, Cambridge University Press, 1994.
20. The 1911 Census and Board of Education reports show that 50 per cent of children attended school till the age of 14. There were 8 per cent of children aged 14 and 15 in schools recognized by the Board of Education, dropping to 2 per cent for 16 and 17 year olds. In addition there were apprenticeships and on-the-job training.
21. Hilary Mantel, *Wolf Hall*, Fourth Estate, 2009.
22. Christopher Hill, *The Century of Revolution, 1603–1714*, Van Nostrand Reinhold, 1961.
23. Eric Hobsbawm, *The Age of Extremes*, Michael Joseph, 1994.
24. Niall Ferguson, 'Wars, revolutions and the international bond market from the Napoleonic Wars to the First World War', paper presented at the Yale International Centre for Finance, October 1999.
25. F. H. Hinsley, *Power and the Pursuit of Peace*, Cambridge University Press, 1962.
26. Paul Kennedy, *The Rise and Fall of the Great Powers*, Fontana, 1989.
27. Ha Joon Chang, *Bad Samaritans*, Random House, 2007.
28. Paul Kennedy, *The Rise and Fall of the Great Powers*, Fontana, 1989.
29. Frank Trentmann, *Free Trade Nation*, Oxford University Press, 2008.
30. Ibid.

2 *June 2014 in Lagos-on-Thames*

1. *Monty Python's Flying Circus*, BBC, 1974.
2. Larry Elliott and Dan Atkinson, *Fantasy Island*, Constable, 2007.
3. Peter Taylor-Gooby, 'Root and branch restructuring to achieve major cuts. the social policy programme of the 2010 UK coalition government', republished in *Social Policy and Administration*, vol. 46, issue 1, pp. 61–8, 2012.
4. Andrew Gamble, *Economic Futures*, British Academy, 2011.
5. McKinsey Global Institute 'Debt and deleveraging: the global credit bubble and its economic consequences', 2010, available at: http://www.mckinsey.com/Insights/MGI/Research/Financial_Markets/Debt_and_deleveraging_The_global_credit_bubble_Update (accessed 20 April 2012).
6. Tim Morgan, *Thinking the Unthinkable*, Tullett Prebon, 2011.
7. Centre for Research on Socio-Cultural Change (CRESC) 'Rebalancing the economy (or buyer's remorse)', CRESC, Manchester University, January 2011.

8   Organisation for Economic Co-operation and Development (OECD), available at: www.pisa.oecd.org/pages/0,2987,en_32252351_32235731_1_1_1_1_1,00.html (accessed 18 April 2012).
9. John Cridland, 'Future champions: unlocking growth in the UK's medium-sized businesses', CBI report, October 2011.
10. Department for Business Innovation and Skills (BIS), *Plan for Growth*, March 2011.
11. Chris Benjamin, *The Lost Origins of Industrial Growth*, Institute for Public Policy Research, 2011.
12. See Larry Elliott, 'UK "missed chance to build up £450bn sovereign wealth fund"', *The Guardian*, 27 February 2008, available at: www.guardian.co.uk/business/2008/feb/27/economics.oil (accessed 20 April 2012).
13. Charles Moore, 'We prevented a Great Depression ... but people have the right to be angry', interview with Sir Mervyn King, *The Daily Telegraph*, 4 March 2011.
14. Adair Turner, speech at Southampton University, September 2011.
15. Adair Turner, *Prospect*, August 2009.
16. Andrew Haldane (Bank of England executive director financial stability), 'The $100 billion question', comments made at the Institute of Regulation and Risk, Hong Kong, March 2010, available at: www.bankofengland.co.uk/publications/Documents/speeches/2010/speech433.pdf (accessed 20 April 2012).
17. Tax Justice Network, *Tackle Tax Havens*, www.tackletaxhavens.com (accessed 20 April 2012).

3   Welcome to the beautiful south

1. Chris Snowdon, *City AM*, 26 March 2012.
2. Department for Business Innovation and Skills (BIS), 'How business can challenge red tape', available at: www.bis.gov.uk/policies/better-regulation-at-bis/how-business-can-challenge-red-tape (accessed 13 April 2012).
3. Department for Business Innovation and Skills (BIS), *Consultation on Modern Workplaces, ii: Flexible working*, May 2011., available at: www.bis.gov.uk/assets/biscore/employment-matters/docs/c/11-699-4-consultation-modern-workplaces-flexible-working.pdf (accessed 16 April 2012).
4. Jill Treanor, 'George Osborne's credit easing to fill gap left by Project Merlin', *Guardian Business Blog*, 3 October 2011, available at: www.guardian.co.uk/business/blog/2011/oct/03/george-osborne-credit-easing-project-merlin (accessed 13 April 2012).
5. HM Revenue & Customs, 'Bringing HMRC's information powers into line with international standards', Consultation document, 7 July 2011.
6. *Mail Online*, 27 August 2011.
7. BBC News Kent, '"Do not disturb" signs taken off Kent nurses' tabards', 31 August 2011, available at: www.bbc.co.uk/news/uk-england-kent-14728114 (accessed 16 April 2012).
8. *Mail Online*, 28 August 2011.

9.   Simon Jenkins, *The Evening Standard*, 28 September 2011.
10. Lynge Nielsen, 'Classifications of countries based on their level of development: how it is done and how it could be done', IMF working paper, 2011.
11. Ibid.
12. *The Economist*, 26 June 2008.
13. David Frost and Antony Jay, *To England with Love,* Hodder Paperbacks, 1967.
14. V. S. Naipaul, *The Return of Eva Peron*, Knopf, 1980.
15. Sebastian Kelly, 'It's bargain Britain ... for foreigners', *Mail on Sunday*, 12 December 2010.
16. National Audit Office (NAO), *Pay Modernisation: New contracts for general practice services in England*, 28 February 2008.
17. 'Cameron plan to import US adviser angers police chiefs', *The Independent on Sunday (IOS)*, 14 August 2011.
18. 'A £155 fine for getting off the train a stop early', *The Daily Mail*, 28 September 2010.
19. 'Britain to boost prices on booze', United Press International (UPI), 23 March 2012.
20. BBC Radio Four, *More or Less*, 18 December 2009, available at: www.bbc.co.uk/programmes/b00p94fp.
21. House of Commons Home Affairs Committee, 'Police Service strength: government response to the Committee's Fifth Report of Session 2009–10', available at: www.publications.parliament.uk/pa/cm200910/cmselect/cmhaff/511/511.pdf (accessed 16 April 2012).
22. Reform (2011) 'Value for money in policing: from efficiency to transformation', report of conference, 29 June, available at: www.reform.co.uk/resources/0000/0316/VfMinPolicing.pdf (accessed 16 April 2012).
23. Matthew D'Ancona, 'All the policies are in place: now it's time for delivery', *The Sunday Telegraph*, 4 March 2012.

4   *A century of failure: the big fixes and why they went wrong*

1   Available at: www.guardian.co.uk/uk/2012/mar/21/budget-speech-2012-full-text (accessed 20 April 2012).
2.   Alec Cairncross, *The British Economy since 1945,* Blackwell, 1995.
3.   Quoted in Robert Skidelsky, *John Maynard Keynes: The economist as saviour 1920–1937*, Penguin, 1995.
4.   Mark Thomas, 'The macro-economics of the inter-war years', in R. Floud and D. N. McCloskey (eds), *The Economic History of Britain since 1700, vol. 2: 1860–1939*, Cambridge University Press, 1994.
5.   Roy Jenkins, *The Chancellors*, Macmillan. 1998.
6.   Roger Middleton, *Government versus the Market: The growth of the public sector, economic management, and British economic performance, 1890–1979*, Edward Elgar, 1996.
7.   John Maynard Keynes, Treasury memorandum 1944, in *The collected writings of John Maynard Keynes: Activities 1944–46, the transition to peace*, ed. D. E. Moggridge, Macmillan, 1979.

8. Ben Pimlott, *Hugh Dalton*, Harper Collins, 1995.
9. David Kynaston, *Austerity Britain 1945–51 (tales of a New Jerusalem)*, Bloomsbury, 2008.
10. Simon Winder, *The Man Who Saved Britain*, Picador, 2011.
11. Quoted in Jad Adams, *Tony Benn: A biography*, Macmillan, 1992.
12. Robert Millward, 'Industrial and commercial performance since 1950', in Roderick Floud and Paul Johnson (eds), *The Cambridge Economic History of Modern Britain, vol. 3: Structural change and growth, 1939–2000*, Cambridge University Press, 2004.

5   Into free-fall: the no-strategy strategy

1. *The Daily Telegraph*, 26 November 2011.
2. *The Financial Times*, 28 November 2011.
3. Queen, 'Bohemian rhapsody', 1975.
4. Neil Kinnock, addressing the Labour Party conference, Brighton, 1987.
5. Anthony Minghella, *On the Line*, Sphere, 1982.
6. Phillip Whitehead, *The Writing on the Wall*, Michael Joseph, 1985.
7. Penelope Lively, *The Photograph*, Penguin, 2003.
8. Ross Clark, *The Road to Southend Pier*, Harriman House, 2007.
9. Ibid.
10. Douglas Hurd, *An End to Promises*, Collins, 1979.
11. HM Government, *The Draft Long-Term Programme*, material to be submitted to the Organisation for European Economic Co-operation, September 1948.
12. Harold Wilson, *Final Term*, Weidenfeld & Nicolson/Michael Joseph, 1979.
13. Demos, *The Go-Ahead Year*, Book Distributors, 1966.
14. Conservative Party, *The Right Approach: A statement of Conservative aims*, Conservative Party Central Office, 1976.
15. Nigel Lawson, *Memoirs of a Tory Radical*, Biteback, 2010.
16. Nicholas Timmins, *Five Giants*, HarperCollins, 1995.
17. Enoch Powell, *Freedom and Reality*, Paperfront, 1969.
18. Ibid.
19. Ibid.
20. Ibid.
21. Ibid.
22. Jock Bruce-Gardyne, *Mrs Thatcher's First Administration*, Macmillan, 1984.

6   Up where we belong: is Britain's economic crisis all in the mind?

1. Vince Cable, speaking to the Policy Exchange, available on the Department for Business website: www.bis.gov.uk/news/speeches/vince-cable-industrial-strategy (accessed 13 April 2012).
2. Russell Hotten, 'CBI chief John Cridland on a mission to explain', BBC News, 18 November 2011, available at: www.bbc.co.uk/news/business-15778641 (accessed 17 April 2012).

3. UK Advanced Engineering Website, www.ukadvancedengineering.com/marketing/manufacturing (accessed 17 April 2012).

4. Work Foundation, quoted in UK Higher Education International Unit (UKHEIU), *International Higher Education in Facts and Figures Summer 2010*, available at: www.international.ac.uk/resources/Int%20facts%20%20figures%20booklet%20FINAL%20FOR%20WEB.pdf (accessed 17 April 2012).

5. Universities UK, quoted in UKHEIU, *International Higher Education in Facts and Figures Summer 2010*, available at: www.international.ac.uk/resources/Int%20facts%20%20figures%20booklet%20FINAL%20FOR%20WEB.pdf (accessed 17 April 2012).

6. Living Countryside, available at: www.livingcountryside.org/index.html (accessed 13 April 2012).

7. TheCityUK, data available at: www.thecityuk.com (accessed 13 April 2012).

8. 'Net migration total up by a fifth', *BBC News*, 25 August 2011, available at: www.bbc.co.uk/news/uk-14663354 (accessed 13 April 2012).

9. Ernst & Young, *European Attractiveness Survey*, May 2011.

10. T. A. B. Corley, *The British Pharmaceutical Industry Since 1851*, Centre for International Business History, University of Reading, available at: http://venuereading.com/web/FILES/business/emdp404.pdf (accessed 17 April 2012).

11. Ibid.

12. Association of the British Pharmaceutical Industry, data available at: www.abpi.org.uk/Pages/default/aspx (accessed December 2011).

13. Arts Council England, data available at: www.artscouncil.org.uk (various dates of access).

14. HM Government, *The Plan for Growth*, HMSO, 2010.

15. Ibid.

16. Ibid.

17. Ibid.

18. Committee on Finance and Industry (CFI) *Report of the Committee on Finance and Industry (Macmillan Report)*, HMSO, 1931.

19. Ibid.

20. Ibid.

21. HM Government, *The Pink Book*, HMSO, 2011.

22. Department of the Environment (DoE), *Engineering Works: Aircraft manufacturing works*, DoE, 1995.

23. Ibid.

24. George Orwell, *The Lion and the Unicorn: Socialism and the English genius*, Secker & Warburg, 1941.

25. Paul Johnson, *A History of the Modern World*, Weidenfeld & Nicolson, 1983.

26. Correlli Barnett, *The Lost Victory*, Macmillan, 1995.

27. Kenneth O. Morgan, *The People's Peace: British history 1945–1990*, Oxford University Press, 1990.

28. D. R. Myddelton, *They Meant Well*, Institute of Economic Affairs, 2007.

29. Margaret Gowing, *Independence and Deterrence: Britain and atomic energy 1945–52*, Macmillan, 1974.
30. D. R. Myddelton, *They Meant Well*, Institute of Economic Affairs, 2007.
31. James Hamilton-Paterson, *Empire of the Clouds: When Britain's aircraft ruled the world*, Faber & Faber, 2010.
32. Ibid.
33. Ibid.
34. Correlli Barnett, *The Lost Victory*, Macmillan, 1995.
35. HM Government, *White Paper on Defence*, Cmnd. 124, HMSO, 1957.
36. James Hamilton-Paterson, *Empire of the Clouds: When Britain's aircraft ruled the world*, Faber & Faber, 2010.
37. Correlli Barnett, *The Lost Victory*, Macmillan, 1995.
38. Simon Hugh Lavington, 'A brief history of British computers: the first 25 years (1948–1973', available at: www.computinghistory.org.uk/articles/18.htm (accessed 17 April 2012).
39. Ibid.
40. Sidney Weighell, *On the Rails*, Orbis, 1983.
41. Michael Edwardes, *Back from the Brink*, Collins, 1983.
42. Kenneth O. Morgan, *The People's Peace: British history 1945–1990*, Oxford University Press, 1990.
43. Peter Donaldson, *10xEconomics*, Penguin, 1982.
44. D. R. Myddelton, *They Meant Well*, Institute of Economic Affairs, 2007.
45. Ian Gilmour, *Inside Right*, Hutchinson, 1977.
46. T. A. B. Corley, *The British Pharmaceutical Industry since 1851*, Centre for International Business History, University of Reading, available at: http://venuereading.com/web/FILES/business/emdp404.pdf (accessed 17 April 2012).
47. *The Daily Telegraph*, 28 December 2011.

7 The great reckoning

1. Trades Union Congress, 'Shrinking wage pool costs workers £60bn a year', 27 January 2012, available at: www.tuc.org.uk/tuc-20547-f0.cfm Need access date (no longer available).
2. Institute for Fiscal Studies, *Autumn Statement*, IFS, 2011.
3. Office for Budget Responsibility, *Economic and Fiscal Outlook*, OBR, November 2011.
4. Ibid.
5. Survey conducted by YouGov in December 2011, results released in January 2012. See http://england.shelter.org.uk/news/january_2012/millions_rely_on_credit_to_pay_for_home (accessed 20 April 2012).
6. Survey, January 2012. See James Hall, 'Six million households have only five days' savings', *The Daily Telegraph*, 9 January, available at: www.telegraph.co.uk/finance/personalfinance/9003467/Six-million-households-have-only-five-days-savings.html (accessed 18 April 2012).
7. Resolution Foundation, 'Squeezed Britain: the 2010 audit of low to middle earners', November 2010.
8. Guy Standing, *The Precariat: The dangerous new class*, Bloomsbury, 2011.

9. Bank of England, *Housing Equity Withdrawal, Quarterly Bulletin*, second quarter, 2011.
10. Bank of England, *Housing Equity Withdrawal, Quarterly Bulletin*, February 2012.
11. McKinsey Global Institute 'Debt and deleveraging: the global credit bubble and its economic consequences', available at: http://www.mckinsey.com/ Insights/MGI/Research/Financial_Markets/Debt_and_deleveraging_The_ global_credit_bubble_Update (accessed 20 April 2012).
12. John Philpott, 'Look ahead 2012', Chartered Institute for Personnel and Development, January 2012, available at: www.cipd.co.uk/podcasts/_ articles/new-year-podcast-2012.htm (accessed 20 April 2012).
13. Chris Grayling, quoted in SKY news interview, 16 November 2011.
14. Interview with the author.
15. Peter Morris and Alasdair Palmer, *You're on Your Own*, Civitas, 2011.
16. Ibid.
17. Aneurin Bevan, speech at Blackpool, May 1945.
18. Royal Academy of Engineering (RAE), *Generating the Future*, March 2010.
19. George Osborne, speaking at UK business lunch at the annual meeting of the World Economic Forum in Davos, 2012.
20. The comment was made in a 2002 speech in which Bernanke referred to a statement made by Milton Friedman about using a 'helicopter drop' of money into the economy to fight deflation.
21. Robert Brenner, *The Boom and the Bubble*, Verso, 2007.
22. The latest is World Economic Forum, *Global Risks 2012*, January 2012, available at: www.weforum.org/reports/global-risks-2012-seventh-edition (accessed 18 April 2012).
23. Lee Howell, speaking at the launch of the World Economic Forum *Global Risks 2012* report.
24. Robin Blackburn, *Age Shock: How finance is failing us*, Verso, 2007.

8   Desperately seeking Sweden, or Freeport Ho! The search for a development model

1. Tony Benn, *Arguments for Socialism*, Jonathan Cape, 1979.
2. Alison Wolfe, *Does Education Matter? Myths about education and economic growth*, Penguin, 2002.
3. US Central Intelligence Agency, *World Factbook*, available at: https://www. cia.gov/library/publications/the-world-factbook/ (various dates of access).
4. Dambisa Moyo, *How the West was Lost*, Penguin, 2011.
5. Trades Union Congress, 'German lessons: developing industrial policy in the UK', January 2012.
6. Evan Davies, *Public Spending*, Penguin, 1998.
7. *The Daily Telegraph*, 22 February 2012.
8. Enoch Powell, *Enoch Powell on 1992*, ed. Richard Ritchie, Anaya, 1989.
9. Deepak Lal, 'Tackling the predatory state: from high tax dirigisme to a new liberalism', in Sheila Lawlor (ed.), *Poverty or Prosperity*, Imprint Academic, 2010.

9   *Hanging on in there: investment during the crisis*

1. *BBC News*, 28 April 2011.
2. Allister Heath, *City AM*, 10 August 2011.
3. Graeme Maxton, *The End of Progress: How modern economics has failed us*, Wiley, 2011.
4. Diane Pearson, *Csardas,* Macmillan, 1975.
5. Max Gunther, *The Zurich Axioms*, Souvenir, 1985.

10   *After the illusions*

1. Mitch Feierstein, *Planet Ponzi*, Bantam Press, 2012.
2. Institute for Fiscal Studies (IFS), *Green Budget,* January 2012.
3. Ibid.
4. *The Guardian*, 16 February 2012.
5. Organisation for Economic Cooperation and Development (OECD), available at: www.pisa.oecd.org/pages/0,2987,en_32252351_32235731_1_1_1_1_1,00.html (accessed 18 April 2012).
6. See Jeevan Vasagar, 'CBI criticises schools over "inadequate" literacy and numeracy', *Guardian*, 9 May 2011, available at: www.guardian.co.uk/business/2011/may/09/cbi-criticises-schools-literacy-numeracy (accessed 20 April 2012).
7. *The Guardian*, 4 February 2012.
8. Ha-Joon Chang, 'Kicking away the ladder', available at: www.paecon.net/PAEtexts/Chang1.htm (accessed 18 April 2012).

Index

Index

'Labour isn't working', 246
leadership election, 64
manifesto, 188
see also individual politicians by name
Lal, Deepak, 297
land and property
as investment, 327–8
London prices, 339–40
rights, 41
see also housing
Land Rover, 54, 191, 224
Larkin, Philip, 235
Lavington, Simon, 225
Lawrence, D. H., 27
Laws, David, 63, 64
Lawson, Nigel, 124, 158, 173, 181, 185–6, 189–90, 295
Lazard, 361
Le Queux, William, 24, 28–9
leadership, search for political, 106–8
leaks (press), 144
Lebanon, 12
Lee Kuan Yew, 284
Legal Services Act, 163–4
legal
practices, ownership regulations, 101, 163–4
services, 213, 229
Lehman Brothers, 258
Liberal Democratic Party, 133, 261
Liberal Party, 12
liberty, constraints/ attacks on, 89, 174, 275–6
Libya, 340
licensing laws, 25, 169, 315

Lichtheim, George, 171
life expectancy, 26, 247–8
limited companies, pros and cons of, 317–20
literacy, 351
Living Countryside, 198
living standards
contemporary, 59
impact of pensions changes on, 247
insulating against political action, 172
as political goal, 178
UK, declining, 237–9, 284
UK, historic pattern, 26–7, 31, 237, 284
UK, recent fall, 7, 55, 83, 87, 237, 258
Lloyd George, David, 19, 20, 22–3, 28, 32, 34, 127, 130–1, 137
Lloyd, John Selwyn, 150
Lloyd's of London, 192, 212
Lloyds Bank, 53, 81, 82, 160
local government, 112, 155, 293–4
London
Barbican, 171
Barking Borough Council, 352
as base for the rich, 110
bombings (7 July 2005), 119
City architecture, 17, 51–2
commuters' attitudes to, 330
Docklands, 163, 172, 193
East, 7
as fin'l centre, 17–18
Great Stench (1858), 26

lord mayor's view, 269
Olympics *see* Olympics
Passenger Transport Board, 137
property market, 339–40
Southall, 316
transport, 8, 94, 137
Wembley, 337
Westminster, 349
world city, 194, 340
Longbridge, 54
Lynn, Jonathan, 1
Lyons, 225

M
Macao, 296
MacDonald, Ramsay, 135, 136
Macmillan, Harold, 149
Macmillan, Hugh
Pattinson/Macmillan Report, 207–8
Made in Dagenham, 54
Mail on Sunday, 110–11
Major, John, 92, 106, 125, 135, 159
Malaysia, 74, 119–20
Mandela, Nelson, 168, 314
Mantel, Hilary, 40
manufacturing
current state of UK, 57, 72–3, 197, 205
decline of UK, 54–5, 134, 159, 353
failure to update, 48–9
foreign-owned firms in UK, 54, 73, 191, 234
hollowing-out of UK, 6, 57, 75, 85, 159, 340
lack of large UK-owned firms, 76